Two Thousand Years Ago

Charles A. Frazee

Two Thousand

Years Ago

The World at the Time of Jesus

WILLIAM B. EERDMANS PUBLISHING COMPANY
Grand Rapids, Michigan / Cambridge, U.K.

Wm. B. Eerdmans Publishing Co.
255 Jefferson Ave. s.e., Grand Rapids, Michigan 49503 /
p.o. Box 163, Cambridge cb3 9pu U.K.
www.eerdmans.com

Printed in the United States of America

07 06 05 04 03 02 7 6 5 4 3 2 1

Library of Congress Cataloging-in-Publication Data

Frazee, Charles A.
Two Thousand years ago : the world at the time of Jesus / Charles A. Frazee.
p. cm.
Includes bibliographical references and index.
isbn 0-8028-4805-2 (cloth : alk. paper)
1. First century, A.D. 2. Bible. N.T.—History of contemporary events. I. Title

D85.F57 F73 2002
930'.5 — dc21
2002033893

A list of photo credits appears on page 248.

This book has been composed in Monotype Ehrhardt and Linotype Univers
Design by Kevin van der Leek Design Inc.

Contents

Introduction

MILLIONS OF PEOPLE read the New Testament privately or hear it proclaimed in Sunday worship without ever putting the events recorded there into the context of world history. This short book attempts to provide a look at other societies contemporary with that of Jesus. It is intended to reach an audience of New Testament readers who would like to know about the world during Jesus' lifetime, to draw some comparisons and contrasts, and to learn a bit about peoples living during the first century.

It may be argued that events occurring in the rest of the world did not play much of a role in the life of Jesus. Yet is it not of some significance that Jesus lived his whole life in a land where a Hellenistic monarch ruled under the surveillance of Roman emperors? It is therefore obvious that both Greek and Roman culture, as well as his own Jewish heritage, had an effect on his mission. It is thought-provoking, too, to wonder how well Jesus' message would have fit into other cultures of his day, or whether we in the twenty-first century would know him at all had he been a member of, say, a Celtic, Pacific, or Native American society.

In the first century, Mediterranean societies were among the few that were literate and have thus left written records. Jesus lived within that world, and for that reason the larger portion of this book deals with the history of Mediterranean peoples. Writing was also known in Parthia, India, and China, but much of the information on the rest of the world comes from anthropologists and archaeologists.

I would like to thank Kathleen Frazee, Sheila Ryan, Brendan Nagle, and James Santucci for their help in the preparation of the manuscript.

Chapter One

Mediterranean Europe

JESUS SPENT HIS ENTIRE life in close proximity to the Mediterranean Sea, a body of water that dominates the geography of southern Europe. Galilee, his homeland, lay at the eastern end of the Mediterranean. The sea's great expanse separates Europe from North Africa, extending over two thousand miles from east to west. Its high salt content, the result of rapid evaporation during the warm summer months, gives it a deep blue color. Cool water flows into it from the Atlantic Ocean at the Strait of Gibraltar, constantly replenishing what is lost. By Jesus' time the Romans, because of their conquests, had made the Mediterranean their lake; they knew it as *mare nostrum,* our sea.

Three peninsulas jut into the sea from continental Europe: the Iberian, the Italian, and the Balkan. Each has its share of mountains; these, over the centuries, have provided excellent stone for building. Many such buildings, constructed before the lifetime of Jesus, are still standing today. The Mediterranean climate offers cool winters, a time when the rains come, and hot, dry summers. Though most of its inhabitants in the first century farmed for a living, harvests were not bountiful. Just the opposite was true, in fact, for the land is rocky and steep and water scarce during the growing season. Mediterranean farmers had to spend long days in the field to provide for their families.

Countless islands dot the Mediterranean, some formed by volcanoes, others the peaks of submerged mountains. The Aegean Sea in particular, off the coast of Greece, is full of islands. The Greeks called them the Cyclades, from their word for circle, believing that they formed a ring around the tiny island of Delos, sacred to them as the birthplace of the gods Apollo and Artemis. It was on these islands that the first European civilization, that of the Minoans, was born. The Minoans eventually moved to Crete, where a succession of monarchs bearing the title of Minos created centers of culture in palaces famous for their architecture and frescoes. Knossos was their capital, and from its port Cretan sailors traded with Egypt and the cities of southwest Asia, bringing back the riches that allowed their rulers to furnish their dwellings in style. Despite its wealth, though, Minoan culture did not last; long before the time of Jesus it was absorbed into Hellenistic Greek society. Because of the conquests of Alexander the Great, all that we know about Jesus comes to us written in the Greek language.

The deep blue color of the Mediterranean comes from its high salt content, the result of rapid evaporation during the summer months.

THE GREEK BACKGROUND

The Lions Gate, built around 1250 B.C. and still standing today, served as the western entrance to the fortified city of Mycenae. The lions are carved on a single block of stone that measures nearly 11 by 13 feet.

Around 1900 B.C. people from the northern Balkans began to settle in the region that became known as Greece. They mixed with the indigenous population there, eventually forming a single people. Four hundred years later, the center of their most advanced society was at Mycenae, a city on the Peloponnesus. Mighty kings built their palace on its height and constructed the Lions Gate, which still stands at the entrance to their fortress home. The Mycenaean Greeks replaced the Minoans as the great seafarers of their age, and with their wealth in gold and silver the kings ordered large tombs to be built for themselves in imitation of the pyramids of Egypt. Though not so huge as those in

Egypt, they were the largest ever seen in the Balkans. Both the Minoans and the Mycenaeans had developed systems of writing, but they were not used for narrative. It was left for Homer, in the *Iliad* and the *Odyssey*, to record the memory of life in Mycenaean times. Mycenae flourished for three centuries before new invaders destroyed it. For hundreds of years thereafter Greece was once again a backwater until, about 750 B.C., civilization appeared again with the birth of the city-state.

Over the next four hundred years, the city-states of Greece produced one of the world's most creative civilizations. Athens led the way, but Corinth and Thebes on the mainland, and Miletus, Ephesus, and Smyrna on the western coast of Anatolia, were also centers of commerce, science, and the arts. Sparta, in its own way, also made a contribution to Hellenic culture. It was not famous for its artists or philosophers, but for a highly structured and disciplined way of life, which has fascinated historians ancient and modern. It was during this period that ancient Athenians invented theater and built the magnificent temples that still stand on top of the Acropolis. Socrates, Plato, and Aristotle walked the streets of Athens, initiating conversations on philosophy, politics, and ethics that continue to this day in the Western world. They built on the work of the scientists of the Anatolian cities, who had preceded them in inquiring about what determines matter and form, motion and space. Writing history also began with the Greeks. Herodotus, called the father of history, recorded the events surrounding the Persian invasion of Greece in the early fifth century, and Thucydides wrote his work on the battles between Athens and Sparta during the Peloponnesian War.

Greek sculptors and painters were extraordinary in their ability to depict their gods and goddesses in bronze and stone and to memorialize their athletes in statues that represent their ideal of the human form. It was the Greeks who conceived of sports as a way to honor their deities, who were thought to enjoy watching a race just as much as mortals did. Their gods and goddesses were regarded as similar to humans in many ways, sharing many of their loves and hatreds, but they had an edge on humans as well: they were immortal, and, among other powers, could become invisible when it pleased them.

In the fourth century, in the region of Macedonia, a very ambitious dynasty was founded when Philip II took the throne. Until then, Macedonia had not made a mark on Greek history, but Philip intended to change that by conquering the surrounding city-states and placing them under his leadership for an invasion of Persia. But although he dominated the Greeks after the battle of Chaeronea in 338 B.C., assassins brought him down before his plans for war against Persia could be accomplished.

ALEXANDER THE GREAT AND THE MACEDONIANS

Philip's son, Alexander, quickly assumed his father's role as leader of the Greeks and Macedonians against the might of the Persians. Alexander marched against the Persian king, Darius III, who, despite great resources, could not stop the invaders and died at the hands of his own generals because of his failure. Within twelve years, Alexander brought most of the southwest Asian world under his rule. Then, in 323 B.C., he died while still a young man of thirty-three. His wife was pregnant with his heir, but his generals intended that they should be Alexander's successors. For several years, there was a contest to see if one of them could take his place, but the battles were inconclusive. As a result, they divided the conquests among them: Ptolemy became king in Egypt; Seleucus governed Syria and the Asian territories taken from Persia; and in Macedonia, actually the poorest part of Alexander's empire, his general Antipater was king. The classical age of Greece was ended, and the period of Hellenistic Greece had begun.

Both Alexander's and Antipater's deaths were taken by many Greeks as signals to revolt, but the Macedonian kings had no intention of letting the city-states of the south escape. Macedonian soldiers garrisoned Athens, which Alexander had treated with leniency, and many of its privileges were revoked. In 279 B.C., the Macedonian kings were unable to halt a Celtic attack on Delphi, which only an earthquake saved from devastation. King Antigonus II Gonatus removed the Celts from Macedonian Greece by promising them tribute, thus persuading them to pass over into Anatolia. Antigonus's rule, from 277 until 239 B.C., was benign, for he had a sincere affection for the culture of ancient Greece.

Then the Macedonian leadership made a fatal mistake. Antigonus's successor, Philip V, chose to ally his nation with Carthage in resisting the growing power of Rome. The Romans responded by encouraging a revolt against the Macedonians. Other wars followed and, in 148 B.C., Macedonia became a Roman province. At the time of Jesus, both Macedonia and the lands of classical Greece, known as Achaia to the Romans, fell into that category.

We must now interrupt the history of Greece to turn to events in Italy. Who were these Romans that had incorporated the Macedonians and Greeks into their world?

THE ROMANS

A Roman author, writing centuries after the foundation of the city of Rome, claimed that the city was begun in 753 B.C., when, according to a long-held legend, twin brothers, Romulus and Remus, decided to settle on the banks of the Tiber River in central Italy. A quarrel about which of the seven hills each should choose to make his home resulted in Remus's death and the newly founded city receiving Romulus's name. An alternate story tells of the Trojan warrior Aeneas establishing the city of Lavinium Longa to the south of Rome, thus beginning the ascent of the Latin-speaking people of the region. But archaeologists, no friends of legends, claim that Rome was occupied by Italian peoples well before 1000 B.C.

Economically speaking, the site of Rome was felicitous, for its location in the center of the Italian peninsula allowed it to benefit from trade between its neighbors: the Greeks in the south and the Etruscans in the north. Greek colonists had arrived in Italy as early as 770 B.C., making their home in the region of the Bay of Naples. They were attracted to Italy for its soil, which was much more fertile than that of their homeland, and for its mineral wealth, which was there for the taking.

Though they lived not far north of Rome, the Etruscans were the only Italians who did not speak an Indo-European language. Herodotus claimed that they had migrated to Italy from Anatolia, but a recent theory asserts that they may well have been the descendants of the Neolithic population of the peninsula. Whatever the case, by the beginning of the seventh century B.C., the Etruscan people had a distinct identity and were noted for their rich farmlands and flourishing cities. Like the Greek city-states, each city had its own political leaders, and each jealously maintained its individuality. When the Etruscans began to expand in the early sixth century, the Romans were in no position to resist, and the city eventually fell under the rule of an Etruscan dynasty.

In 509 B.C., the Roman aristocrats, known as patricians, revolted against Tarquin the Proud, their Etruscan king, driving him from the city. The patricians formed a republic under the direction of an assembly known as the Senate. On an annual basis the Senate chose two consuls as the major administrative officials of the city. Other magistrates were also elected to serve the city's needs, but always with colleagues and only for a yearly term, for the ancient Romans had developed a great fear of the concentration of power in a single individual.

It was considered beneath Roman patricians to engage in business, with the sole exception of buying and selling land.

Service in the army was the key to Roman citizenship. Rome and the area that surrounded it, known as Latium, lay in a plain that was subject to raids from the peoples who lived in the Apennines, the mountain chain that runs down the spine of Italy. For this reason, the army always had to be on the alert, because Rome lacked natural defenses. Every able-bodied man was expected to serve a tour of duty in the military. Each found a position in a century, which was captained by a centurion. Sixty centuries made up a legion.

The government of Rome was an oligarchy; power was concentrated in the hands of several ruling families. The remainder of the population fell into the plebeian class. Like the Brahmans, their counterparts in India, the patricians justified their rule by appealing to their knowledge of sacred texts and their priestly functions. The plebeians, though, who made up the bulk of the army, eventually began to resent their lack of status. After decades of political struggle, they won the right to enter the Senate, stand for election to the magistracies, and have their own convention, the Plebeian Assembly, recognized as a legal entity with legislative powers. Its officers, the ten tribunes, over time became important figures in the Roman government.

ROMAN LIFE

During the lifetime of Jesus, Roman society was divided into classes determined by birth and wealth. At the top were the patricians, the great landowners descended from noble families, whose incomes were large enough to allow them to spend their time in politics and military commands and to pursue the lives of gentlemen farmers. It was considered beneath them to engage in business, with the sole exception of buying and selling property. Over time, a class known as *equites* emerged; they were an upper middle class whose members had attained rank because of their wealth, if not their birth into patrician families. Merchants, artisans, and professionals also composed a large group of citizens. Included in this class were freedmen and -women, former slaves who had purchased their liberty or were emancipated by benevolent masters.

DAILY LIFE

To conquer cities, the Romans used catapults they referred to as "wild asses" for the way their rears kicked up under the force of recoil. These machines could hurl a fifty-pound stone over four hundred yards.

Slaves, both male and female, were very numerous, most of them serving the upper classes as domestics. They had no legal rights, could not marry without permission, and could be bought or sold. Many were prisoners of war; others were simply the children of slave parents. The government owned many of the slaves who worked in the mines or served in the galleys, while private individuals leased others on contract. Roman slaves led a miserable existence, and runaway slaves could expect death by crucifixion.

Men in the upper classes wore togas. These were pieces of cloth, eighteen feet long and seven feet wide, draped over the shoulder and fastened with a pin. It was almost impossible to perform physical labor in such a garment; therefore it quickly became a symbol of status. Women wore *stolae,* long dresses that reached to the ankles.

The father of a family had absolute authority over his household. All property was at his disposal, and all decision-making his prerogative. He arranged his children's marriages, usually with the intent of increasing his family's wealth and status. Roman women, although hardly equal to men, enjoyed much more freedom to participate in public life than did women in Greece. Girls were given in marriage when about thirteen; boys were generally closer to twenty. The Romans were serious about educating their sons, for advancement in society depended on their written and oral skills and on acquaintance with the literary classics. Teachers of rhetoric were always in great demand.

> *No greater virtue was esteemed in Rome than* pietas, *the veneration that individuals and the officials of the city paid to the divinities who protected Rome and led it to victory.*

When the Romans came into contact with the Greeks, they simply matched the Greek divinities with their own. As a result, Zeus became identified with the Romans' Jupiter, Hera with Juno, Aphrodite with Venus, and so on. But the Romans, unlike the Greeks, always treated their gods and goddesses with reverence. No greater virtue was esteemed than *pietas,* the veneration that individuals and the officials of the city paid to the divinities who protected Rome and led it to victory. Janus, the god who guarded doors, was the most popular deity of early Rome. His temple in the Roman Forum stood open in times of war, but was closed in times of peace. Despite the fact that less attention was paid him in later times, he was always invoked first during prayer. Jupiter, originally a god of the oak forest and the sky, came into prominence later. He was Jupiter, "the greatest and the best," because of the esteem in which the Romans held him. Juno, his wife, and Minerva, goddess of war and wisdom, also had their share of temples. Mars, the god of war, received continual sacrifices in his honor, as did Venus, patron of love, and Diana, goddess of fertility and the hunt. Vesta, the goddess of the hearth, also had her temple in the Forum, where vestal virgins kept her sacred fire.

Every town had its temples to the gods and goddesses. These were generally rectangular buildings, with columns either in front of or around the whole perimeter of the building. Altars stood in front of the temples for the offering of sacrifices to the gods and goddesses. They were placed where they could be seen, for only priests had the right to enter temples. Certain temples offered the right of asylum, meaning that criminals and debtors could escape punishment if they fled to one of them before their arrest.

Upper-class Romans honored the gods in formal celebrations, but preferred to look to philosophy for their ethics. Stoicism became the favored guide to the good life, because it was so much in harmony with the instincts of the educated. Nearly everyone sought the advice of astrologers when planning their days; despite their interest in philosophy, the Romans were extremely superstitious.

ROMAN EXPANSION

Rome claimed that its army existed for the sake of defense, but as the population climbed and the demand for farmland became more pressing, politicians looked for opportunities to use the army for expanding the city's borders. First to fall was a nearby Etruscan town. A setback occurred, however, when in 390 B.C. an unexpected Celtic force swept into Latium, placing Rome itself under a seven-month siege. Once delivered from this threat, the Romans became even more conscious of the need for military preparedness. The Senate commissioned attacks on the Etruscan towns to the north and then set the army against the Greek city-states in the south of Italy. Their ambitions turned next to the island of Sicily, where both Greeks and Carthaginians sat atop the wealth in grain that came from the land's great bounty.

In 264 B.C., Rome was drawn into a quarrel between two rival cities in Sicily, thereby initiating a conflict with Carthage, which felt threatened by the Romans' intervention. Three wars with Carthage followed. All were Roman victories. For a time, Rome was threatened by a Carthaginian army in Italy, led by the general Hannibal, but the loyalty of Rome's allies dissipated the strength of the invaders. With

Carthage driven from the land, the Romans inherited the Carthaginian territory of Spain.

The Romans' usual procedure in conquered territories was to set up a provincial governor, called a proconsul or prefect, to administer the region and to oversee the collection of taxes. Ten senators, in consultation with the general who had conquered the region, drafted a constitution that was submitted to the entire Senate, spelling out the obligations and rights of the province. In the provinces, the local people kept their language, customs, and religion without Roman interference, but they also had to furnish conscripts for the Roman army, and they had no say in foreign affairs, which was the sole prerogative of the Senate.

Though the proconsuls had only a limited staff of young men and a small garrison of troops to assist them, their duties were significant. It was their responsibility to keep the peace and to settle all judicial disputes. The Senate initially appointed them for yearlong terms, but their tenure could be extended, and often it was. The best of them were honest men, but too many were unscrupulous in demanding money and accommodations from the provincials they governed. They kept splendid courts, with entertainers and a variety of hangers-on filling their palaces. Because they were usually senators who, after their tour of duty was over, would return to the Senate, very little was done by their fellows to hold them accountable. To enrich themselves, they often confiscated the estates of those accused of disloyalty, or collected fines out of all proportion to the offense. Local people were terrified of provoking them, for the proconsuls could inflict the death penalty on anyone accused of a crime.

Because citizens paid no taxes, the Senate was quite willing to impoverish the provinces so that the city of Rome might flourish. The provincials paid two principal taxes: a poll tax, the *tributum capitis,* and a land tax, the *tributum soli.* The land tax was set anywhere from one-tenth to one-twentieth of the annual income of a piece of property. It was not paid each year, but after a period of time known as the *indictio,* which might extend for as many as fifteen years. In addition to these regular payments, proconsuls could assess extraordinary levies in times of real or contrived emergencies in a completely arbitrary manner. The money they raised allowed the Romans to finance their armies, to offer the officers of the state magnificent incomes, and to provide bread and oil to the lower classes.

Because gathering taxes was so difficult for the proconsuls, they often resorted to tax farming. Wealthy individuals, usually from the equestrian class, bid for the right to collect taxes in return for a set sum of money to be turned over immediately to the treasury. They formed companies of publicans, whose grasping ways made tax collecting the most despised profession in all the Roman provinces.

THE RISE OF THE GENERALS

By the close of the second century B.C. the Roman republic was the undisputed master of much of the Mediterranean, but affairs in Rome itself had turned nasty. Small farmers could no longer compete with large landowners, whose estates were cultivated by slaves. They therefore sold their lands and poured into the city, hoping to find work, but there were simply too few jobs. As a result, huge numbers of unemployed crowded the streets of Rome, living as clients of the rich and famous and spending their time attending plays, gladiatorial contests, and other public entertainments.

Civilian control of the republic faltered because ambitious generals like Gaius Marius, Lucius Cornelius Sulla, and Gnaeus Pompeius (better known as Pompey) could easily manipulate the Senate through their allies there. While previously the army had been composed of citizen farmers who enlisted for a limited number of days, Rome's new role as policeman of the Mediterranean required a professional force with skilled leaders. Military command had become the gateway to a political career, and this required new lands to conquer. The Iberian Peninsula beckoned to the west, as did the Balkans to the east.

The Spanish people were not easily persuaded to acquiesce to Roman control. It took from 218 to 16 B.C. to completely subdue the country. Resistance to the Romans ran deep, and despite their diversity — the land was a mixture of Iberians, Celts, Greeks, and Phoenicians — the

Spaniards were united in their distaste for Rome. Rebellions were constant, giving the Roman armies in Spain little time to rest.

Roman generals, more confident than ever, also directed their attention eastward, marching against the Macedonians to punish them for their alliance with Carthage. In 167 B.C., the Romans dictated the breakup of the Macedonian state into four parts after a battle that brought down Perseus, the last Antigonid king. Roman respect for Athens allowed the city to keep its own government, but, in 146 B.C., when a Macedonian rebellion erupted, the general Lucius Mummius ordered all of Greece put under the direct rule of the Romans. The rebellion gave Mummius an excuse to destroy Corinth, a potential commercial rival in the eastern Mediterranean, and dozens of other Greek cities. From Epirus alone he took a hundred thousand captives.

"No one can call himself a man unless he's been to Corinth." – Horace

The Roman push toward the east accelerated, eventually reaching Anatolia. In 133 B.C., the king of Pergamum died heirless, leaving his lands to Rome, and in 74 B.C., Bithynia, a kingdom in Anatolia south of the Sea of Marmara, was incorporated into Rome's territories. More Greeks now came to Italy as war captives or by choice, bringing their culture with them. The Roman upper class gradually became enamored of Hellenistic culture, envious of its great architects, artists, philosophers, playwrights, and authors. Thus Greek culture not only survived but, ironically, significantly impacted its conquerors.

ROMAN GREECE

Roman Philhellenism meant that the Greeks were allowed considerable freedom to run their local affairs while Jesus was on earth. Athens in particular was held in high esteem; major legal cases continued to be tried at its Areopagus, and many young Roman aristocrats came to study under its teachers, who introduced them to the thought of Plato and Aristotle. In return for offering hospitality to their sons, the Romans treated the Athenians with respect. Though Sparta was reduced to less than a thousand citizens, its assembly, the Gerousia, held regular sessions. The city-states that oversaw the sacred precinct at Delphi continued to serve in that capacity, and the Athenians were permitted to keep a garrison on Delos. While most of the region of classical Greece suffered from depopulation, Rhodes, thanks to past allegiance to Rome, prospered as a free city. The athletic games in honor of the gods and goddesses at Olympia, Delphi, and the Isthmus of Corinth continued to be held regularly.

DAILY LIFE

Julius Caesar is credited with founding the *Acta Diurna* ("Daily Events") in 59 B.C. A precursor to modern newspapers, it was a daily journal posted in prominent places in Rome and major provincial towns with the intent of disseminating official information. A typical issue would report official news as well as astrological omens, significant births and deaths, and outcomes of major trials and gladiatorial contests. Whatever people of Jesus' day knew of the world events would have come from the *Acta Diurna*.

Roman expansion into Anatolia brought a reaction from Mithradates VI, who was king of Pontus, a region south of the Black Sea in modern Turkey. In 89 B.C., Mithradates captured the Roman provinces of Anatolia, reportedly killing eighty thousand Roman citizens, and sailed his fleet into the Aegean, sacking the sacred island of Delos in retaliation for its loyalty to Rome. He called on all Greeks to join him in ridding themselves of foreigners, not an easy decision because, at least for the upper class, prosperity had accompanied Roman occupation. In 86 B.C., the Athenians, pushing aside their misgivings, declared for Mithradates. Within months a Roman army, captained by Sulla, descended on Greece.

When Athenian negotiators met with Sulla, they reminded him of the Athenian victory at Marathon in 490 B.C. Sulla responded that he had come to Greece to put down a rebellion, not to learn about history. He easily defeated the Greek armies allied to Mithradates, after which he burned down their homes and the harbor at Piraeus, and looted the Athenian temples. Athens and its neighbors did not recover for several decades. During Jesus' lifetime the damage was still under repair and Athens had lost its commercial importance, which it would not regain until modern times.

While Athens stagnated, Corinth was in the process of rebuilding, for Julius Caesar established a Latin colony there, which soon grew to be a

The island of Delos was reputed to be the birthplace of the gods Apollo and Artemis and was therefore a very sacred place for the Greeks. At the time of Jesus it had become a great slave market. Traders built lavish houses on the island like the one in the foreground, and ships landed at the harbor in the distance.

major commercial center. On the tall acropolis behind the city, the cult of Aphrodite's devotees became so well known that the Roman poet Horace could say: "No one can call himself a man unless he's been to Corinth." Thessalonike replaced Athens as the political and commercial capital of Macedonia.

JULIUS CAESAR

In the last half-century before Jesus' birth, Julius Caesar rose to power, a man whose goal was to dominate the Roman government. Caesar maneuvered to gain military commands in Spain and southern Gaul, where his victories made him more popular than any other general. A jealous Pompey challenged him for the leadership of Rome, and a four-year civil war resulted in a total victory for Caesar.

In the text of the *Antiquities of the Jews* by Flavius Josephus, a Jewish historian living in Rome, a Christian editor at some point inserted this passage concerning Jesus. For many Romans, it was probably the first that they learned of Jesus.

Source: Flavius Josephus, Antiquities of the Jews *18.63-64. Trans. L. H. Feldman*

ABOUT THIS TIME THERE LIVED JESUS, A WISE MAN, IF INDEED ONE OUGHT TO CALL HIM A MAN. FOR HE WAS ONE WHO WROUGHT SURPRISING FEATS AND WAS A TEACHER OF SUCH PEOPLE AS ACCEPT THE TRUTH GLADLY. HE WON OVER MANY JEWS AND MANY OF THE GREEKS. HE WAS THE MESSIAH. WHEN PILATE, UPON HEARING HIM ACCUSED BY MEN OF THE HIGHEST STANDING AMONGST US, HAD CONDEMNED HIM TO BE CRUCIFIED, THOSE WHO HAD IN THE FIRST PLACE COME TO LOVE HIM DID NOT GIVE UP THEIR AFFECTION FOR HIM. ON THE THIRD DAY HE APPEARED TO THEM RESTORED TO LIFE, FOR THE PROPHETS OF GOD HAD PROPHESIED THESE AND COUNTLESS OTHER MARVELOUS THINGS ABOUT HIM. AND THE TRIBE OF THE CHRISTIANS, SO CALLED AFTER HIM, HAS STILL TO THIS DAY NOT DISAPPEARED.

After the fall of Pompey, Caesar tried to win over his remaining enemies rather than eliminate them. He attracted many of the equestrians to his side, as well as officials serving in the Italian towns outside Rome, thus creating a party of Caesarians who were willing to tie their fortunes to him. In 45 B.C., he supervised a wide range of senatorial legislation and had himself declared perpetual dictator, so that he enjoyed unlimited authority. Those in the Senate who opposed him, led by Marcus Junius Brutus and Gaius Cassius Longinus, stabbed Caesar to death on the Ides of March (March 15, 44 B.C.) with daggers they had hidden in their togas. They claimed that they acted in the name of freedom to save Rome from a monarchy.

Marc Antony, Caesar's chief of staff, claimed the body and had it placed on a funeral pyre in the Forum. He gave an oration that stirred up the populace against Brutus and his accomplices, forcing them to flee the city. Caesar's will determined that his sole heir should be Gaius Octavius, better known as Octavian, his adopted son and grand-nephew. Only eighteen years of age, Octavian was completing his education in Apollonia in Illyricum. He hurried back to Rome, where he found that Antony had already appropriated Caesar's wealth. He had little choice at the time but to ally himself with Marc Antony and Marcus Aemilius Lepidus, another of Caesar's generals. First they purged their enemies, three hundred senators and two thousand *equites,* among whom was Marcus Tullius Cicero, Rome's most famous orator. They then made for Greece, where Brutus and Longinus had gathered an army. In 42 B.C., at the battle of Philippi, Caesar was avenged when the army of Brutus and Cassius collapsed.

For the next several years Octavian consolidated his power in Italy, while Marc Antony went to the east, where he allied with Cleopatra, the queen of Egypt. By 31 B.C., Octavian was ready to challenge Antony for the leadership of Rome. At Actium, off the west coast of Greece, the fleet of Octavian intercepted that of Antony and Cleopatra. Octavian won the battle, and, not wanting to be taken captive, Antony and Cleopatra committed suicide.

→

In statues such as this one, Augustus appears a model of physical perfection. But according to the historian Suetonius, "[Augustus's] teeth were small, few, and decayed. . . . Julius Marathus, Augustus's freedman and recorder, makes his height five feet seven inches, but this is an exaggeration, although, with body and limbs so beautifully proportioned one did not realize how small a man he was. . . . His body is said to have been marred by blemishes of various sorts — a constellation of seven birthmarks on his chest and stomach exactly corresponding in form, order, and number with the Great Bear; and a number of hard, dry patches suggesting ringworm, caused by an itching of his skin and a too frequent and vigorous use of the scraper at the Baths. He had a weakness in his left hip, thigh, and leg, which occasionally gave him the suspicion of a limp. . . ."

By 29 B.C., Octavian had removed all his enemies from the scene, leaving him in complete control. He was wise enough to keep the forms of the republic in place while ensuring that ultimate authority lay in his own hands. He announced to the Senate that he wanted to relinquish all the extraordinary powers he had assumed, and to return the government to the Senate and to the people of Rome. Flattered, the senators acclaimed him "Augustus" and gave him the title of *Princeps,* "First Citizen."

Augustus lived simply enough. Although small in stature and subject to a host of illnesses, he never doubted that he had a special destiny. His residence was in downtown Rome in an ordinary house, where he lived with his wife, Livia Drusilla, and daughter, Julia, who sewed clothes for the family with their own hands. Augustus knew that the Romans were tired of war and welcomed the peace his rule brought them. The Senate, over which he served as presiding officer, continued to add to his titles and never challenged the proposals he put before them. He reduced the size of the army from 60 to 28 legions, but established the Praetorian Guard to be an elite corps directly serving him. He embarked on a huge building program in Rome and financed public works all over the Mediterranean. Hoping to restore the ancient religious celebrations, Augustus supervised the construction of new temples, restored the old ones, and subsidized the priesthoods that served them. In A.D. 13, Augustus commissioned the Altar of Peace, a monument that exists to this day, to memorialize his accomplishments.

One reason for his interest in restoring old religious traditions was that Augustus was wary of the foreign mystery religions that had come into Rome from the East. Very different from Roman public worship, as those who joined them were sworn to secrecy, they could, he feared, become the nucleus for dissent against the government. Marked by purification rituals and devotion to particular gods or myths, they attracted initiates from all classes, who were promised blessings in the afterlife, and, in this life, a bond of fellowship with all who belonged. The most popular of the cults were those devoted to the Egyptian goddess Isis, and the Eleusinian mysteries, imported from Greece, which celebrated the return of Persephone to her mother, Demeter. Other mysteries involved rituals so licentious that Roman authorities put stringent controls on their practice. Such was the worship of Cybele, the Great Mother Goddess of Anatolia, and that of Dionysos of Greece, the Lord of Wine. Dionysian festivals were invitations to throw off all social restraint in an effort to reach an ecstatic state in which Dionysos himself was thought to enter participants. Most upper-class Romans looked upon such behavior as unseemly, to say the least, and Augustus hoped that the mystery religions would disappear if people returned to the traditional Roman gods and goddesses.

To strengthen family life, Augustus legislated against adultery, drew up new laws on marriage, and tried to limit the extravagant lifestyles of the rich. He centralized the state treasury for the more effective collection and dispersal of revenues, and established the monetary value of gold and silver. He governed Spain, Gaul, Dalmatia, Syria, and Egypt directly, appointing all the civilian and military officials stationed there. He was commander of all Roman armies wherever they were found and unilaterally made decisions on how they should be used in both peace and war.

PROVINCIAL ADMINISTRATION

Augustus closely integrated the two Spanish provinces, Nearer Spain and Further Spain, under Roman administration. At the time of Jesus, the Spaniards were well on their way to assimilating Roman culture. From the time of Julius Caesar, Rome sent out colonies of veterans to farm the country's public lands, and a migration of civilians poured into the cities. Twenty-three colonies set down roots in Spain in the following century, as Spain's strategic position, its great mineral wealth, and its fertile lands attracted thousands of Italian settlers. Excellent roads facilitated communication and transportation between cities and served the unstated purpose of making rebellions less probable. Within the towns, Roman builders erected temples, theaters, amphitheaters, baths, and administrative centers. Spain, they decided, was to look like another Italy, with Roman-style cities dotting the countryside. During Jesus' lifetime, its two provinces were among the wealthiest of all Roman lands.

Roman deities absorbed the local gods and goddesses in Spain or were identified with them. Temples were built to the divine Augustus; the one at Augusta Emerita, modern Mérida, still stands as a monument to the imperial cult. On Augustus's birthday and on the anniversaries of his accession and victories, huge amounts of money were spent to provide gladiatorial games, chariot races, and public banquets. During these days of celebration, the priests and priestesses, *flamines* and *flaminicae,* chosen by the city councils, carried statues of Augustus in processions that ended in the amphitheaters where the games would take place.

In the towns, a Hispano-Roman elite of landowners formed local assemblies, led by two city magistrates known as *duovirs.* Reporting to them were two deputies and treasurers and their staffs. These assemblies collected the taxes that sustained Roman revenues. Society mirrored that of Rome itself, consisting of rich landowners, a middle class of army officers, professionals, merchants, a large number of peasant farmers, and, at the very bottom, the slaves who worked in the mines. The mines exported silver, copper, and lead, and made their owners immensely wealthy. As in Rome, poorer people sought patrons to aid them with financial and legal problems.

In 19 B.C., Augustus traveled to Greece, where he found that the Athenians still jealously guarded their democratic form of government. He therefore chose to make his residence on the nearby island of Aegina, much to the chagrin of the Athenians. Nevertheless, Augustus confirmed Athens' privileges as a free city, exempt from Roman taxation. Wealthy landowners dominated the local legislature, the Council of Six Hundred, and only a small number of its members were consistently elected to the offices of the state. Many of these belonged to the Gephyraei, a religious society made up of the old aristocracy that claimed descent from ancient families. Augustus tried to strengthen the authority of this elite, for he feared the Athenian lower classes. His fears were confirmed when, in A.D. 13, those at the bottom of the social ladder revolted against the monopoly the landowning families held in the government. In addition to his involvement with Athens, Augustus also sent out colonists to Greece: one group to Nicopolis, the other to Patrae.

THE IMPERIAL FAMILY

Augustus was necessarily concerned with finding an heir to his throne, but in this area of his life he was met with continuous disappointment. He was sincerely devoted to Livia Drusilla and to his daughter, Julia, whose mother was Augustus's first wife, Scribonia. It was also Livia's second marriage, and she brought with her two sons from the first, Drusus and Tiberius. Augustus chose one of his nephews to be Julia's first husband, but the young man died prematurely. He then committed her to his deputy and friend, Marcus Agrippa, twenty years her senior. Agrippa and Julia had four children, and Augustus adopted the two boys, Gaius and Lucius, as his own, moving them into his house and personally teaching them to read and write. Without doubt, he intended that they should be his heirs.

Livia Drusilla, Augustus's wife, was officially deified by her grandson, the Emperor Claudius. She was the first woman in Roman history to be so honored.

The attention that Augustus lavished on his grandchildren was not at all to the liking of Tiberius, who, until then, had been Augustus's favorite. In 11 B.C., Tiberius had agreed to divorce his first wife on Augustus's orders, to marry Julia after the death of Agrippa. Unknown to Augustus, though, Julia had made a career of infidelities while Tiberius was absent from Rome. On Augustus's orders he had also spent long years fighting on Rome's borders in difficult campaigns, and now it was evident that he was to be passed over. In 6 B.C., he sailed off to Rhodes in self-imposed exile to show his resentment. He did not ask Augustus for permission, and he did not take Julia with him. While Tiberius was spending his days looking out to sea in boredom, Jesus was born.

Augustus's grandson, Gaius, became, without doubt, his pride. In

Augustus ordered this account of his reign, known today as the "Deeds of the Divine Augustus," to be inscribed on bronze pillars outside his tomb.

IN MY TWENTIETH YEAR, ACTING ON MY OWN INITIATIVE AND AT MY OWN CHARGES, I RAISED AN ARMY WHEREWITH I BROUGHT AGAIN LIBERTY TO THE REPUBLIC OPPRESSED BY THE DOMINANCE OF A FACTION. THEREFORE DID THE SENATE ADMIT ME TO ITS OWN ORDER BY HONORARY DECREES, IN THE CONSULSHIP OF GAIUS PANSA AND AULUS HIRTIUS. AT THE SAME TIME THEY GAVE UNTO ME RANK AMONG THE CONSULARS IN THE EXPRESSING OF MY OPINION; AND THEY GAVE UNTO ME THE IMPERIUM. IT ALSO VOTED THAT I, AS PROPRAETOR, TOGETHER WITH THE CONSULS, SHOULD "SEE TO IT THAT THE STATE SUFFERED NO HARM." IN THE SAME YEAR, TOO, WHEN BOTH CONSULS HAD FALLEN IN BATTLE, THE PEOPLE MADE ME CONSUL AND TRIUMVIR FOR THE RE-ESTABLISHING OF THE REPUBLIC. :: THE MEN WHO KILLED MY FATHER I DROVE INTO EXILE BY STRICTLY JUDICIAL PROCESS, AND THEN, WHEN THEY TOOK UP ARMS AGAINST THE REPUBLIC, TWICE I OVERCAME THEM IN BATTLE. :: I UNDERTOOK CIVIL AND FOREIGN WARS BOTH BY LAND AND BY SEA; AS VICTOR THEREIN I SHOWED MERCY TO ALL SURVIVING CITIZENS. FOREIGN NATIONS, THAT I COULD SAFELY PARDON, I PREFERRED TO SPARE RATHER THAN TO DESTROY. ABOUT 500,000 ROMAN CITIZENS TOOK THE MILITARY OATH OF ALLEGIANCE TO ME. RATHER OVER 300,000 OF THESE HAVE I SETTLED IN COLONIES, OR SENT BACK TO THEIR HOME TOWNS WHEN THEIR TERM OF SERVICE RAN OUT; AND TO ALL OF THESE I HAVE GIVEN LANDS BOUGHT BY ME, OR THE MONEY FOR FARMS — AND THIS OUT OF MY PRIVATE MEANS. I HAVE TAKEN 600 SHIPS, BESIDES THOSE SMALLER THAN TRIREMES. :: TWICE HAVE I HAD THE LESSER TRIUMPH; THRICE THE CURULE TRIUMPH; TWENTY-ONE TIMES HAVE I BEEN SALUTED AS "IMPERATOR." AFTER THAT, WHEN THE SENATE VOTED ME MANY TRIUMPHS, I DECLINED THEM.

2 B.C., when Jesus was still an infant, Augustus gave him a command on the Danube frontier, starting his career with a military command that would provide him entrance to high political office. A year later Augustus sent him on a mission to negotiate a settlement with the Parthians over the kingship of Armenia. Having successfully completed this task, Gaius journeyed through the eastern Mediterranean lands, but, returning to Antioch, suddenly took ill and died. In the meantime, his brother, Lucius, had drowned in the sea off the coast of Gaul.

These tragedies forced Augustus to look once again to Tiberius and to reluctantly permit his return to Rome. Augustus adopted him as his son, and the Senate voted him the titles that he required to take up his duties as presumed heir. For the next few years, Tiberius was again busy on Rome's borders, leading the legions against the Germans who constantly threatened the Rhine and Danube frontiers.

The Augustan Age was one that produced many notable authors: Livy, the historian; Virgil, the poet; and his contemporaries, Horace and Ovid. While Virgil was a friend and admirer, Augustus had little use for Ovid, whose lyrics praised the very opposite of Augustus's plans for a more moral society. In A.D. 8, Augustus banished Ovid to Tomis, a city on the Black Sea, where he lived out the rest of his life.

In the summer of A.D. 14, when Jesus was in his late teens, Augustus reached seventy-five years of age. He was tired; the years weighed heavily on him, so he virtually shut himself off from public life. In the spring of that year, he had deposited his will in the temple of the vestal virgins. During a stay at one of the imperial villas, he became ill and left for the island of Capri, then crossed over to the mainland and on August 19, in Nola, a city near Mt. Vesuvius, he died. Livia waited to see if the Praetorian Guard would support Tiberius before announcing her husband's death. When she learned that it would, the people of Rome were given the news. Within the month, the Senate declared Augustus a god, ordered Agrippa Postumus, a grandson, killed, and recognized Tiberius's succession to the principate.

Throughout the Roman world, the announcement of the emperor's death could hardly be believed. Most of the people alive had known no other ruler. None of the Gospel writers tells us how the people in

Nazareth reacted to the news, but it must surely have been a topic of conversation at the dinner table of the family of Mary and Joseph.

Augustus began the Roman Empire in fact, if not in name. His administrative skills put it on such a firm foundation that it would survive all challenges for centuries to come. He established the *Pax Romana,* which knit the Mediterranean into a whole, allowing the early Christian Church the best conditions possible for the spread of the new faith. Without the prosperity and peace that Augustus bequeathed to the Mediterranean world, the first Christian missionaries, especially St. Paul, would have found their task infinitely more difficult.

TIBERIUS CAESAR

Tiberius began his rule on a moderate note. He decided that Rome's borders were large enough that the army should be used only for defense. He appointed honest officials to important posts and cut government spending. He ordered an end to the gladiatorial contests. When the Senate wanted to honor him by giving his name to a month of the year, he declined; thus today we have September rather than Tiberius. After ten years in office, however, Tiberius's temperament turned sour. Perhaps this change occurred due to the death of Drusus, one of his sons. Or perhaps it was because of the influence of Sejanus, the head of the Praetorian Guard, who may well have had something to do with the death of Drusus. Tiberius continued to listen to his stories of plots to overthrow him without investigating their validity. Since it made no provision for public prosecutors, Roman law encouraged private accusations against a person for the commission of a crime. Known as *delatio,* the process was constantly being abused, for the delator was rewarded with part of the fine paid to the state upon a conviction. Sejanus and his accomplices used *delatio* to amass huge fortunes from false accusations.

Believing himself surrounded by enemies, Tiberius abandoned Rome and secluded himself on the island of Capri. He had developed a skin ailment, which apparently was sufficiently disfiguring that he was embarrassed to appear in public and spent much of his time brooding over his

affliction. He commissioned several new villas on Capri, well endowed with prisons and dungeons for suspected conspirators. The emperor lived in these homes surrounded by entertainers, poets, and musicians to keep him amused. At Passover in A.D. 30, Jesus' execution passed as just one more day in the constricted life of Tiberius Caesar.

Jesus' lifetime spanned the years of Augustus and Tiberius Caesar, but it is doubtful that either of them ever learned of his existence. Events in Galilee and Judea were not immediate concerns of Rome's two leaders. Furthermore, the values that he espoused were far removed from those held dear by the ruling classes of Rome. For them, the accumulation of

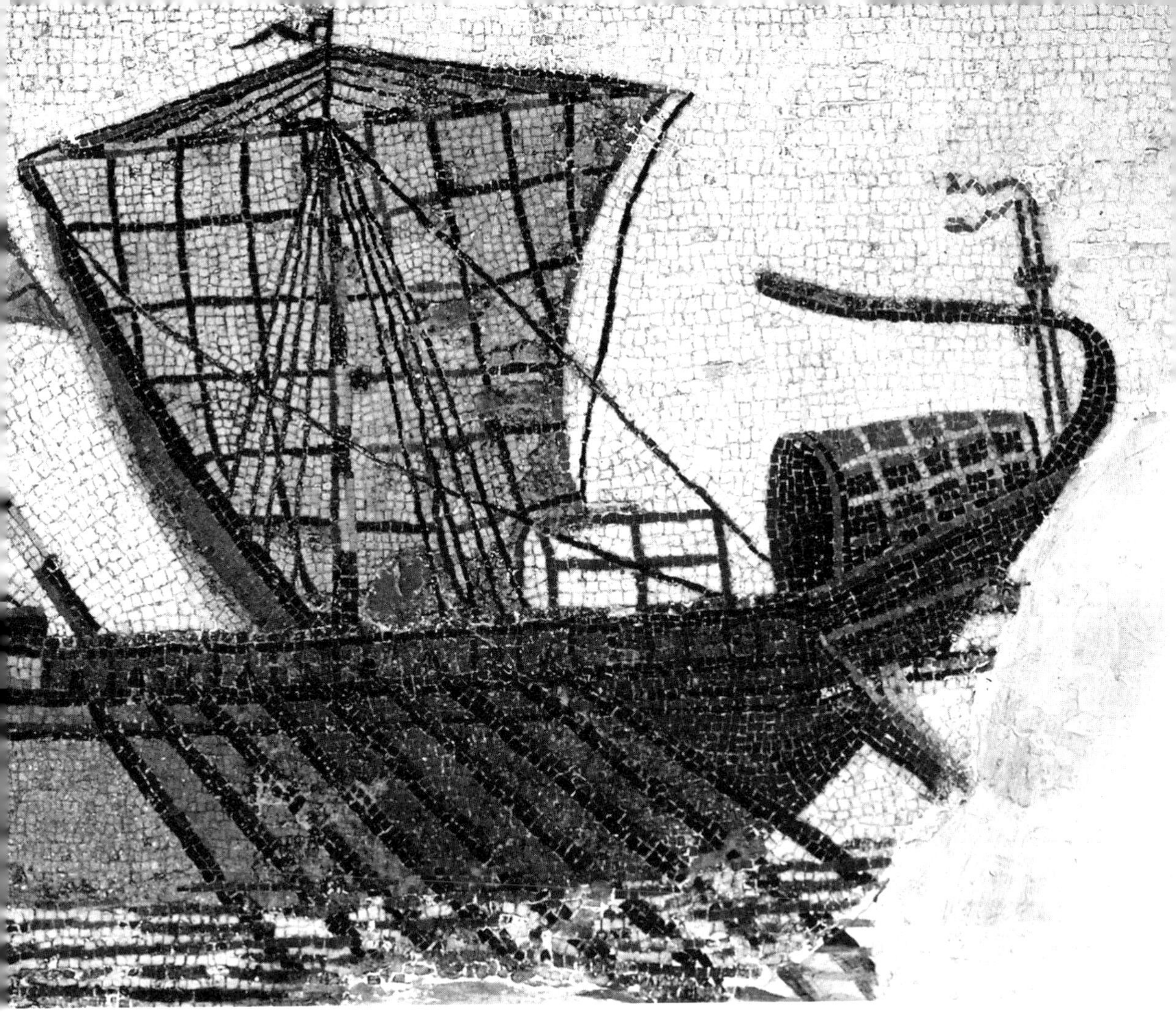

Roman merchants in Jesus' day traveled in nine-oared sailboats like the one depicted on this mosaic. The bow has a decorative metallic spur in the form of a dolphin; the eye painted on the side was intended to bring good fortune.

wealth, military fame, and political power were all-important; the poor were useful at best and dangerous at worst. The Roman leaders had little regard for human life, as the gladiatorial games aptly demonstrate. How different was Jesus' teaching to live simply, to practice kindness, to show compassion for those who suffered, to work for peace, and to ask the Father for just enough bread to get through the day!

It is possible to find echoes of Jesus' teachings in Roman Stoicism; it did, after all, call for ethical living and the development of moral sensitivity. But though the Stoics did not believe that wealth was essential for human happiness, none of them ever described the poor as blessed. Furthermore, they would have found Jesus' death as a criminal extremely difficult to understand; it was not something of which a Roman would approve.

Jesus obviously came into contact with the power of Rome every time he went to Jerusalem for the Jewish holy days, for its soldiers constantly patrolled the streets of the city. The Gospels tell us that he once healed the son of a Roman centurion; it would be fascinating to know how the two men spoke to one another. Was it in Latin? It would have been extremely unlikely that a Roman officer would have learned Aramaic. Did the centurion come to believe the message of Jesus? Did they keep in touch after the boy was healed? We cannot know the answers to these questions; all we know for certain is that Roman rule certainly affected the destiny of Jesus. For though he stood apart from Roman concerns, content to "render unto Caesar that which is Caesar's," and intent on preaching his message of the coming of the kingdom of God, he died by crucifixion because of the powers delegated by Rome to the prefect of Judea.

When the Senate wanted to honor the new emperor by giving his name to a month of the year, he declined; thus today we have September rather than Tiberius.

Chapter Two

North Africa and Egypt

At the time of Jesus, North Africa and Egypt were part of the Roman Empire, home to the richest cities of the Mediterranean region. Together they also had the largest populations anywhere in the Roman world: over seven million in Egypt and close to five million in North Africa. Both were very important to the city of Rome, because the grain that fed the populace of the city was grown in the rural areas of the two regions.

North Africa consists of a long, narrow strip of land along the southern coast of the Mediterranean Sea. The shoreline is rugged and difficult, and deep harbors are few. The Atlas Mountains, a coastal chain, rise about 40 miles inland, splitting the area into many diverse sections, a succession of small pockets of level land nestled within the highlands. Between sixty and three hundred miles inland the great Sahara Desert begins, the most arid region in the world — a vast empty land of sand and rocky, arid soil. Today as two thousand years ago, rainfall is the key to life in coastal North Africa: it is generally abundant near the sea, but unreliable at best farther inland.

THE BERBERS

The native people of North Africa were the Berbers; anthropologists believe them to be indigenous to the region. They were divided in the ancient world, as they are today, into hundreds of small bands held together by kinship and a common nomadic or seminomadic economy. Until recent times, Berber was not a written language, so what is known of their history has been told by others.

As late as five thousand years ago, rains still reached the Sahara, making it a vast grassland where large animals and their human hunters lived. The ancestors of the Berbers left remarkable petroglyphs on the walls of canyons in southern Algeria depicting a way of life that progressed from hunting to herding as cattle were first imported from Egypt. The dromedary, the one-humped camel often associated with the desert, was unknown in Berber culture until Roman times.

CARTHAGE

As early as 1000 B.C., immigrants from Phoenicia put down settlements on the North African coast in order to enhance their trading network, which extended the length of the Mediterranean Sea. Utica was the first of these, but around 810 B.C., colonists from Tyre on the Lebanese coast established themselves at Carthage. The excellence of the site, with its deep harbor, attracted more and more settlers, making it the largest city of the western Mediterranean, its citizens defended by a huge wall that encircled the city. New settlers were welcomed so long as they did not emigrate from Greece, for the Carthaginians rightly regarded the Greeks as competitors. In a great sixth-century naval battle between the two peoples, the Carthaginians emerged victorious, allowing them to control the sea as far as Gibraltar and beyond. It was now the Carthaginians' turn to establish colonies on the Balearic Islands, Sicily, and Corsica. Expansion was necessary, for the city's population was approaching two hundred fifty thousand people by the fourth century.

A Carthaginian merchant oligarchy, which elected the town magistrates, emphasized the development of commerce. Unlike the Romans, Carthaginian businessmen who dictated policy had little interest in building a land empire, but preferred to put all their energy into economic development and into providing a citizen navy to protect it. The political elite were quite content to let Berber farmers grow the food that sustained the city population, and to enlist young Berber men in the army to serve under an officer corps of Carthaginians.

FURTHER FACTS

The name Hannibal means "favored by Baal."

The Carthaginians continue to worship the Phoenician gods of their forbears: Baal Hammon, Tamit, and Melqart. The latter was a god who died, was cremated, and then rose again. Offerings of infant sacrifices to Baal Hammon were considered a necessary component of Carthaginian worship.

In the third century B.C., Carthage found itself challenged by the growing power of Rome. Before that time there had been cooperation between the two, for Rome was then exclusively a land power. In 264 B.C., however, as mentioned in Chapter 1, Rome took one side and Carthage the other in a dispute between two Sicilian cities. This dispute escalated into the first of the Punic Wars. The Romans for the first time built a navy, cut off supplies to Carthage's forces in Sicily, and ultimately proved victorious. Carthage sought to regroup in the following decades by expanding into Spain, bringing on a second Punic War. Hannibal, the North African city's most able general, recruited an army in Spain that included an elephant corps, and marched over the Alps into Italy. He won a series of victories over incompetent Roman generals sent out to challenge him, but never felt he had the resources to attack Rome directly. Recalled to Africa because of a Roman army making its way toward Carthage, in 202 B.C., Hannibal's forces collapsed at the battle of Zama.

Carthage's potential to rebuild brought on the third and last Punic War. Again Carthage was beaten. This time the Romans completely destroyed the city, laying it waste for more than a century. Its territory became a Roman province called Proconsular Africa, with a governor sitting in Utica. His authority extended over all the former Carthaginian lands in the region of Numidia in northwest Africa. During the third Punic War, about half the Numidian towns, Cirta (now Constantine

Ruins of a Roman amphitheater in Tunisia.

in Algeria) among them, had allied with Rome, and the Senate rewarded these cities for their loyalty. A Numidian kingdom came into existence as a Roman client state, but after it made a serious attempt at breaking its dependence on Rome, the Senate reduced it to a Roman province. Vestiges of Carthaginian culture survived up to the time of Jesus among the Berber population that had come under the sway of Carthage.

ROMAN NORTH AFRICA

The excellent port around which Carthage was built (today the site is just outside modern Tunis) caused Julius Caesar to order the city to be rebuilt in 44 B.C. as a Roman settlement. Caesar was assassinated before the first emigrants left Italy, but in that year Carthage received its first contingent of Romans. Later, Augustus transported three thousand veterans of the army to Proconsular Africa and offered the Carthaginians the right to choose their own magistrates and coin their own money. During the time of Jesus, Carthage was second only to Alexandria in Egypt as the most important city in North Africa, but it was a city where there was a great gulf between the Latins and the natives.

Generous grants were given to Roman immigrant families — normally 125 acres of land to each farmer. Usually a family could effectively tend no more than fifteen, which meant that the other 110 acres could be rented out to native Berbers, making it very attractive to land-hungry Italians to move to Africa. Within several generations much of the farmland passed into the estates of wealthy senators and equestrians. Overseers hired natives or used slaves to produce crops and tend cattle for absentee landlords. Roman Africa had little industry.

With the lands of Carthage under their authority, Roman legionaries began expanding southward with the goal of bringing the Berber peoples living there under control. Initially it was extremely difficult to turn nomads into settled farmers growing grain. Forts had to be built on the perimeters and roads constructed to ensure the Roman presence. As the legions advanced, more land became open for Roman settlement. This colonization went rather smoothly, for the Berbers proved too disunited to put up any sustained resistance. One Roman commenting on the natives complained thus: "Their way of life is primitive, and they lack comforts."

Only one legion needed to be stationed in Africa because of the relative peace that prevailed. Its main duty was to maintain domestic order, and there was only one major exception. During the lifetime of Jesus, from A.D. 17 to 24 one Berber nation, the Musulami, under their chieftain Tacfarinas, fought the Romans because Tiberius had refused to let his people settle within Roman Africa.

The Cyrenaeans must also have shared with the Athenians a love of wisdom, for, according to Plutarch, they requested that Plato be the one to draw up a constitution for their city.

In Africa and Numidia, the Romans did not mix with the natives. A man could legally marry only a woman who was also a citizen or someone from a town that had the right of intermarriage with Romans. Therefore Roman administrators and merchants married the daughters of other civil servants and businessmen and lived in their own parts of town. Nevertheless, a Berber middle class formed and sought to imitate Roman ways, even if it was excluded from Roman society. Its members constructed towns that probably used the same Roman architects and engineers, and the wealthier among them developed a lifestyle that mirrored that of the Latins. North African people therefore had their public baths, central heating, and wine shops just as the Romans did.

The larger North African cities at the time of Jesus were well known for their prosperity. Great gates welcomed visitors into the towns. All had one or more forums, a senate chamber where the city *curia* met, a basilica for legal matters, temples, theaters, amphitheaters, and baths. Augustus himself financed the building of a large theater in Carthage. Towns were full of statues of the emperors and local politicians who had made donations to the citizenry. The Romans forbade human sacrifice, but allowed the worship of Baal Hammon to continue without them, for they identified him with their god Saturn.

The biblical story of Jesus' crucifixion, which mentions Simon of Cyrene.

Source: Matthew 27:32-37 (RSV)

AS THEY WERE MARCHING OUT, THEY CAME UPON A MAN OF CYRENE, SIMON BY NAME; THIS MAN THEY COMPELLED TO CARRY [JESUS'] CROSS. AND WHEN THEY CAME TO A PLACE CALLED GOLGOTHA (WHICH MEANS THE PLACE OF A SKULL), THEY OFFERED HIM WINE TO DRINK, MINGLED WITH GALL; BUT WHEN HE TASTED IT, HE WOULD NOT DRINK IT. AND WHEN THEY HAD CRUCIFIED HIM, THEY DIVIDED HIS GARMENTS AMONG THEM BY CASTING LOTS; THEN THEY SAT DOWN AND KEPT WATCH OVER HIM THERE. AND OVER HIS HEAD THEY PUT THE CHARGE AGAINST HIM, WHICH READ, "THIS IS JESUS THE KING OF THE JEWS."

The Holy Family's flight into Egypt

Source: Matthew 2:13-23 (RSV)

NOW WHEN THEY HAD DEPARTED, BEHOLD, AN ANGEL OF THE LORD APPEARED TO JOSEPH IN A DREAM AND SAID, "RISE, TAKE THE CHILD AND HIS MOTHER, AND FLEE TO EGYPT, AND REMAIN THERE TILL I TELL YOU; FOR HEROD IS ABOUT TO SEARCH FOR THE CHILD, TO DESTROY HIM." AND HE ROSE AND TOOK THE CHILD AND HIS MOTHER BY NIGHT, AND DEPARTED TO EGYPT, AND REMAINED THERE UNTIL THE DEATH OF HEROD. THIS WAS TO FULFILL WHAT THE LORD HAD SPOKEN BY THE PROPHET, "OUT OF EGYPT HAVE I CALLED MY SON." :: THEN HEROD, WHEN HE SAW THAT HE HAD BEEN TRICKED BY THE WISE MEN, WAS IN A FURIOUS RAGE, AND HE SENT AND KILLED ALL THE MALE CHILDREN IN BETHLEHEM AND IN ALL THAT REGION WHO WERE TWO YEARS OLD OR UNDER, ACCORDING TO THE TIME WHICH HE HAD ASCERTAINED FROM THE WISE MEN. THEN WAS FULFILLED WHAT WAS SPOKEN BY THE PROPHET JEREMIAH.

> "A VOICE WAS HEARD IN RAMAH,
> WAILING AND LOUD LAMENTATION,
> RACHEL WEEPING FOR HER CHILDREN;
> SHE REFUSED TO BE CONSOLED,
> BECAUSE THEY WERE NO MORE."

BUT WHEN HEROD DIED, BEHOLD, AN ANGEL OF THE LORD APPEARED IN A DREAM TO JOSEPH IN EGYPT, SAYING, "RISE, TAKE THE CHILD AND HIS MOTHER, AND GO TO THE LAND OF ISRAEL, FOR THOSE WHO SOUGHT THE CHILD'S LIFE ARE DEAD." AND HE ROSE AND TOOK THE CHILD AND HIS MOTHER, AND WENT TO THE LAND OF ISRAEL. BUT WHEN HE HEARD THAT ARCHELAUS REIGNED OVER JUDEA IN PLACE OF HIS FATHER HEROD, HE WAS AFRAID TO GO THERE, AND BEING WARNED IN A DREAM HE WITHDREW TO THE DISTRICT OF GALILEE. AND HE WENT AND DWELT IN A CITY CALLED NAZARETH, THAT WHAT WAS SPOKEN BY THE PROPHET MIGHT BE FULFILLED, "HE SHALL BE CALLED A NAZARENE."

MAURITANIA AND CYRENAICA

The situation of Mauritania — modern Morocco — differed from that of Proconsular Africa. The ubiquitous Roman army had of course conquered it, but allowed a Mauritanian client king, Bocchus, to continue to govern his nation. In Jesus' lifetime Bocchus's son, Juba II, occupied the Mauritanian throne. He ruled from 25 B.C. to A.D. 23 from his capital of Tingis, known today as Tangier. Juba's wife, Cleopatra, was of noble ancestry, a surviving daughter of Marc Antony and Cleopatra VII, the Egyptian queen. The king himself was a man of letters, collecting books in Latin, Greek, and Syriac, and proving himself a great admirer of Rome.

To the east of Proconsular Africa, in what is now Libya, lay Cyrenaica. Because it was isolated geographically from the great centers of civilization, we know nothing of its history before the seventh century B.C., when Greeks on the island of Thera dispatched a colony to settle on its coast. Here the colonists built the city of Cyrene. The local Berbers were pleased to exchange the products of the desert with the newly arrived Greeks. Prosperity came to the city because of trade with Crete and Egypt, and much of its wealth went into the construction of a huge temple to Zeus, begun about 520 B.C. The temple was so large that visitors compared it to the Parthenon of Athens. The Cyrenaeans must also have shared with the Athenians a love of wisdom, for, according to Plutarch, they requested that Plato be the one to draw up a constitution for their city.

During the Hellenistic period, the Ptolemies of Egypt claimed sovereignty over Cyrene and the four other nearby cities that comprised the Pentapolis, and Egyptian garrisons were stationed there to ensure compliance with their rule. Subsequently, in 96 B.C., Ptolemy Apion in his will transferred Cyrenaica to Rome. The Senate voted to accept the gift and promised the Pentapolis cities local self-government. But in 63 B.C., Rome assumed direct control, making the region a province, and Roman troops arrived to guard the frontier. Twice during Jesus' lifetime Roman generals were deployed into the desert to check the raids of native peoples. In A.D. 14, Leptis Magna, once a Phoenician city, was one of the

→

This mosaic offers one of the few surviving images of the Pharos. According to legend the huge mirrors in the lighthouse could be used as weapons to concentrate the sun and set enemy ships ablaze as they approached. Another tale purports that they were large enough and set at such an angle that activity in the city of Constantinople, hundreds of miles away, could be monitored from Alexandria. Neither story is plausible, but both illustrate the magnificence of the lighthouse.

The author of the Gospel of John was clearly influenced by the work of Philo of Alexandria, as these sample passages suggest.

Sources: John 1:1-5, 9-13 (RSV); Philo, Who Is the Heir of Divine Things? *42 (205-6).*

"IN THE BEGINNING WAS THE WORD, AND THE WORD WAS WITH GOD, AND THE WORD WAS GOD. HE WAS IN THE BEGINNING WITH GOD; ALL THINGS WERE MADE THROUGH HIM, AND WITHOUT HIM WAS NOT ANYTHING MADE THAT WAS MADE. IN HIM WAS LIFE, AND THE LIFE WAS THE LIGHT OF MEN. THE LIGHT SHINES IN THE DARKNESS, AND THE DARK HAS NOT OVERCOME IT. . . . THE TRUE LIGHT THAT ENLIGHTENS EVERY MAN WAS COMING INTO THE WORLD. HE WAS IN THE WORLD, AND THE WORLD WAS MADE THROUGH HIM, YET THE WORLD KNEW HIM NOT. HE CAME TO HIS OWN HOME, AND HIS OWN PEOPLE RECEIVED HIM NOT. BUT TO ALL WHO RECEIVED HIM, WHO BELIEVED IN HIS NAME, HE GAVE POWER TO BECOME CHILDREN OF GOD; WHO WERE BORN, NOT OF BLOOD NOR OF THE WILL OF THE FLESH NOR OF THE WILL OF MAN, BUT OF GOD."

"TO HIS WORD, HIS CHIEF MESSENGER, HIGHEST IN AGE AND HONOR, THE FATHER OF ALL HAS GIVEN THE SPECIAL PREROGATIVE, TO STAND ON THE BORDER AND SEPARATE THE CREATURE FROM THE CREATOR. THIS SAME WORD BOTH PLEADS WITH THE IMMORTAL AS SUPPLICANT FOR AFFLICTED MORTALITY AND ACTS AS AMBASSADOR OF THE RULER TO THE SUBJECT. THE WORD REJOICES IN THE GIFT AND, EXULTING IN IT, ANNOUNCES IT AND BOASTS OF IT, SAYING, "AND I STOOD IN THE MIDST, BETWEEN THE LORD AND YOU" (NUMBERS 16:48); NEITHER BEING UNCREATED LIKE GOD, NOR CREATED LIKE YOU, BUT BEING IN THE MIDST, BETWEEN THESE TWO EXTREMITIES, LIKE A HOSTAGE, AS IT WERE, TO BOTH PARTIES: A HOSTAGE TO THE CREATOR, AS A PLEDGE AND SECURITY THAT THE WHOLE RACE WOULD NEVER FLY OFF AND REVOLT ENTIRELY, CHOOSING DISORDER RATHER THAN ORDER; AND TO THE CREATURE, TO LEAD IT TO ENTERTAIN A CONFIDENT HOPE THAT THE MERCIFUL GOD WOULD NOT OVERLOOK HIS OWN WORK. . . ."

most flourishing towns of North Africa, thanks to the favors it received from the Emperor Augustus.

Large numbers of Jews settled in the Cyrenaican cities, most of them spilling over from Egypt. Others were frontier guards receiving farmland in return for military service. Simon, a Jew from Cyrene, appears in the New Testament as the man drafted by the Romans to carry Jesus' cross.

ANCIENT EGYPT

Readers of the Old and New Testaments will certainly know at least a few details about ancient Egypt. Matthew's Gospel tells of the Holy Family's flight there to escape the wrath of Herod the Great. Just as their ancestors, the ancient Israelites, sought refuge from famine in Egypt, and then were led by Moses back to their homeland, so Jesus' family stayed for a time in Egypt. New Testament writers made the parallel: Jesus was both the new Israel and the new Moses.

By the time of Jesus' birth, the Egypt of the pharaohs was long gone. The great pyramids of Giza were already over two thousand years old, and even the knowledge of how to build a pyramid was lost, for Egypt in the first century, like the rest of North Africa, had become part of the Roman world.

↗

From her image on coins such as this one, dating from about 40 B.C., it is hard to explain the spell Cleopatra seemed to cast over Julius Caesar and Mark Antony.

The geography of Egypt, of course, remained the same. The great Nile River still flooded each year, laying down a rich layer of silt in its valley, which enabled the country's farmers to reap harvests unknown in any other part of the Roman Empire. Human settlement was found in the three areas of the country that could be cultivated: upper Egypt, extending from just below the first cataract to Memphis; lower Egypt, the delta region; and the Fayum, a depression to the west of the river that received water from one of the channels connected to the Nile. To the east and west of the Nile, with the exception of a few oases, all was desert, the home of a few nomadic peoples.

At the time of Jesus' birth, Egypt was a country of three cultures and three peoples. The most numerous were the native Egyptians, the indigenous inhabitants of the land; then the Greeks, who were the elite of the country; and the Romans, who now provided the civil administrators and soldiers to govern and secure it. Relatively few Italians wanted to make their home in Egypt, so the Greeks actually set the tone for the cultural life of the country.

The Ptolemies, though Greeks, practiced brother-sister marriage in imitation of several ancient pharaohs.

The Greek presence in Egypt began in classical times, when a colony was settled at Naukratis, but it was conquest by Alexander the Great that set the stage for Egyptian culture in the first century. In 332 B.C., his war against the Persians brought him to Egypt. The native Egyptians welcomed him, for the Persians, who had occupied their country for several decades, were difficult taskmasters.

Alexander planned to ensure the Greek presence by constructing a great city on the Mediterranean that would bear his name. After choosing the site on one of the delta channels and outlining its dimensions, he left Egypt never to return. A Greek architect planned the city on a rectangular grid, with major streets crossing at right angles, unlike any other city in Egypt. There were five quarters, each named after a letter of the Greek alphabet.

HELLENISTIC EGYPT

Upon Alexander's death, his general Ptolemy brought his corpse back to Alexandria for burial there. This gave Ptolemy the right to claim the succession, but other generals claimed their own portions of Alexander's empire, and the Ptolemies had to content themselves with Egypt and neighboring countries. In 305 B.C., Ptolemy added *Sōtēr* (Savior) to his name and announced the beginning of his own, independent rule. He began a dynasty that lasted until the coming of the Romans and Egypt's annexation, just thirty years before the birth of Jesus. The dynasty was somewhat unusual in that the Ptolemies, though Greeks, practiced brother-sister marriage in imitation of some of the ancient pharaohs. Only the very last Ptolemy, Queen Cleopatra VII, bothered to learn the Egyptian language.

Ptolemaic Egypt became the wealthiest of the Hellenistic kingdoms that inherited the legacy of Alexander. Alexandria soon dominated the commerce of the eastern Mediterranean, growing to an estimated five hundred thousand people. For six centuries it was a commercial and cultural center, enduring long after Rome itself had gone into a slump. Other new cities appeared in the delta, and old ones expanded. The country's resources allowed its rulers to initiate an immense building program. The palace complex, known as the Brucheion, filled one-third of the area inside the city's walls. Around and within it were majestic gardens, fountains, baths, administrative buildings, and the living quarters of the royal family. Inside the city, the Ptolemies built gymnasiums, theaters, amphitheaters, and temples dedicated to both Egyptian and Greek gods and goddesses. The largest of the temples was the Serapion, dedicated to Serapis, who combined features of both Egyptian and Greek divinities. One column of the Serapion still stands in modern Alexandria, where it is known as Pompey's Pillar.

At the juncture of Alexandria's two harbors, the Ptolemies built a lighthouse called the Pharos, which is now known as one of the Seven Wonders of the Ancient World. Mariners far out at sea could sight the city because of the light it gave. On its top floor at night burned a constant fire whose light, with the aid of mirrors, was reflected for miles out into the Mediterranean.

The Ptolemies also wanted Alexandria to be the center of intellectual life in the eastern Mediterranean and to replace Athens as the center of Greek thought. This was the reason for Ptolemy I's decision to build the Museon, which has given its name to collections of antiquities and art ever since. Scholars, scientists, and doctors from all over the Greek world descended on Alexandria, lured by generous fellowships and free room and board.

Ptolemy's son and successor, Ptolemy II Philadelphos, not to be outdone by his father, financed the construction of Alexandria's great library. His ambition was to have a copy of every book in the world in Greek translation; the library eventually held over five hundred thousand scrolls. The Serapion also was home to a library, but it was a smaller collection. Thanks to Ptolemy II, Jewish translators were put to work rendering the Hebrew Scriptures into Greek, a translation known as the Septuagint. It was this translation that the Gospel writers used, rather than the original texts, when referring to the Hebrew Scriptures.

Unfortunately, just before Jesus' birth, a fire set during the war between Julius Caesar and Pompey destroyed much of the great library's contents. However, Marc Antony made up for the loss by seizing about two hundred thousand scrolls from the library at Pergamum and transferring them to Alexandria as a gift to Queen Cleopatra. This collection survived until about A.D. 270, when another fire destroyed it completely.

All of these buildings were extant at the time of Jesus, and certainly the magnificence of Alexandria was a topic of conversation for Jesus, Mary, and Joseph. Alexandria was the largest city near their home, and it was likely they would have had relatives or friends living there.

JEWS IN EGYPT

Beginning in the second century B.C., a large number of Jews began to emigrate to Alexandria, so that by the first century Jews occupied one whole quarter and much of a second. This community maintained ties to its homeland, sending a half-shekel per household for the upkeep of the Temple, and traveling regularly back and forth on the relatively easy journey to Jerusalem.

The Jews of Ptolemaic and later Roman Egypt had their own internal organization. Elders of the community administered justice according to Jewish law and custom. They provided welfare to needy members and supervised cemeteries. Their synagogues were centers of social as well as religious life; rabbis offered religious services on the Sabbath and conducted the festivals that were a part of worship. Roman law exempted Jews from the adoration of the Hellenistic deities or of the deified emperors, from serving in city magistracies, and from appearing in court on the Sabbath. Greek Alexandrians resented the privileges the Jews enjoyed and often stirred up riots against them; the majority of the populace had no understanding of how a people and a religion could become so identified.

The outstanding Jewish scholar of Alexandria was Philo, a contemporary of Jesus, who lived from about 13 B.C. to A.D. 45 or 50. He came from a family of Hellenized Jews, probably of the same social class as St. Paul. Philo set himself the task of reconciling the Hebrew Scriptures with the Greek philosophers, particularly Plato, and he also played a role in the political life of the Alexandrian Jewish community. It is impossible to know if Jesus was familiar with his work, but it is almost certain that the author of John's Gospel knew of it. It was Philo who first developed the theology of Logos (the Word) as an intermediary between God and humanity. The well-known introduction of John's Gospel owes much to Philo's thought.

THE ROMAN PRESENCE

The growing weakness of the later Ptolemies, coupled with the country's great riches, was an open invitation for Rome to become involved in Egyptian affairs. The Roman Senate became the self-appointed protector of Egyptian independence. In 164 B.C., Antiochos IV, the Hellenistic king of Syria, invaded Egypt with the intent of adding it to his own empire. He was met by the Roman ambassador to Egypt, Popillius Laenas, who warned him of the consequences of such an action. Antiochos asked for time to consider, prompting Popillius to draw a circle on the ground around him, demanding that he answer before he stepped out. Antiochos wisely withdrew. Thereafter, Roman advisors to the Ptolemies were the real power behind the Egyptian throne.

It was not surprising, therefore, when in 55 B.C. the Roman general

This obelisk, known as Cleopatra's Needle, was probably erected around 1500 B.C. by Pharaoh Thutmose III. It guarded the entrance to the Caesareum in Alexandria in Jesus' day; it was brought to London in 1879 and today stands on the Thames Embankment there.

Pompey intervened directly to ensure that his protégée, Ptolemy XIII, was chosen to take the throne. Several years later, while Ptolemy was in the midst of a dispute with his wife-sister, Cleopatra VII, in theory his co-ruler, the battle between Julius Caesar and Pompey for control of Rome spread to Egypt. Caesar arrived there in hot pursuit of Pompey, only to discover that he had been murdered treacherously by the Egyptians. Caesar then threw his army behind Cleopatra's efforts to become sole ruler of Egypt, and in 47 B.C. her goal was attained. The Roman general and the Greek queen soon became lovers. Their son was named Caesarion.

Afterward, Caesar brought Cleopatra to Rome, where he had a statue of her erected for the admiration of the Romans. Exactly the opposite occurred, however; the upper class of Rome was outraged at the presence of a foreign queen in their midst. After Caesar was assassinated, Cleopatra sailed back to Alexandria, where she had a second chance to shape Roman policies. There she associated the young Caesarion with her, making him co-ruler of Egypt.

In her grief, Cleopatra commissioned a large temple to be built to honor the memory of the now deified Caesar. This was the Caesareum, a huge complex with two obelisks from pharaonic times placed at its entrance. The building itself was still unfinished at the time of Cleopatra's death, so Augustus had to pay for its completion. (The two obelisks still exist: one in New York's Central Park, the other on the Thames Embankment in London.)

This time it was Marc Antony who formed a lover's alliance with Cleopatra, for her charms cast a spell over Roman generals that is hard to explain from looking at the image on her coins. In 31 B.C., Octavian's ships at the battle of Actium defeated the combined fleets of Antony and Cleopatra and both chose suicide rather than face capture by Octavian. Caesarion was ordered killed. This victory allowed Octavian, later Caesar Augustus, to proclaim, "I added Egypt to the empire of the Roman people."

EGYPT AND AUGUSTUS

Augustus made Egypt an imperial province, and such was its status throughout the lifetime of Jesus. Augustus personally appointed its governor, who had the title "Prefect of Alexandria and All Egypt." This position was reserved for members of the equestrian class; senators were forbidden to enter the country without the emperor's permission. Augustus and later Tiberius were determined to keep Egypt as their personal estate and to enjoy all of its immense wealth. Augustus stationed first three, then two legions at Nicopolis, just outside Alexandria, to keep order. Many soldiers were put to work cleaning the waterways of the country, which had become full of silt during the wars.

The Roman prefects of the first century had many duties. Their first and most important task was to make sure that the grain harvest was collected and shipped to Rome as efficiently as possible. Each also had to serve as chief judge, deal with the edicts, petitions, and prescripts that came from Rome, and make sure that the waterways, dikes, and reservoirs were kept in good repair. Prefects also had the obligation to oversee the building programs that the emperors financed. It appears that the prefects were, like the ancient pharaohs, isolated from direct contact with the general public. One prefect's wife, during the reign of Tiberius, was famous for having never left the palace grounds in over sixteen years, and for never having allowed a native Egyptian to come into her residence.

When official visitors came to Egypt, it was the prefect who had to greet them and make them comfortable. Nearly everyone wanted to visit Upper Egypt and the Colossi of Memnon, actually two statues of Amenhotep III, which "sang" when the morning sun first struck one of the statues. (Apparently this phenomenon occurred when the morning wind blew through a crack in the stone of the statue.) In A.D. 19, during Jesus' lifetime, Germanicus, the adopted son of Tiberius, visited Alexandria. His reception in the Alexandrian hippodrome was the largest and most tumultuous ever given a Roman general.

The Roman army was in charge of transporting grain up the Nile and seeing to its storage in the merchant ships destined for the capital. Soldiers also were stationed at the mines to make sure the ores brought to the surface were put to use as the government required. The prefects had to deal with a large bureaucracy of officials, nearly all of them Greeks, who were pleased to find jobs under the Romans.

Ownership of property was the key to privilege in Roman Egypt. While private property had been rare in Ptolemaic Egypt, the Romans actively promoted the building up of large estates. Many were held by women — about one-third of the total. A tax fell on these lands, paid in grain to the state. Other taxes, often leased to publicans to collect, were assessed in coin.

The Romans allowed local elections to fill municipal offices from a list of candidates who met certain property qualifications. Those elected, however, had to administer the town under the watchful eyes of the prefect's own officials, usually army officers. Holding municipal office could be expensive, because city officials had to provide for religious festivals and entertainments out of their own pockets. The prefects also expected them to provide manual laborers to work on state projects such as the repair of the roads and canals that crisscrossed the land. In return for fulfilling their responsibilities, the upper class of Greeks and the Egyptians who had assumed administrative positions had a good chance of obtaining Roman citizenship. The authorities, however, fiercely guarded the number of applicants, because citizenship allowed people political, legal, and economic privileges that the Romans preferred to keep for themselves.

The extended family was all-important in Egyptian society, whether its members were rich or poor. Often living together under the same roof, families thought in terms of collective welfare rather than of individual happiness. Homes of the poor were always of mud brick; only the very wealthy could afford stone. Houses were designed as rooms surrounding a courtyard, which rich people used for socializing and the poor for keeping their animals. In the towns, native Egyptians and Greeks lived apart from one another, mingling only in public life.

Life in large cities provided a wide range of entertainment. The hippodrome and the theater drew large crowds, and parades on festival days were eagerly attended. Singers, mimes, acrobats, and jugglers performed more frequently in smaller towns. City officials appreciated these entertainers because Alexandria, like Rome, had a large population of unemployed who could be dangerous when provoked. From time to time they rioted, forming mobs that could not be controlled. Prefects employed soldiers to guard them, but even trained soldiers could not always stand up to mobs. During Augustus's rule, one Alexandrian prefect was killed, stoned by a throng of angry protestors.

Religion played a large role in Roman Egyptian culture. While Serapis was the Greeks' favorite god, native Egyptians preferred the worship of Isis. The myth attached to her cult held that her husband, Osiris, had been hacked to death, but then restored to life. Osiris then became the god of the underworld and Isis mother of the universe. Almost the whole pantheon of Greek gods had eventually found their way to Egypt, where many were identified with local deities. A great procession to honor Dionysos was one of Alexandria's favorite festivals.

The Ptolemies and the Romans financed the extension of old temples and the building of new ones. Begun by the Ptolemies and finished by the Romans, the temple of Isis at Philae on the Nile River was one of the most impressive. On the local level, popular concern for worship meant that even small towns had up to a dozen places of worship, and the larger cities held hundreds. The art of mummification of dead animals as well as people was still popular during Jesus' lifetime. Rich Romans wanted to be buried in large stone sarcophagi.

The Greek and Roman concept of priesthood demanded that civil officials should assume the roles of clerics; thus, relatively few cults had a permanent group of priests. This stood in sharp contrast to the Egyptian concept of a priestly class that went about with shaved heads and long white garments, following an ascetic way of life and serving as full-time officials of the temples. In Jesus' time, the Egyptian priests retained little of the respect and wealth that they once commanded, and their occupation was no longer prestigious. They were replaced by popular spirituality, of which magic, amulets for healing and warding off the evil eye, and a constant search for the advice of oracles were all a part.

Jesus, had he so chosen, could have made an impression in Roman Egypt. If he had identified himself with the native Egyptians, it would have been his miracles that attracted people. Magic was a favorite entertainment of the Egyptian masses, and they would certainly have placed any wonders he worked into that category. Unfortunately, it is entirely likely that the spiritual dimension of his miracles would have been lost on an Egyptian audience. They were so used to magicians whose goal was simply to awe large crowds that it would have been difficult for him to use them to elicit faith in God.

On the other hand, it is possible that he could have reached the Egyptians not as a miracle worker but as one of the many academics who made their home in Alexandria. There was certainly no lack of teachers there. If he had possessed a good command of Greek and an interest in philosophical questions, perhaps he could have attached himself to the scholars of the Museon. A group of disciples could have formed about him, as they did around other teachers, to carry on his work. But the great social gap between Greek and Egyptian cultures would have limited his message to the elite.

Chapter Three

Southwest Asia

SOUTHWEST ASIA EXTENDS from the Mediterranean Sea in the west to the Indus River in the east. The Black Sea and the Caucasus Mountains border it on the north, and the Indian Ocean and the Persian Gulf on the south. The region is geographically diverse, ranging from deserts to high mountains to fertile valleys, but in general it suffers from aridity and thin soil. The deforestation that began almost as soon as human civilization arrived here caused erosion to increase over the centuries, making the problem of insufficient water even more acute. Where once in the ancient world large cities stood, today there are only ruins covered by desert sands.

Anatolia lies in the far northern corner of the region, the land that now forms modern Turkey. Compared to other parts of Southwest Asia, Anatolia is remarkably productive. The east is very mountainous, but the Aegean region has fertile plains for farming and gentle hills for pasturing animals. And while the Black Sea region is less favored, excellent harbors can be found on the western coastline.

ANATOLIA IN THE ANCIENT WORLD

Long before the birth of Jesus, in the New Stone Age, the largest city in the world was situated at a place now known as Çatal Hüyük, its remains dating from about nine thousand years ago. Six thousand people may have lived here, sustained by exchanging the obsidian that they mined for food brought them by hunters and gatherers. It was the Anatolian people who carried the knowledge of farming and herding into Europe, when they and their inventions crossed the Dardanelles, reaching Greece around 6000 B.C.

Archaeology indicates that burial customs were unique at Çatal Hüyük: the dead were interred in their own houses, just a foot below the surface of the platforms where they had slept in life.

Over the millennia, new people entered Anatolia from both the east and west. One of these, the Hittites, built the first empire in Anatolia. They were also the inventors of ironworking, a technology from which the rest of the world profited immensely. About twelve hundred years before the birth of Jesus, the Phrygians replaced the Hittites as the dominant people of Anatolia, locating their capital at Gordion. The wealth of their nation is recalled in the story of Midas, the king whose touch turned everything to gold. The Phrygian religion centered on Cybele, the Great Mother Goddess, long a deity of Anatolian peoples. The Phrygians subsequently passed her cult on to their neighbors. The priests of Cybele, self-castrated, were so frenzied in their worship that when their religion arrived in Rome, the Senate ordered that they remain confined at all times to the temple area. The worship of the Great Mother Goddess was still very much alive during the lifetime of Jesus.

While the Phrygians were creating an inland empire, Greeks from the Balkans began emigrating across the Aegean to colonize the Anatolian coastline, establishing major cities in Ionia. The products of the Greek cities and the ships that carried them throughout the Mediterranean made their wealth known far beyond their shores. Ephesus, Miletus,

The Asklepion at Pergamum, in the foreground of this photograph, was famous as a healing shrine.

Phokea, Smyrna, Pergamum, and Priene, the most important Greek cities in Anatolia, promoted their culture throughout Southwest Asia.

When the Phrygians began to fade, the Lydians picked up their mantle. Sardis was the Lydian capital, situated about forty miles inland and home to a massive citadel and a luxurious palace for its ruler. The last of these was Croesus, another ruler in the tradition of golden monarchs, but his end was not a happy one. In 546 B.C., the Persians besieged and took his city and absorbed Lydia into their empire. Nor did they stop with the conquest of Lydia; they also placed the Ionian Greek cities under their sovereignty. Sardis continued to exist for many more centuries, but misfortune continued to plague it. In A.D. 17, during Jesus' lifetime, a great earthquake leveled the city.

The wealth of the Phrygians is recounted in the story of Midas, the king whose touch turned everything to gold.

The Persians were still in power in 334 B.C., when Alexander the Great appeared on the scene and wrested Ionia into his control. Upon his death, Anatolia passed to his general Seleucus, but his heirs lacked the resources to hold their possessions intact. As a result, several small kingdoms broke away from the Seleucid state.

The largest of these kingdoms was Pergamum, where a Macedonian dynasty known as the Attalids ruled from the city acropolis. They began a great building program that included all the edifices expected in a Hellenistic capital. Two of these made Pergamum of the Attalids remarkable: its library and a monumental altar dedicated to Zeus (now in the Berlin Museum). A huge and very steep theater was built into the hillside of the Pergamum citadel, seating up to thirty thousand spectators. Near the city was an Asklepion, a healing shrine dedicated to the god Asklepios, which drew men and women from all over the Mediterranean in search of cures.

"Asia is so rich and prosperous that it surpasses all lands in the fertility of its soil, the variety of its products, the size of its pastures, and the number of its objects for export abroad." — Cicero

In Hellenistic times, Galatia formed a separate region in the center of Anatolia. Its origins date from the third century, when a large group of Celtic peoples, the Gauls, crossed over into Anatolia, wreaking havoc wherever they went. In 230 B.C., Attalos I of Pergamum at last defeated the Gauls, and added their lands to his kingdom. Enough of the Celtic population remained to lend the region the name it had in Jesus' day, and St. Paul would later write his most personal letter to its inhabitants.

During the Hellenistic era in Anatolia, thousands of Greeks left their Balkan homeland to pursue opportunities in central and western Anatolian cities, strengthening their culture's long-standing presence on the Aegean coast. They brought with them skills in building temples, theaters, baths, gymnasiums, and parks to serve communities of several thousand residents. A rich merchant oligarchy formed city assemblies and elected local magistrates.

At Ephesus, citizens constructed a temple to Artemis (who eventually became the Romans' Diana) that drew pilgrims from all over the eastern Mediterranean. An arsonist destroyed the first temple of Ephesus on the night that Alexander the Great was born, so it had to be rebuilt. When finally completed, it was three times the size of the Parthenon of Athens. Today a single pillar remains of this enormous structure, which has become known as one of the Seven Wonders of the ancient world.

Anatolia's small kingdoms proved no match for the growing power of Rome, a situation that was best recognized by Attalos III of Pergamum. After his death in 133 B.C., Attalos willed his kingdom to the people of Rome. Two years later the Senate accepted this addition to their empire, establishing the territories of Pergamum as the province of Asia.

ROMANS IN ANATOLIA

The annexation of Pergamum was a major gain for Rome because it opened the door to further expansion and brought the wealthy Ionian Greek cities into the Roman economic network. According to the renowned orator Cicero, "Asia is so rich and prosperous that it surpasses all lands in the fertility of its soil, the variety of its products, the size of its pastures, and the number of its objects for export abroad." Pergamum remained the province's capital, but Ephesus was home to the governor's residence. Smyrna grew larger because of its thriving export market: olive oil, wine, dried fruit, timber, and marble shipped from its excellent harbor.

To the north and east of Asia, bordering the Black Sea, the kingdom of Pontus proved to be a competitor to Rome. Since Alexander's conquest it had gone its own way, but like other Hellenistic states of Anatolia, Pontus looked with dismay as Rome came closer to its lands. Eventually, in the first century B.C., the Pontian king Mithradates VI felt strong enough to challenge the Romans for supremacy over Anatolia and the Greek mainland. After several attempts to move beyond his borders, in 89 B.C. he invaded Bithynia with an army better trained and better equipped than the world had ever seen before. While his fleet scoured the Aegean, he called on the cities of Asia to drive out the Romans. In a gigantic massacre, the natives slaughtered eighty thousand Italians who had settled in their midst. For a time it appeared that Mithradates was on the way to success, until Sulla's legions drove him from Greece. Forced back to Pontus, Mithradates was allowed to keep his throne, but he lost all his gains. After the Mithradatic Wars, Sulla laid an indemnity of twenty thousand talents, a crippling sum, on each city that supported him, nearly bankrupting local governments.

DAILY LIFE

In Jesus' day, the process by which coins were made was similar throughout the world: small metal disks of gold, silver, or bronze were cast by pouring the molten alloy from a crucible onto a flat surface, where they cooled into a lens shape. Striking the blanks, as they were called, was simple: they were placed in between two dies on an anvil and struck two or three times with a hammer. As many as 100 coins per hour could be made this way.

With Mithradates presumably no longer a threat, from 78 to 74 B.C. the Romans continued to expand their authority over the Hellenistic kingdoms of Anatolia: Bithynia, Lycia, Pisidia, and Lycaonia, regions St. Paul would visit on his missionary journeys in the next century.

There was now a new competitor to Rome's ambitions in Anatolia, the kingdom of Armenia. About 800 B.C., the Armenians are first mentioned as a people living in the mountains of eastern Anatolia. For centuries they lived under Persian influence, adopting the Persians' national religion, Mazdaism, as their own, but late in the second century B.C. they broke free to chart an independent path. By 83 B.C. their monarch, Tigranes I, reigned over a kingdom that extended from the Euphrates River to the Mediterranean seacoast of Syria, with his capital at Tigranocerta. It was Tigranes who put an end to the Seleucid dynasty of Antioch.

The Romans responded to the Armenian expansion by dispatching an army against Tigranes and his father-in-law, the ever-persistent Mithradates, who, they were convinced, must have had a hand in directing the offensive. In 66 B.C., Lucius Licinius Lucullus defeated Tigranes's army and permitted him to retain his kingdom, but only on condition that he recognize he was now a client of the Romans. Over the next several decades, Armenia was torn between one faction that was comfortable under kings who pledged loyalty to Rome, and another that favored a Parthian allegiance. Throughout Jesus' lifetime, Armenia experienced times of independence punctuated by periods in which kings willingly sent tribute to Rome.

FURTHER FACTS

The famous Roman roads varied in their composition according to what was locally available, but nearly all were made of three separate layers: a thick foundation, a layer of sand to provide firmness, and a pavement of stone, gravel, or iron slag. Ditches on either side of the roads provided drainage, ensuring that they retained their firmness.

In 66 B.C., the Senate commissioned Pompey to proceed with another army to the East, to deal once and for all with Mithradates. One more time the cold steel of Roman swords prevailed. Four years after Pompey's expedition, the Senate established Pontus as a province directly ruled from Rome. There would be no more Mithradates. During his march through the East, Pompey also added Cilicia, Pamphylia, and Isauria to Roman sovereignty. During Jesus' lifetime, Tiberius annexed Cappadocia in the central area of the Anatolian plateau to Rome, and by 25 B.C. the king of Galatia had turned over his realm to the Romans. A generation before the time of Jesus, Rome was close to rounding out its control of Anatolia, with its accumulation of the former patchwork of individual Hellenistic states. Unfortunately Roman administration did not always mean an improvement in quality of life for many of its new subjects. Too many administrators were corrupt, and the financial burdens they imposed very heavy, especially while the Roman civil wars were in progress.

Once Augustus consolidated his authority over Rome, a new era of peace ushered in a period of prosperity for Anatolia that was well underway during the lifetime of Jesus. Excellent roads connected the cities with one another. Every town was filled with its citizen assemblies, trade associations, and clubs for every age and interest group. The town fathers were very anxious to ingratiate themselves with Roman authorities. It is still possible to see an inscription of Augustus in modern Ankara, detailing all the wonderful deeds of the deified ruler. His birthday became the opening day of the New Year.

On the fringe of eastern Anatolia, there were a number of independent states which managed to fend off Roman control until after Jesus' lifetime. Such was Osroene with its capital at Edessa (modern Urfa in Turkey). Two centuries after the death of Jesus, it became a center of Syrian Christianity. The Georgians lived in a mountainous country at the far end of the Black Sea. An indigenous people, they called themselves Kartveli, and their land Sakartvelo. Beginning in the third century, Georgian kings kept their capital at Mtskheta. The Azeri were a Turkic-speaking people who made their home next to the Caspian Sea. Persian influence dictated much of their culture. During the lifetime of Jesus, Baku, Gança, and Naxçivan were important for trade in silk and lamp oil.

PHOENICIA

To the south of Anatolia, on the Mediterranean coast, lay the ancient cities of Phoenicia: Tyre, Sidon, Byblos, and Aradus, all of which were incorporated into the Roman province of Syria. Once the greatest sea traders of the Mediterranean, the Phoenicians in Jesus' lifetime were but a fraction of the population in their own homeland because of an influx of Greeks, Syrians, Jews, and Roman administrators and settlers.

By the first century, Tyre had recovered from its destruction, which had been ordered by Alexander the Great. For eight months the city had resisted his army. When it did fall, in his wrath Alexander ordered Tyre razed, its men killed, many by crucifixion, and its women and children sold into slavery. The Ptolemies began its rebuilding, so that during Jesus' lifetime the city was again a center of manufacturing and trade.

Augustus offered Berytus, before Roman times a rather insignificant place, special privileges as a Roman colony. Both Herod the Great and Herod Agrippa financed many of its buildings. The businessmen of these cities exported textiles to all parts of the Mediterranean world, and Phoenician dye works produced the special scarlet color that graced aristocratic attire throughout the empire. About thirty years before the birth of Jesus, the art of glass blowing was invented here, greatly increasing the selection of goods that could be exported from the cities of the coast.

The Phoenician cities developed a relationship with Galilee, where Jesus grew up, for they depended on it to supply them with grain, as the coastal plain on which they were located was too narrow for extensive farming. Timber for building the roof of the Temple in Jerusalem was imported from Mt. Lebanon in the Phoenician hinterland.

The religions of Phoenicia and Syria are mentioned frequently in the Bible. Baal and Asherah, gods of fertility, were seductive deities for the Israelites, who had become farmers and who depended on fertile harvests for their livelihood. The Israelite prophets considered them dangerous competitors of Yahweh. Adonis, who later became a popular god of the Greeks, was also a deity who belonged to the Phoenician pantheon. According to myth, Adonis had died of a wound from a boar, but Astarte, known to the Greeks as Aphrodite, so loved him that her grief over his loss persuaded the gods of the underworld to allow him to return to earth for six months each year.

Jesus visited the cities of Phoenicia, for they were quite close to Galilee. And people came from Tyre and Sidon to listen to him, for his reputation as a wonder-worker became known along the Phoenician coast. Mark's Gospel (7:24-30) tells of one such visit, in which Jesus healed the daughter of a Phoenician woman who sought his help.

SYRIA

Since 66 B.C. Syria was also a Roman province with important trading centers at Damascus, Aleppo, and Palmyra, where the products of the desert were exchanged for those of the Mediterranean. Antioch on the Orontes River was the Syrian capital, the Romans having inherited it from the Seleucids. Augustus settled some of his veterans on the estates confiscated from the Seleucids, but Greek was the language of the vast majority of urban citizens, and Hellenistic values and culture dominated their society. In the countryside, on the other hand, the ancient Semitic culture continued, little touched by events in the cities.

In Jesus' lifetime, Antioch was the largest city of Southwest Asia, renowned for its magnificent buildings, temples, parks, hippodrome, and colonnaded streets. Its wealth came from its connection to the Great Silk Road that started in China and ended in the ports of the Mediterranean.

A story of Jesus' travels to Phoenicia

Source: Mark 7:24-30 (RSV)

"AND FROM THERE HE AROSE AND WENT AWAY TO THE REGION OF TYRE AND SIDON. AND HE ENTERED A HOUSE, AND WOULD NOT HAVE ANY ONE KNOW IT; YET HE COULD NOT BE HID. BUT IMMEDIATELY A WOMAN, WHOSE LITTLE DAUGHTER WAS POSSESSED BY AN UNCLEAN SPIRIT, HEARD OF HIM, AND CAME AND FELL DOWN AT HIS FEET. NOW THE WOMAN WAS A GREEK, A SYROPHOENICIAN BY BIRTH. AND SHE BEGGED HIM TO CAST THE DEMON OUT OF HER DAUGHTER. AND HE SAID TO HER, "LET THE CHILDREN FIRST BE FED, FOR IT IS NOT RIGHT TO TAKE THE CHILDREN'S BREAD AND THROW IT TO THE DOGS." BUT SHE ANSWERED HIM, "YES, LORD, YET EVEN THE DOGS UNDER THE TABLE EAT THE CHILDREN'S CRUMBS." AND HE SAID TO HER, "FOR THIS SAYING YOU MAY GO YOUR WAY; THE DEMON HAS LEFT YOUR DAUGHTER." AND SHE WENT HOME, AND FOUND THE CHILD LYING IN BED, AND THE DEMON GONE."

The fertility god Baal was a seductive deity for the ancient Israelites; prophets of Yahweh spent a great deal of time warning them away from his worship.

Source: Jeremiah 2:7-9 (RSV)

"AND I BROUGHT YOU INTO A PLENTIFUL LAND
TO ENJOY ITS FRUITS AND ITS GOOD THINGS.
BUT WHEN YOU CAME IN YOU DEFILED MY LAND,
AND MADE MY HERITAGE AN ABOMINATION.
THE PRIESTS DID NOT SAY, 'WHERE IS THE LORD?'
THOSE WHO HANDLE THE LAW DID NOT KNOW ME,
THE RULERS TRANSGRESSED AGAINST ME;
THE PROPHETS PROPHESIED BY BAAL,
AND WENT AFTER THINGS THAT DO NOT PROFIT.
THEREFORE I STILL CONTEND WITH YOU, SAYS THE LORD,
AND WITH YOUR CHILDREN'S CHILDREN I WILL CONTEND."

Much of the silk, jade, glass, and carpets that found their way to Rome reached there by way of Antioch.

The Romans brought to Syria a level of prosperity for three hundred years that it has never since attained. A wealthy upper class had leisure to build summer villas in the mountains, where men could spend their days in sports and hunting. In the cities, theaters, baths, odeons for musical productions, and amphitheaters for gladiatorial contests kept the urban population content. Four legions were stationed in the country to fend off the raids of desert nomads — an essential task if caravans were to travel with security. In fact, the Romans had their own camel corps to patrol the main roads that went from Aleppo to Antioch and from Damascus to the Red Sea.

In Jesus' lifetime, Syrians were frequent travelers into Galilee. Jesus spoke their language, Aramaic, which had spread throughout inland Southwest Asia because of its importance in trade. Baalbek and Emesa were celebrated religious sanctuaries that drew pilgrims into the country. A large number of Jews made their homes in Phoenicia and Syria, and many aspects of early Christianity took shape in this part of the world.

THE JEWS UNDER HELLENISTIC RULERS

Jesus was born in Southwest Asia, and its culture provided the setting for his entire life and work. It is significant that he was born into a Jewish family that had been worshiping the One God, Yahweh, for well over twelve hundred years. Jesus would claim to have a unique relationship with Yahweh, whom he called his Father. He would also speak of an Advocate or Intercessor, known to Christians today as the Holy Spirit, who was distinct from the Father. It is this revelation that eventually gave birth to the Christian doctrine of the Trinity, a concept quite foreign to traditional Judaism. Early Christians, who were nearly all Jews, considered Jesus to be the long-awaited Messiah, and it was this belief that within seventy years after his death caused the two religions to take different historical paths. To the gentile peoples of the Mediterranean, for whom the notion of a Messiah meant nothing, Christian missionaries emphasized the belief that Jesus was the Son of God.

The Jewish people during the millennium before Jesus' birth had weathered a vast array of historical events. Their traditions, in good times and bad, had enabled them to preserve their identity while other nations much more numerous and powerful disappeared. They had survived persecutions and exile, and had emerged the stronger for it. The Hebrew Bible, known to Christians as the Old Testament, chronicles these events.

DAILY LIFE

If Jesus had any education at all, it would have consisted of learning to read and write at the local synagogue. The Hebrew Scriptures would have been his text, and the local rabbi his teacher in informal sessions.

At the core of the Jewish faith was worship at the Temple in Jerusalem, where priests and Levites carried out a daily round of prayers, songs, and sacrifices. Built after the return of the Jews from their Babylonian captivity in the sixth century B.C., the Second Temple was not as grand as the one built by Solomon. The Holy of Holies, once home to the sacred Ark of the Covenant, was now just an empty room, but to pious Jews it was still the place where God's presence rested. The Temple dominated the skyline of Jerusalem, and huge crowds visited it on a daily basis. During the major festivals of the religious calendar, Jerusalem overflowed with pilgrims, and the New Testament makes a point of telling about Jesus joining the processions that went up to Jerusalem during the three great feasts of Passover, Shabuot (Pentecost), and Sukkot (Tabernacles).

The Jews lived under Persian rule from the time of their return from Babylon until the coming of Alexander the Great in 332 B.C. After Alexander had successfully completed the siege of Tyre, units of his army advanced into Galilee and Judea, meeting no resistance. In between Galilee and Judea was Samaria, which was home to an ethnically mixed population whom the Assyrians had moved into the region after transporting the Jewish population of ancient Israel to the Euphrates region. Although most of them were worshipers of Yahweh, the Samaritans' ancestry meant that they were rejected by the Jews and were forbidden entry into the Temple in Jerusalem.

From 323 until 175 B.C., Jews and Samaritans were the subjects of Hellenistic kings, either the Ptolemies of Egypt or the Seleucids of

Syria. The high priests, the chief religious figures of the Jewish religion, represented the Jews to the monarchs and as much as possible supervised local government. The Ptolemies, who ruled for the first hundred years of this period, did not concern themselves with events in Judea so long as tribute payments from Jerusalem arrived on a regular basis.

Jesus claimed to have a unique relationship with Yahweh, whom he called his Father. He also spoke of an Advocate or Intercessor, known by later Christians as the Holy Spirit, who was distinct from the Father. It is this revelation that eventually gave birth to the Christian doctrine of the Trinity.

The situation for the Jews took a dramatic turn when, in 223 B.C., the Syrian king Antiochus III defeated the Ptolemies and annexed Galilee, Samaria, and Judea to his realm. He treated his new subjects with respect until he experienced a severe military defeat at the hands of the Romans, which left him with a devastating indemnity to pay. Syrian tax collectors descended on the region with a vengeance. His successor, Seleucus III, went so far as to plunder the Temple treasury, but the worst was yet to come.

When Antiochus IV began his rule, he implemented a plan to Hellenize all of his subjects, a goal which fell especially hard on the Jewish people. In 169 B.C. and again two years later, he led his army into Jerusalem, plundering the city of whatever wealth it held. In the Temple precinct, where the Altar of Burnt Offerings stood, he ordered the erection of a statue of Zeus, which for pious Jews was the "abomination of desolation" spoken of by the prophet Daniel.

Efforts to eradicate the Jewish faith soon provoked resistance. Mattathias, a priest from the town of Modin, raised a force to resist the foreigners. For thirty-five years a conflict ensued between the Syrian forces and Mattathias's sons until the Jewish army, at last, proved successful. Known as the Maccabean Revolt, its high point came in 164 B.C. with the rededication of the Temple, now commemorated in the feast of Hanukkah.

Jonathan, one of the sons of Mattathias, assumed the office of high priest and took over the leadership of the Jewish people, ousting the Syrian garrison from Jerusalem. Under Jonathan's son, John Hyrcanus I, the last battles of the conflict were fought. To bolster Jewish claims, Hyrcanus sought and obtained Roman recognition. He also destroyed the Samaritan temple on Mt. Gerizim to demonstrate his power, a move that embittered the Samaritans toward the Jews even further. A dynasty known as the Hasmonean was now in place, making it easy for the succession to pass to members within the family. During the short rule of Hyrcanus's son, the high priest Aristobulus took the title of king. In 103 B.C. the succession fell to Alexander Jannaeus, whose reputation was tarnished by terrible acts of cruelty. On one occasion, the king slaughtered six thousand of his subjects for objecting to his holding both the priesthood and the kingship. Jannaeus was also bent upon a policy of expansion; it was his army that marched northward and reclaimed Galilee from the Seleucids.

DAILY LIFE

To travel from Galilee to Jerusalem on foot, as Jesus did several times, was a journey of approximately 120 miles and at least three or four days.

Jannaeus's widow was Salome Alexandra, who ruled in her own name until her sons, Hyrcanus II and Aristobulus II, came of age. The rivalry between them was to doom the Hasmonean dynasty, for each sought to hold both the high priesthood and kingship to the exclusion of the other. Their quarrels once more allowed the Romans to intervene, favoring the weak Hyrcanus II over his more able brother.

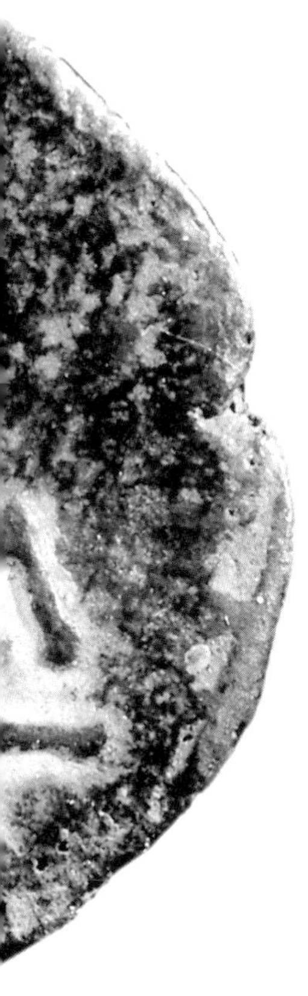

↑

That this bronze coin of Alexander Jannaeus contains inscriptions in both Hebrew and Greek illustrates the Hellenism which many of his subjects resented.

HEROD THE GREAT

Hyrcanus had among his close advisors an Idumean named Antipater. (Living in the Sinai region, the Idumeans were people of Arab descent who were forced to become Jews by the Hasmoneans.) Antipater became the power behind the throne, which allowed him to fashion policy and guaranteed that his son, Herod, should have high office. Around this time, Pompey declared that the Hasmonean kingdom should be made an ethnarchy ruled by the legate of Syria. The legate directed that Galilee form a separate political unit from Judea with Sepphoris as its capital.

The city was a natural fortress and the obvious choice for the honor. Most of the towns of Galilee were given a certain amount of local self-government, but Herod held real power as governor of the region.

While holding this position, Herod came under attack from Antigonus, the last descendant of the Hasmonean dynasty. For three years the contest continued, with Antigonus appealing for aid from the Parthians, and Herod counting on Roman legions to support his cause. It was their assistance that enabled Herod to occupy Jerusalem, so that by 37 B.C. the contest was over. Through massive confiscation of the royal lands of the Hasmoneans, Herod rewarded his supporters, who then became the landholding class in Galilee, Samaria, and Judea. It is quite evident from Jesus' parables how this new elite treated the peasant farmers who worked on their estates; the story of Lazarus and the rich man recorded in Luke 16:1-6 is a striking example. By 37 B.C., Herod was undisputed ruler in Judea, Galilee, and Samaria, but in fact a client king of Rome. History now knows him as Herod the Great.

FURTHER FACTS

"Herod despaired of recovering, for he was about the seventieth year of his age; he grew fierce, and indulged the bitterest anger upon all occasions; the cause whereof was this, that he thought himself despised, and that the nation was pleased with his misfortunes."

— *Flavius Josephus*

Becoming a servant of the Romans proved to be no great problem for Herod, who was every bit the Hellenistic monarch. He lived very much like an Oriental despot, taking ten wives during his lifetime, but allowing only one, Mariamne, whom he eventually put to death, to be called queen. Herod built fortresses throughout his territories, which he trusted would provide him security. One of these was the Antonia, which overlooked the Temple in Jerusalem. He also commissioned a new palace of massive proportions in Jerusalem along with a hippodrome for chariot races. Every four years, athletic contests were held in imitation of the games provided by other Hellenistic sovereigns. Herod's bodyguard was comprised of four hundred Gauls who had once served Cleopatra in Egypt. The king's extravagance stood in marked contrast to Jerusalem's beggars, who had to live on charity even amid the city's splendors.

In 20 B.C., to ingratiate himself with the Jews, Herod began the reconstruction of the Second Temple. Eighteen thousand workmen were

Although he was probably a teenager when it happened, the author of the Gospel of Luke connects the census with Jesus' birth.

Source: Luke 2:1-7 (RSV)

"IN THOSE DAYS A DECREE WENT OUT FROM CAESAR AUGUSTUS THAT ALL THE WORLD SHOULD BE ENROLLED. THIS WAS THE FIRST ENROLLMENT, WHEN QUIRINIUS WAS GOVERNOR OF SYRIA. AND ALL WENT TO BE ENROLLED, EACH TO HIS OWN CITY. AND JOSEPH ALSO WENT UP FROM GALILEE, FROM THE CITY OF NAZARETH, TO JUDEA, TO THE CITY OF DAVID, WHICH IS CALLED BETHLEHEM, BECAUSE HE WAS OF THE HOUSE AND LINEAGE OF DAVID, TO BE ENROLLED WITH MARY, HIS BETROTHED, WHO WAS WITH CHILD. AND WHILE THEY WERE THERE, THE TIME CAME FOR HER TO BE DELIVERED. AND SHE GAVE BIRTH TO HER FIRST-BORN SON AND WRAPPED HIM IN SWADDLING CLOTHS, AND LAID HIM IN A MANGER, BECAUSE THERE WAS NO PLACE FOR THEM IN THE INN."

called into Jerusalem to contribute their skills to the project. Herod's wealth allowed the importation of the finest materials for the building: gold, marble, and timber from Mt. Lebanon. Despite this effort, most Jews regarded him with horror, and toward the end of his life, Herod's paranoia verged on insanity. Matthew's account of the slaughter of the children of Bethlehem reflects Herod's moods very accurately.

THE SONS OF HEROD THE GREAT

In 4 B.C. Herod died, leaving the country he governed much poorer and more dispirited than it was when he first came to power. His prodigal spending and extravagant building program had been accomplished on the backs of the rural population. Riots broke out on the news of his death, and the Syrian legate, Publius Quintilius Varus, had to deal with numerous challenges. Confusion was compounded in that Herod had left four separate wills. Delegates went off to Rome to settle the matter, where Augustus ordered his three sons to divide their father's inheritance. Archelaus, then eighteen years old, became ethnarch of Judea, Samaria, and Idumea; his younger brother, Herod Antipas, tetrarch of Galilee and part of the region east of the Jordan River; and Philip, a half brother, the northeastern quarter of Herod's old territories.

Archelaus proved so incompetent and tyrannical that in A.D. 6 a delegation of Jews went to Rome to petition Augustus to remove him. At one Passover, Archelaus had ordered four thousand demonstrators killed for protesting the execution of two well-known scribes. The emperor agreed to remove Archelaus, exiling him to Gaul. Augustus then decreed that Judea should become a province directly under Roman control.

To learn the status of this addition to his rule, Augustus commissioned the legate of Syria to take a census of Judea. This census, which the writer of the Gospel of Luke links to the appearance of the Holy Family's presence in Bethlehem, would have occurred while Jesus was in his early teenage years. In Judea it caused considerable opposition, which eventually broke out into open rebellion. Leader of the revolt was Judas the Galilean, but his forces were no match for those of Rome. Roman legions put down the rebellion, and Judea saw no more violence during the remainder of Jesus' lifetime.

Herod Antipas fared much better than his brother. Galilee harbored no political revolutionaries during his long tenure as tetrarch, so there was no need to station Roman soldiers there during Jesus' lifetime. Antipas recognized that he governed only so long as the Romans were content with his decisions, so he pursued a cautious policy. Noted for cleverness (Jesus calls him a fox in Luke 12:30), his answer to trouble was simply to eliminate troublemakers.

Antipas had ample resources, some of which he used to rebuild Sepphoris, which he restored for his capital. Later he decided to build a second residence on the Lake of Galilee at Tiberias, named for the emperor. The lake, thirteen miles long and seven miles wide, was a natural scenic spot for this new palace. While in residence at Tiberias, Antipas ordered the death of John the Baptist, although the beheading actually took place at the fortress of Machaerus (Matt. 14:1-12)

Antipas was as ruthless as his father in collecting taxes from the long-suffering peasantry of Galilee. He employed his own agents, however, rather than using publicans, thus increasing the amounts that went into his treasury. The farmers of Galilee, whom the tax collectors sought out, grew wheat and barley in the valleys, and, fortunately, rain was dependable, in contrast to the aridity of Judea, where terracing the mountainsides was necessary to hold moisture in the ground. Olive orchards and vineyards covered the mountains of Galilee. The poor who are so often mentioned in the Gospels were those who worked at a subsistence level on the estates of large landowners or were free farmers whose amount of land was barely sufficient to feed their families. Debt was a serious problem in Jesus' lifetime for the farmers of Galilee, a fact attested to in the phrases of the Bible's most well-known prayer, the Our Father.

For the most part, the Jewish people living in Galilee were the men and women whom Jesus knew best. It was to them that he delivered his teachings on the Kingdom of Heaven. Jesus loved to teach at the beach, or from a boat moored a bit offshore, where a crowd of people would be able to hear him. Galilee was an isolated region cut off from its spiritual

↗

The Qumran caves, home to the Essenes or some other separatist sect in Jesus' day, are where the Dead Sea Scrolls were discovered in 1947.

center of Jerusalem by Samaria, and the Galileans must have felt it a special opportunity to hear Jesus' religious instruction.

In Judea, Augustus, and later Tiberius, appointed prefects, or procurators: Valerius Gratus and Pontius Pilate. Each was subordinate to the legate of Syria, and each held his appointment for ten years, a testament to the relative calm that lay over Judea at the time. Relations between Pilate and Herod Antipas were not good, a fact noted in Luke 13:1 and 23:12, where their cooperation in the prosecution of Jesus furthered a reconciliation between them. Pilate remained in office until A.D. 36, when the Syrian legate removed him for too severe a repression of a Samaritan outbreak of violence.

JUDAISM IN THE FIRST CENTURY

The Judaism of Jesus' lifetime was far from monolithic. All who practiced it could agree on the importance of the worship of Yahweh and obedience to the Torah, the books of the law which now comprise the first five books of the Bible. But different groups held different interpretations of the law. Leadership was invested in the high priest, the religious head of the Jewish faith, who alone was allowed into the Holy of Holies once a year on the Day of Atonement. The high priest's council of advisors, which was also the supreme court on internal affairs within Judaism, was known as the Sanhedrin. Because Herod insisted on appointing several different men to the office in the last years of his life, there may have been eight different high priests during Jesus' lifetime. Joseph Caiaphas figures prominently at Jesus' trial, as does Annas, who by that time had been deposed.

In the first century, three major parties existed on the religious horizon of Judaism. The Sadducees formed a group whose leadership was composed of the priests who performed the Temple liturgy. Conservative in their theology, the Sadducees rejected much of the oral tradition of Judaism. They had allies among those Jews who adopted Hellenistic culture as a positive force in national life.

The Essenes were their opposites. This group of Jews vigorously resisted any accommodation of Hellenistic culture and of the priests of the Temple who had compromised with it. Although the date of their origin is not certain, apparently they came into existence about 150 B.C. during the struggle among the Hasmoneans over the high priesthood. One group of rigorists settled at Qumran and produced the texts now known as the Dead Sea Scrolls. At Qumran they lived a monastic life, guided by the Spirit of Truth as taught by a Teacher of Righteousness. Their vision was apocalyptic, for in their view the coming of the Messiah was imminent.

Pharisees made up the third and largest distinct party of Jews during Jesus' lifetime. Like the Essenes, they were disillusioned by the Hasmonean priesthood and sought to distance themselves from it. To become a Pharisee, a candidate had to go through a period of probation to see how well he kept the strict tithing rules and the laws of ritual cleanliness. In addition to the Torah, the Pharisees accepted the oral traditions of the Jewish religion — for example, a belief in angels and in the resurrection of the body, both of which were notions rejected by the Sadducees. Contemporary sources report that the Pharisees were highly respected as devout laypersons, in contrast to reports in the New Testament, where a much different picture of them is presented. Who can forget Jesus' condemnation of the legalism that had come to taint their ranks? "Alas for you Pharisees!" he laments in Luke 11:42, "You pay tithes of mint and rue and every herb, but you pay no attention to justice and the love of God!" There is no evidence for believing that Jesus allied himself with either the Sadducees, the Essenes, or the Pharisees.

The Gospels often speak of a group called the scribes and associate them with the Pharisees. Essentially the scribes were interpreters of the Law who gathered disciples about them. Three eminent scribes were contemporaries of Jesus: Hillel, his grandson Gamaliel (who was Saul of Tarsus's instructor), and Shammai. Hillel was originally from Babylon and was well known for having walked all the way to Jerusalem to begin his work. Both Hillel and Shammai served as officers in the Sanhedrin.

In addition to those of the Jewish faith, first-century Judea also had its share of Syrian, Greek, and Roman settlers, who came as merchants, artisans, administrators, and soldiers. The Decapolis, across from the Sea of Galilee, held almost entirely Hellenistic cities. According to St. Luke,

Jesus visited these cities, or at least the countryside around them, at least once. The people who lived there brought with them their own religious traditions, and certain cities were well known for temples dedicated to foreign gods.

JESUS

The evangelists speak of Jesus as a *tektōn,* a woodworker. This was a person who made doors for houses (which were otherwise constructed of mud brick or stone) as well as tables, chests, and chairs for their furnishing. A *tektōn* would also fashion yokes for oxen and plows for farmers, as well as boats for fishermen. It is tempting to think that Peter and Andrew and the sons of Zebedee got to know Jesus when he crafted their boat.

Nazareth, Jesus' hometown, was a very small village made up of interrelated families. A single spring served everyone living there. Archaeologists have discovered a few silos for storing grain, cisterns, presses for olives and grapes, and some millstones in Nazareth, none of them showing that any but poor people made their home in the town.

Women in Nazareth would have lived an extremely restricted life, never leaving their houses without wearing two veils. Girls were engaged when they reached twelve or thirteen, and a year later married men who were generally much older. They received little or no education, and their days were long and difficult.

Jesus' occupation was determined for him, for Jewish law required a father to teach his son his craft. Because families sought to be self-sufficient, Joseph and Jesus probably had to spend a good deal of time away from home on jobs commissioned at distant locations. The fact that Sepphoris, only four miles away from Nazareth, had been destroyed at the time of Herod's death must have given the carpenters of the town many years of employment in rebuilding it.

About A.D. 20, new opportunities arose for laborers in Tiberias, thanks to Herod Antipas's constructions. The town had both a synagogue for its Jewish population and a stadium for the Greeks and Romans. Although there is no certain evidence of Jesus' presence in either Sep-

The Roman historian Strabo on the religion of the Persians, which was quickly adopted by the Parthians.

Source: Strabo, Geography. *Trans. H. L. Jones.*

THE PERSIANS DO NOT ERECT STATUES NOR ALTARS, BUT, CONSIDERING THE HEAVEN AS JUPITER, SACRIFICE ON A HIGH PLACE. THEY WORSHIP THE SUN ALSO, WHOM THEY CALL MITHRAS, THE MOON, VENUS, FIRE, EARTH, WINDS, AND WATER. THEY SACRIFICE, HAVING OFFERED UP PRAYERS, IN A PLACE FREE FROM IMPURITIES, AND PRESENT THE VICTIM CROWNED. :: AFTER THE MAGUS, WHO DIRECTS THE SACRIFICE, HAS DIVIDED THE FLESH, EACH GOES AWAY WITH HIS SHARE, WITHOUT SETTING APART ANY PORTION TO THE GODS; FOR THE GOD, THEY SAY, REQUIRES THE SOUL OF THE VICTIM, AND NOTHING MORE. NEVERTHELESS, ACCORDING TO SOME WRITERS, THEY LAY A SMALL PIECE OF THE CAUL UPON THE FIRE. :: BUT IT IS TO FIRE AND WATER ESPECIALLY THAT THEY OFFER SACRIFICE. THEY THROW UPON THE FIRE DRY WOOD WITHOUT THE BARK, AND PLACE FAT OVER IT; THEY THEN POUR OIL UPON IT, AND LIGHT IT BELOW; THEY DO NOT BLOW THE FLAME WITH THEIR BREATH, BUT FAN IT; THOSE WHO HAVE BLOWN THE FLAME WITH THEIR BREATH, OR THROWN ANY DEAD THING OR DIRT UPON THE FIRE, ARE PUT TO DEATH. :: THEY SACRIFICE TO WATER BY GOING TO A LAKE, RIVER, OR FOUNTAIN; HAVING DUG A PIT, THEY SLAUGHTER THE VICTIM OVER IT, TAKING CARE THAT NONE OF THE PURE WATER NEARBY BE SPRINKLED WITH BLOOD, AND THUS BE POLLUTED. THEY THEN LAY THE FLESH IN ORDER UPON MYRTLE OR LAUREL BRANCHES; THE MAGI TOUCH IT WITH SLENDER TWIGS, AND MAKE INCANTATIONS, POURING OIL MIXED WITH MILK AND HONEY, NOT INTO THE FIRE, NOR INTO THE WATER, BUT UPON THE EARTH. THEY CONTINUE THEIR INCANTATIONS FOR A LONG TIME, HOLDING IN THEIR HANDS A BUNDLE OF SLENDER MYRTLE RODS. :: IN CAPPADOCIA (FOR IN THIS COUNTRY THERE IS A GREAT BODY OF MAGI, CALLED PYRAETHI, AND THERE ARE MANY TEMPLES DEDICATED TO THE PERSIAN DEITIES) THE SACRIFICE IS NOT PERFORMED WITH A KNIFE, BUT THE VICTIM IS BEATEN TO DEATH WITH A LOG OF WOOD, AS WITH A MALLET.

phoris or Tiberias, it is a strong possibility that his occupation, his toolbox under his arm, took him there and on other journeys looking for work. This may help in understanding why so many people instantly were willing to follow him: Jesus was already their friend.

Jesus probably received no formal education, for rabbinical schools did not yet exist in Galilee. He could read Hebrew, which suggests that his family had enlisted a teacher for him. Possibly an instructor at a nearby synagogue offered classes, for Jesus' spoken language was Aramaic. Surprisingly, there is little evidence of Greek schools in Judea or Galilee. Probably Greeks and Latins offered him jobs that would have introduced him to the phrases in those languages needed to carry on his occupation. The Jews of Nazareth would have looked on the Greeks and Romans as distinctly foreign and, other than sharing the same land, would have had little to do with them.

During his lifetime, as often as possible, Jesus visited Judea on the three great feasts of the year that required the presence of Jewish men in Jerusalem. He would also have paid the half-shekel for the upkeep of the Temple and the additional ten percent of his income that was demanded during the time pilgrims spent in Jerusalem. It is thought that Jerusalem was a city of twenty-five thousand people in the first century, but on feast days the city had to provide accommodations and food for ten times that number. Probably pilgrims from Galilee had to live in tents outside the city walls during the festivals, and it was in one of these pilgrim processions that Jesus entered Jerusalem on Palm Sunday.

The accusations brought against Jesus at his trial are indicative of the tensions existing among the Roman authorities, who on the one hand cared little about Jewish law, and on the other were greatly concerned that there be no threat to Caesar's rule. Caught as Jesus was between his challenge to the religious establishment and Roman political concerns, it is easy to see how his fate was sealed. His death by crucifixion, a common Roman punishment for sedition, was all but inevitable.

The art of glassblowing was invented in Phoenicia around the time Jesus was born, when craftspeople discovered that glass that had been softened by heat could be shaped by air blown into it through a tube. Simple round vessels were made freehand; more complicated designs required the use of molds. The glassblowing techniques that were developed in Jesus' day remain largely unchanged today. The cup in this picture was discovered in Iran and dates from about two centuries after Jesus' death.

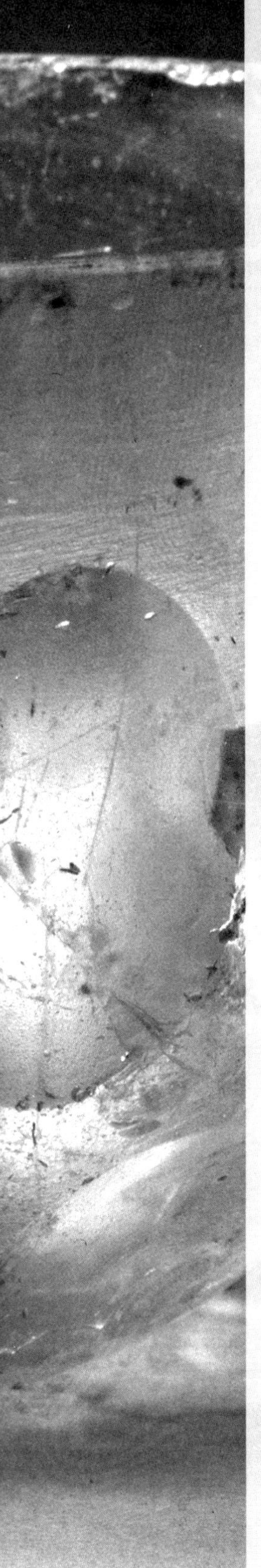

ARABS

The Arab world began just south of Judea on the Sinai Peninsula. Starting around 900 B.C., Arab kingdoms began to spread northward from Yemen, a region the Romans called Arabia Felix to distinguish it from the great desert of the peninsula. Throughout their history, the Arabs had made their living through specialty trade, bringing in huge profits to merchants dealing in frankincense, myrrh, and spices from the Orient, and Augustus believed Rome should have a hand in this luxury commerce. As a result, in 26 B.C. a Roman expedition under Aelius Gallus crossed the Red Sea from Egypt to add Arabia Felix to Rome's eastern possessions. Desert heat, hunger, and thirst melted the resolve of the legionnaires, however, and they withdrew the following year. During Jesus' lifetime, the border between Judea and the Arab world was quiet.

THE PARTHIANS

The Roman world extended to only a very small corner of Mesopotamia in Jesus' day. Crossing the Euphrates River brought travelers into the land of the Parthians, who now controlled a large part of Southwest Asia. Mesopotamia, the region where the Sumerians had first developed civilization, was but one more part of the world that time had passed by.

The origins of the Parthians (originally known as the Parni) were in the mountains of Khorasan, today in the northeastern corner of Iran. Possibly they were of Scythian origin; certainly they had perfected the cavalry charges identified with warfare on the steppes. About 238 B.C., a chieftain named Arsaces united the Parthians into a mighty fighting force that overwhelmed the Seleucid armies stationed in Persia. The Parthians then assumed the leadership of the country, dividing it, as the Persians had, into territories called satrapies. Over the next several decades, the Parthians pushed into Babylonia and Mesopotamia as the fortunes of the Seleucids continued to decline. The Romans began to worry over Parthian gains, for they were interested in adding Babylonia and Mesopotamia to their own empire. Eventually the Parthians and Romans met on the Euphrates to discuss the division of the region between them.

Another place where both the Parthians and Romans had clashing interests was Armenia. Who would have the final say over the choice of a king there? In 55 B.C., Marcus Licinius Crassus, a member of the first Roman triumvirate, thought to make a name for himself as a general. He raised an army to fight the Parthians, although there was no real reason for doing so. His army marched from Syria, following the Euphrates, planning to reach the capital of the Parthians at Ctesiphon. At Carrhae (modern Haran in southeastern Turkey) the Parthian cavalry dealt the Romans a crushing blow. Crassus became a Parthian prisoner and was later executed. Marc Antony tried to avenge Crassus's defeat, but was defeated himself in turn.

In 20 B.C., the situation between Rome and Parthia took a dramatic turn for the better when the Parthian king, Phraates IV, in an effort to put the animosity between the two states behind him, returned the standards of the Romans captured in the past to Augustus and freed all Roman prisoners still in captivity. In response to this gesture, Augustus sent Musa, an Italian woman, to join the harem of the Parthian king.

Musa so enchanted the king that she persuaded Phraates to send four of his sons to Rome with their families. In 2 B.C., she killed her husband and placed their son, Phraataces, on the Parthian throne. Much to the horror of the Greeks living in Parthia, Phraataces married his mother. In A.D. 4, when Jesus was still a child, Phraataces was overthrown, and Musa disappeared, her fate unknown. After the three-year reign of an unpopular king, Vonones, the Parthian throne was seized by Artabanus III, formerly king in Media. His kingship was contemporaneous with the lifetime of Jesus.

Though the Parthians were the victors over both the Seleucids and the Romans, they remained culturally the heirs of Persia. At their capital of Ctesiphon, on the banks of the Tigris River, their monarchs called themselves "King of Kings," the former Persian title. Parthian kings claimed to own all the land of the country and kept massive courts and harems. Seven great families shared in the wealth of the kingdom, whose revenues came from taxing the peasantry and merchants. This brought enough money to Ctesiphon for the Parthians to finance their military forces and to create a capital befitting their rulers' extravagant tastes.

The Parthian economy was divided between farmers, herders, and businessmen. The farmers were always under stress because rainfall was so unpredictable. As a result, they dug long underground tunnels, *qanats*, for carrying water from the mountains to their fields. Without irrigation, farming would have been impossible. Parthian merchants were in a much more favorable position. They served as the middlemen between China and Rome on the Great Silk Road and made a monopoly of their enviable position.

Despite Persian influence, the number of Europeans living within Parthian borders was so significant that Greek was the official language, followed by Aramaic, and Parthian taking only third place. Coins issued by the Parthian rulers have Greek inscriptions. The large Greek community in Ctesiphon erected temples to the gods of Olympus, where ceremonies that had their origins in ancient Athens were still carried out in detail for the protection of the Parthian monarch.

The Parthians had adopted the Persian religion of Ahura Mazdaism. Originally this faith was part of the old Indo-European worship, but in the sixth century a reformer named Zarathustra came on the scene. Little is known of his personal life, but Zarathustra was apparently able to convince the Persian monarch to accept his teachings. Zarathustra proposed a dualistic faith that pitted a good god, Ahura Mazda, against an evil one, Ahriman. He affirmed that after death a just god would pass judgment on a man's or a woman's life, awarding a place of happiness to the good and a place of suffering to the bad. It was through Zarathustra's teachings that the concepts of heaven and hell eventually became part of Pharisaic Judaism.

Priests of the Ahura Mazda religion were called Magi. Among the Greeks and Romans, they had a bad reputation for practicing "magic," but were respected for their study of the heavens, which was not so much for the sake of learning astronomy as it was for predicting the future through astrology. The worship of Ahura Mazda was carried on in fire temples, for it was thought that fire was the purest of substances. The fires in these temples were extinguished only at the death of a king, and it was the first duty of the new Parthian king to rekindle the flame. Along with fire, earth was sacred to the Parthians; thus the dead were not buried but left exposed for birds of prey to dispose of.

Mithras, the god of light, was the favorite of Persian and later Roman soldiers. Only men could be candidates for entry into his cult, and those who did were initiated in a ceremony that required them to be baptized in the blood of a bull. His devotees worshiped in cave sanctuaries, each of which was adorned with a statue of Mithras slaying a bull. For several centuries, Mithraism was a serious competitor to Christianity for the devotion of the Roman people.

Such was the world of Southwest Asia two thousand years ago, a region of great diversity in peoples, rulers, and religions. Jesus was a member of this world where Rome and Parthia dictated the political scene, Hellenism provided the cultural backdrop, and Judaism offered the religious framework for his teachings.

Chapter Four

Europe beyond the Alps

DESPITE ITS SMALL SIZE, the European continent is geographically very diverse. The far north, where modern Norway and Sweden are situated, is a land of rugged mountains. Finland, though nearly as far north, is a flat land dotted with many lakes, the last part of Europe to experience glaciation. The Baltic Sea separates Scandinavia from central Europe, which is characterized by rolling hills and lowlands that geographers call the Great European Plain. This region contains some of the most fertile land on earth, and in the time of Jesus it was heavily forested. It extends from southern England to the Ural Mountains of Russia. Below the Great European Plain is an area of uplands where the soil is less fertile and often rocky, making up for its relative aridity with its huge stores of mineral wealth. To the south of the uplands, the Alps cut across Europe. Their peaks are among the most picturesque anywhere in the world.

PEOPLES OF ANCIENT EUROPE

Today, the nations that lived north of the Alps in the first century are classified according to language families. In Jesus' time, with only a few exceptions, these languages all belonged to the Indo-European family.

There is still no agreement among archaeologists as to when the Indo-Europeans arrived in Europe. Some argue for a date about 6000 B.C., while others think that it was much later, closer to 2000 B.C. Whenever they came, they overran the Neolithic peoples who had populated Europe before them, absorbing them into their own culture. One plausible theory is that the Indo-Europeans crossed into Europe from Anatolia as farmers and slowly moved westward among the Stone Age hunters. Only the Basques of northern Spain and southwestern France were able to resist assimilation, explaining why their language has no relationship to any other. In addition to a number of similar languages, the Indo-Europeans brought with them distinctive pottery and burial practices, and a dependence on horses in both peace and war. At the time of Jesus, the largest linguistic groups were Celtic, Germanic, and Baltic

The men and women of Urnfield cultures cremated their dead and sealed them in ceramic urns such as this one.

↗

Polished stone axes and hammers such as these, unearthed from sites in Austria, Hungary, and the Czech Republic, were used by the Battle-ax people over two millenia before Jesus' birth.

in the north of Europe, Slavic in the east-central region, and Greek, Latin, Illyrian, Thracian, and Iberian in the southern peninsulas of the continent.

Archaeologists have located some Indo-European settlements dating from about 2500 B.C. in the Danube basin. Here, they suspect, lived the ancestors of many of the populations that later occupied Europe. One particular culture is known as Battle-ax because of the distinctive metal and stone axes that were buried in mounds along with the remains of their dead chieftains. In the Iberian Peninsula, grave gifts of distinctive bell-shaped cups have given the men and women there the name of the

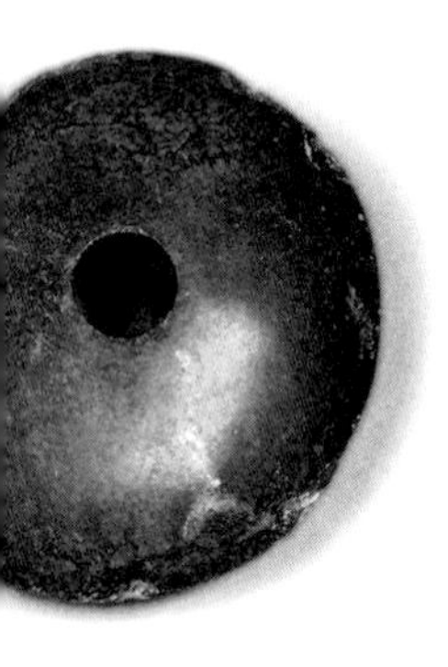

"THE ENTIRE RACE WHICH NOW GOES BY THE NAME OF GALLIC, OR GALACTIC, IS WARLIKE, PASSIONATE, AND ALWAYS READY FOR FIGHTING, BUT OTHERWISE SIMPLE AND NOT MALICIOUS. IF IRRITATED, THEY RUSH IN CROWDS TO THE CONFLICT, OPENLY AND WITHOUT ANY CIRCUMSPECTION; AND THUS ARE EASILY VANQUISHED BY THOSE WHO EMPLOY STRATAGEMS. FOR ANY ONE MAY EXASPERATE THEM WHEN, WHERE, AND UNDER WHATEVER PRETEXT HE PLEASES; HE WILL ALWAYS FIND THEM READY FOR DANGER, WITH NOTHING TO SUPPORT THEM EXCEPT THEIR VIOLENCE AND DARING. NEVERTHELESS THEY MAY BE EASILY PERSUADED TO DEVOTE THEMSELVES TO ANY THING USEFUL, AND HAVE THUS ENGAGED BOTH IN SCIENCE AND LETTERS. THEIR POWER CONSISTS BOTH IN THE SIZE OF THEIR BODIES AND ALSO IN THEIR NUMBERS. THEIR FRANKNESS AND SIMPLICITY LEAD THEM EASILY TO ASSEMBLE IN MASSES, EACH ONE FEELING INDIGNANT AT WHAT APPEARS INJUSTICE TO HIS NEIGHBOR. AT THE PRESENT TIME INDEED THEY ARE ALL AT PEACE, BEING IN SUBJECTION AND LIVING UNDER THE COMMAND OF THE ROMANS, WHO HAVE SUBDUED THEM; BUT WE HAVE DESCRIBED THEIR CUSTOMS AS WE UNDERSTAND THEY EXIST IN FORMER TIMES, AND AS THEY STILL EXIST AMONGST THE GERMANS. THESE TWO NATIONS, BOTH BY NATURE AND IN THEIR FORM OF GOVERNMENT, ARE SIMILAR AND RELATED TO EACH OTHER. THEIR COUNTRIES BORDER ON EACH OTHER, BEING SEPARATED BY THE RIVER RHINE, AND ARE FOR THE MOST PART SIMILAR. GERMANY, HOWEVER, IS MORE TO THE NORTH, IF WE COMPARE TOGETHER THE SOUTHERN AND NORTHERN PARTS OF THE TWO COUNTRIES RESPECTIVELY."

Bell Beaker culture. About 1800 B.C. these two groups merged, forming the Unetician culture, identified by their widespread use of bronze instruments and weapons.

The Uneticians were expert miners who not only fabricated bronze, copper, and tin objects for their own use, but also traded with their neighbors for the commodities they lacked. They lived in small villages surrounded by timber stockades. When a leader of prominence died, his body was interred with his weapons and gold jewelry in a wood-lined shaft grave, and then a mound was constructed over it.

The development around 1250 B.C. of a new method for burying the dead has given the name of Urnfield to the culture of northern Europe. As their name indicates, the men and women who lived during this period cremated their dead and sealed the ashes in clay urns before burying them in collective graves. The Urnfield people built large houses of logs, and, like the Uneticians, were skilled metalworkers. Their smiths forged huge cauldrons for boiling meat eaten in large communal meals. The weapons of the Urnfield warriors were bronze slashing swords, always buried with their owners. During this period, a characteristic art began to appear, full of abstract designs with swirls, spirals, circles, and dots. The artists especially favored images of animals and birds in their work.

The next development in northern European civilization was the arrival of iron-making skills around 600 B.C., among people now identified as early Celts. This new metal offered a great improvement in farming techniques, for a plowshare of iron could dig into the clay soils of Europe; wooden plows could only scratch the surface of the ground. The resultant surplus of food spurred a population boom, bringing prosperity to farmers and cattle herders as well as to craftspeople. With their iron axes they cleared forests to expand their fields, in which they grew the cereal grains that women made into bread. Between their villages, which were fortified with earthen ramparts and timber palisades, teams of farmers cooperated to build roads, sometimes using stone or planks of wood as pavement. Smiths learned how to fit iron tires snugly over the rims of wooden wheels while the metal was still hot, a development which further aided transportation between villages.

In this excerpt from *Cooley's Cattle Raid,* Cuchulain — one of the great heroes of Celtic mythology — laments with his childhood friend Ferdiad that they must fight each other to the death.

CUCHULAIN:

"WE WERE HEART-COMPANIONS ONCE;
WE WERE COMRADES IN THE WOODS;
WE WERE MEN THAT SHARED A BED,
WHEN WE SLEPT THE HEAVY SLEEP,
AFTER HARD AND WEARY FIGHTS.
INTO MANY LANDS, SO STRANGE,
SIDE BY SIDE WE SALLIED FORTH,
AND WE RANGED THE WOODLANDS THROUGH,
WHEN WITH SCATHACH WE LEARNED ARMS!"

FERDIAD:

"O CUCHULAIN, RICH IN FEATS,
HARD THE TRADE WE BOTH HAVE LEARNED;
TREASON HATH O'ERCOME OUR LOVE;
THY FIRST WOUNDING HATH BEEN BOUGHT;
THINK NOT OF OUR FRIENDSHIP MORE,
CUA, IT AVAILS THEE NOT!"

THE CELTIC WORLD

The most important age of the Celts lasted for about eight centuries, from 700 B.C. to A.D. 100. During that time, the Celtic population extended in a band several hundred miles wide from Ireland to the Black Sea and even beyond, into Galatia in Anatolia. They reached their largest expanse about 250 B.C., with the most heavily populated area being the Rhône region of modern France; soon thereafter, thanks to the Roman army, they began to recede. Just fifty years before Jesus' birth, Julius Caesar incorporated the Rhône valley into Roman territory, and Latin colonists from Italy started building cities among the Gauls. The people in these towns were Roman, but the countryside was predominantly Celtic for many more centuries.

The use of iron weaponry allowed the Celts to expand in many directions. The Boii and Scordisci moved into Bohemia and Moravia. The first Celts to reach Ireland may have arrived before 500 B.C., with more waves of settlers following for the next four hundred years. Hoping to loot the temple of the famous Delphic Oracle, Celtic warriors charged into Greece in 279 B.C. and subsequently passed into Anatolia.

Roman writers were fascinated by the Celts, so what is known about them during their age of expansion is found in Latin authors. For while some Celts, in contact with the Romans, learned to read and write Latin, they never put those skills to work in their own languages. Roman authors were impressed with the Celts because of their large bodies and flaming red hair. On the other hand, the clean-shaven Romans commented disparagingly on the men, who wore great mustaches and beards. They also found the polygamy of the Celts offensive and had little use for the clothing of Celtic women, into which small decorative bells were often sewn.

In addition to farming and herding cattle, the Celts mined gold and silver as well as the more accessible iron ore. Skilled miners sought out sources of salt hidden deep beneath the earth. Some mines tunneled twelve hundred feet into mountains, forcing workers to carry torches made of pine branches for light. Less productively, young men also spent long hours training for war. Great warriors were revered by the Celts,

Before a battle, Celtic soldiers took off their clothes to show their contempt for armor and fought naked except for torques like the ones here, often made of gold, worn around their necks. They also washed their hair in lime so it would stand up in spikes, giving them a frightening appearance.

and a successful fighter had to bring home the heads of those he had killed and nail them to the front of his house for all to admire.

Gallic Celts, once they discovered the pleasures of wine, could hardly get enough of it. The Roman historian Diodorus of Sicily, writing a few decades before the birth of Jesus, remarked, "The Gauls are very fond of drinking wine, and fill themselves with what merchants bring into their country. They drink it unmixed." The Romans were well aware of the extreme individualism of Celtic leaders. It was the rare charismatic chief who could hold an alliance together for very long. The one exception was Vercingetorix, the leader who tried to rally the Gallic peoples to resist Julius Caesar. In 52 B.C., the Gauls agreed to unite in an alliance to repel the Romans. For seven years Vercingetorix did everything in his power to hold the line against the Romans, but finally failed. Taken prisoner, he was paraded in triumph around the streets of Rome and then executed.

↑

Legend has it that both Vercingetorix and St. Peter were held captive in this jail cell in the Forum in Rome.

The death of Vercingetorix did not mean the total end of resistance, but never again were the Celts of Gaul independent of Roman occupation. The great advantage that the Roman army had over them was their military formation. The Romans marshaled their infantry into a square bristling with spears and marched forward, each man's shield linked to that of the person next to him. Every Roman soldier wore protective armor and a helmet to ward off any blows. The Celts, on the other hand, thought of warfare as a way for the individual to prove his bravery. Before a battle, soldiers took off their clothes to show their contempt for armor and fought naked except for torques, often made of gold, worn around their necks. They also washed their hair in lime, so it would stand up in spikes, giving them a frightening appearance. Druids, the Celtic religious leaders, urged them on, as did groups of women who ran back and forth among the ranks, carrying torches and yelling out curses against the enemy. Shouting at the tops of their voices, like men gone mad, the Celtic soldiers threw themselves with their long slashing swords against the lines of disciplined Roman warriors.

FURTHER FACTS

Vercingetorix's guerrilla warfare tactics came close to getting the better of Julius Caesar. The Celtic chieftain staged brief, fierce attacks and then retreated to heavy natural fortifications, and took to burning Gallic villages so that the Romans could not live off their resources.

IRELAND

While the Gauls had been under Roman occupation for fifty years before the birth of Jesus, the Celtic peoples living in the British Isles were still independent. Ireland was home to five major kingdoms, Connaught, Ulster, Leinster, and Munster, and, for a short time, Meath, but there were dozens of other clan chieftains who also claimed to be kings. Possibly there was already a high king at Tara in the first century.

The king's duty was to provide for the protection and well-being of his people and to represent them in dealings with their neighbors. He lived in a settlement surrounded by a wooden palisade and possibly an earthen ditch, with a wooden dining hall and several houses inside; each complex had to be large enough for his subjects to use as a place of refuge in time of danger. According to Celtic tradition, anyone in the royal family could be elected to the kingship. Usually the choice fell upon the strongest warrior. The Celts believed their gods inspired the electors, who were drawn from a council of the large landowners. A special ritual attended the king taking office.

Ordinary men and women lived in circular wooden houses with thatched roofs, possibly having stone foundations. Living conditions were crowded, for polygamy was the norm and most men had to provide shelter for numerous wives and children. This was the closest Ireland ever came to town life during Jesus' lifetime and for centuries afterward.

The Irish economy was based on farming and cattle herding. The large landowner had clients who watched over his cattle and lived off their products, but who had certain obligations of service. Some clients were freemen and women; others were on contract to provide service for a set number of years. A class of slaves did much of the hard work. Cattle rustling was one way young Irish men proved themselves; the earliest surviving work of Irish literature is entitled *Cooley's Cattle Raid.*

FURTHER FACTS

"The immense power of the druids was the weakness of the Celtic polity. No nation that is ruled by priests drawing their authority from supernatural sanctions is capable of true progress."

— Julius Caesar, in his memoirs

After a successful campaign, Irish warriors would enjoy a great banquet, where the best warriors were honored with a special portion of meat. These feasts were held in a royal dining hall, where the soldiers sat on hides spread over the floor. Heroes were encouraged to recount their exploits for everyone's admiration, and as the beer and ale flowed, so did the length of the story. Some celebrations lasted for days until all the food and drink were gone and the guests exhausted.

Celtic society was patriarchal, and a wife who did not please her husband could be returned to her father's house in disgrace. The usual pattern of the Irish upper class was to send their sons and daughters to other families to be reared. They, in turn, received children from those families. Having foster parents forged a bond between the two households. Girls remained until they were fourteen, boys until seventeen, and when they returned home they were expected to bring with them all the skills of young men and women in Irish society.

Irish druids performed the most important legal and religious functions. They also kept track of the calendar, which revolved around the four seasons and which reserved the first day of each for feasting and games. The powers of the druids to deal with the unseen world were especially needed the night before the New Year, the feast of Samhain, when the spirits of the dead were released on the earth and great danger was abroad for the living; from this feast was born our celebration of Halloween.

The druids had many privileges because of their duties, but access to their ranks took twenty years of training. This required memorizing the rituals of the Irish religion and the law codes. Nothing was ever written down for fear of compromising the purity of the law. Druids paid no taxes, did not bear weapons, and could move about freely all over Ireland. There were dozens of Irish gods that the druids had to venerate and to whom sacrifices and prayers needed to be offered. The major deities were those common to all Celtic people: Imbolc, Brigit, Belenos, and Lug. They were patrons of war and fertility, the two major concerns of the Irish at the time of Jesus. The largest religious festival of the year, the Beltaine, combined sports, dancing, and sacred rituals. Cattle were led between two fires so that the smoke would purify them. More gruesome sacrifices required the offering of heads or skulls to the gods. Irish belief in the head as the repository of life made these sacrifices essential for the good of the worshipers. Unlike many peoples of their day, the first-century Irish believed in a life after death, in which men and women were thought to receive rewards or punishment according to their earthly existence.

→

This shield, known as the Battersea Shield, is made of bronze and was used by the Britons in Jesus' day for ceremonial purposes. Shields used by warriors in battle would have been less lavishly decorated.

THE BRITONS

Many peoples made their home in Britain, which still bears the name of the largest of the Celtic nations, the Britons. Like the Irish, they crossed the Channel about 500 B.C., and in Britain they built on the traditions of the Stone Age people who had preceded them. Britain's first inhabitants reached the island about 7000 B.C. and were responsible for the construction of large stone megaliths, the most famous of which we call Stonehenge. Apparently this edifice had some astronomical purpose, but no one today can be certain what it was. Evidently leaders of this era commanded a great deal of political power; how else could they have organized large numbers of people to work on a project that had no apparent economic value? When the Celts arrived in Britain, Stonehenge was already several thousand years old. By the time of Jesus, the Celtic migration from the continent was finished; about 100 B.C., the last to arrive, the Belgae, came from the region on the mainland that now bears their name.

The Britons and all the other Celts on the island built hill forts throughout the country. Archeologists have identified more than fifteen hundred of them. They employed a unique construction in their fortifications, interlacing timber and stone, and in the process strengthening the walls of their towns. One of these, Maiden Castle in Dorset, had room enough for five thousand inhabitants.

From 100 B.C. until A.D. 100, the Celts in modern Scotland, known

↘

The stones used to build Stonehenge, some weighing as much as four tons, were transported from the Prescelly Mountains in Wales, some 240 miles away, and from Avebury, 20 miles away. It is estimated that its construction required over 30 million hours of labor.

as Picts, constructed round towers, called *brochs,* using dry stone. The brochs had interior stairways, which would have required professional builders to construct them. These may have served as watchtowers or as homes for large landowners, symbols of their residents' importance in the Celtic society of Scotland. Scottish archaeologists have also unearthed timber houses built on islands in the many lakes of the country, as well as homes that were built half buried beneath the surface of the ground to protect their occupants against the winter cold.

From the Celtic feast of Samhain was born our celebration of Halloween.

Celtic society in both Scotland and Britain was, as in Ireland, always turbulent. Much of the energy of young men went into training for war. The wealthier rode into battle riding horse-drawn chariots, which had to be very sturdy since roads were nonexistent.

ROMAN BRITAIN

↑

Brochs such as this one may have served as watchtowers or as homes for large landowners, symbols of their residents' importance in Pict society.

In 54 B.C. Julius Caesar, in search of yet another conquest, brought his troops across the English Channel for an invasion of Britain. His memoirs tell how deeply he was impressed with the size of the population, which may have numbered one million men and women, and note the efficient farming and cattle-herding methods of the Celts. Most of Caesar's campaigns were in Sussex and Essex, where he forced the people to pay him tribute. The Romans were especially interested in the tin nuggets that came from Cornwall, where people panned the rivers to find them, for tin mixed with copper produced bronze.

Because Caesar had other interests, he abandoned Britain within a year and returned to the continent. It remained for the Roman army, on the orders of Emperor Claudius, to invade Britain a second time in A.D. 43, twelve years after the death of Jesus. Toward the end of the first century, a Roman general occupied the Scottish Lowlands, but no Roman armies ever reached the Highlands or Ireland, allowing Celtic culture to thrive there until the eighteenth century.

THE GERMANS

Historians are fortunate that both Greek and Roman authors possessed an interest in the Germanic peoples, and that there were Mediterranean merchants who, in times of peace, would cross over into Germania in order to market their goods. Naturally, neither Greeks nor Romans saw the Germans as anything but barbarians, living outside civilization, without cities, roads, law, writing, and the arts, resulting in a very one-sided account of the peoples with whom they came into contact.

At the time of Jesus, the Germans, unlike the Celts, were increasing in numbers and importance. While Roman armies had signaled the end

↗

German warriors who could afford them wore bronze helmets such as this one; most, however, went into battle wearing only trousers. While the dome covering the head offered substantial protection, the horns were largely decorative, intended to make the wearer look intimidating.

of independent Celtic nations on the European mainland, the Germanic people on many occasions were able to hold their own against the forces of Rome, thanks in part to the aid of geography. The Germans lived to the north of the Celts in what is now northern Germany, Denmark, the Netherlands, and southern Scandinavia. The distance between the Romans and Germans was simply too great. When Roman armies were on campaign, they always traveled with huge baggage trains, which made it very difficult for them to move into German territory, where roads were mere footpaths, bridges were nonexistent, and forests covered much of the land.

In the first century, the Germans, like the Celts, did not comprise a single nation, but many diverse peoples, some large and some small, who occupied a certain region, worshiped in the same way, and followed a common leader. Contemporary with Jesus the largest of the German nations were the Suebi and the Vandili. Because of frequent wars and constant migration, there were never any stable boundaries among the Germans.

Archaeologists are still debating the origins of the Germans. Certainly they formed part of the great Indo-European migration into Europe and spoke a common language until as late as 750 B.C. Settling in the far north of Europe where there was but a thinly scattered Neolithic population, they probably met little resistance from their predecessors and easily absorbed them into their own groups. The Germans brought with them domesticated cattle, sheep, and pigs and the seeds of cereal grains, particularly barley, which can survive in cold and moist climates. The early Germans also used plows, which teams of oxen pulled through the soil in preparation for planting.

When the Bronze Age arrived in northern Europe around 1800 B.C., German smiths learned how to hammer the metal into daggers, spearheads, axes, and jewelry. Many of these objects were buried with their owners in graves of hollowed-out logs. Clearly grave gifts were important to these peoples: in Sweden, one early German captain was interred with his boat.

By the eighth century B.C., the amount of arable land could no longer keep pace with the growth in the German population, resulting in significant expansion that continued up to the time of Jesus and beyond. Climate change is thought to have contributed to these centuries of wandering. For around this time, northern Europe entered into a period of much cooler and rainier weather, with a rise in sea level along the Baltic coastline. Constant flooding of their villages and fields no doubt encouraged many men and women to seek new homes in an effort to escape the ever-present mud that threatened to engulf them. Their war bands now had another advantage: iron weaponry that had passed to them from the Celts.

The German expansion eastward was made at the expense of various Illyrian peoples who made their homes in that part of Europe. When they moved southward, it was the Celts who were pushed out of the way. A prime example of the Germanic migrations after the eighth century can be followed in the history of the Basternae. Leaving their homeland in northern Germany, they began to head south, arriving about 230 B.C. at the Black Sea. For the next two hundred years they roamed around what is now Romania, on occasion forcing out the Dacians, the original settlers of the lower Danube. The Romans became concerned that the Germans were threatening their security and sent a force against them. In 29 B.C., they challenged them to a battle that crushed the Basternae and forced the survivors to become Roman subjects, a status they maintained through the time of Jesus. Later, the Goths eliminated them altogether.

In addition to the Basternae, the Romans were worried about the movements of other Germans. In the middle of the second century B.C., the Burgundians left their constricted home of Bornholm, an island off the Swedish mainland, and advanced southward until, centuries later, they settled in the region of modern France that today bears their name. About the same time, the Goths of Götaland in Sweden decided to embark on a similar journey toward the Mediterranean.

When not called out to fight Romans, the Germanic people fought one another. Like the Celts, Germans placed the highest value on learning military skills.

The Teutones and Cimbri were originally based on the Danish peninsula of Jutland. About 120 B.C., the Cimbri descended into the province of Noricum, around modern Austria, challenging the Roman hold over the Danubian valley. The Teutones joined them there and sent a request to the Roman Senate that they be given lands in this lightly populated region. The Senate not only rejected their appeal, but also sent several armies to push them back into Germania; none of their campaigns proved successful. Now in southern Gaul, Rome's most able general, Gaius Marius, met the Teutones at Aquae Sextiae, modern Aix-en-Provence, and dealt them a crushing blow. A year later he disposed of the Cimbri in northern Italy. The Germans, however, kept coming. In one of his campaigns in Gaul, Julius Caesar had to fight a hundred twenty thousand Suebi who had crossed the Rhine River. German-Roman hostilities continued through the lifetime of Jesus, battles that are well documented by contemporary authors.

In 12 B.C., Caesar Augustus took up the battle against the Germans on the Rhine. Although it is possible that he wanted to extend the border between the Romans and Germans from the Rhine to the Elbe River, it is more likely that his motivation was simply defensive: he wanted to punish the Germans for their constant raids across the Rhine. Whatever the reason, he sent his adopted son and the brother of Tiberius, Nero

Claudius Drusus, on five campaigns against the Frisians and Saxons. In 9 B.C., the Romans camped alongside the Elbe, but during his return from the expedition, Drusus died after breaking a leg in a fall from his horse.

In A.D. 4, when Jesus was still a young boy in Nazareth, Augustus commissioned another army to scour the Danube frontier. A major threat to that border came from an alliance of Germans formed under the leadership of a chieftain named Maroboduus. This time the Roman command was entrusted to Tiberius. Before he could dispose of Maroboduus, though, he was called away to put down a revolt in Illyria, essentially leaving the Germans in place. Augustus then deputed Quintilius Varus to pacify the Germans threatening the Roman Rhine frontier. Varus was an unfortunate choice. Before his new appointment, he had held the governor's post in Syria, where his greed had alienated nearly everyone. In A.D. 9, Varus led his army into a trap set by the Germans at Teutoburg Forest, located in modern Westphalia. The disaster was nearly complete. Twenty thousand Roman legionnaires fell in battle. Wiped out were Legions XVII, XVIII, and XIX; they were never reconstituted. Survivors either killed themselves, like Varus, or were taken prisoner. Some of the latter were buried alive as sacrifices to the German gods for the victory. All Roman settlements in Germania except Aliso, a site near modern Haltern, were soon overrun. The commander at Aliso had to break through a siege to escape the slaughter.

Hunting wild animals, surprisingly, was so infrequent an activity for the Germans of Jesus' day that wild game made up less than two percent of the German family's diet.

For Caesar Augustus, the Roman debacle at Teutoburg Forest was enough. During the five remaining years of his life, no more armies were sent into Germania. Jesus was in his early teens when Teutoburg's battle took place. How much the news of the Roman defeat was talked about in Nazareth is impossible to know. Certainly anything that made life difficult for the Romans would have been welcomed by the nationalists among Jesus' Jewish companions and would have encouraged them in their resistance to Rome.

After the death of Augustus in A.D. 14, Tiberius became the new emperor. He had vivid personal memories of his own wars against the Germans and felt that Teutoburg cried out for revenge. Only months after he became emperor, Tiberius dispatched Germanicus Caesar, his nephew and the son of Drusus, to avenge the Roman defeat. Three times Germanicus plunged into Germania, and in A.D. 15 he reached Teutoburg Forest, where he ordered religious rites celebrated for the soldiers who had fallen five years earlier. In the course of his third expedition, Drusus had to fight the forces of a German coalition led by Arminius, himself a former legionary and therefore well acquainted with the Roman army's tactics. Arminius's experience, however, was not enough to bring him victory. Germanicus defeated his force of eighty thousand men and the Romans recovered two of the three legions' standards lost at Teutoburg Forest.

Disaster followed this stunning victory for Roman arms. After Germanicus put his soldiers aboard ships at North Sea ports for the return to Italy, a terrible storm wreaked havoc on the fleet, sending many of the ships and their men to the bottom. Germanicus's victory was therefore a tarnished one. The following year, Tiberius refused to allow him to mount another campaign in Germania. Instead, the emperor was content to make the Rhine and upper Danube rivers a permanent border between Germans and Romans. He stationed eight legions along the frontier, but they were purely defensive. Two Roman provinces, Germania Superior in the north and Germania Inferior in the south, served as the Rhine frontier for the next several centuries.

It was not so stable on the Danube, where hostilities continued between Romans and Germans for years to come. In these battles with the Romans, the Germans fought as foot soldiers, for only a very few chieftains could afford a horse. The soldier's principal weapons were thrusting spears and javelins that were light enough to be thrown. Neither swords nor bows and arrows were common, nor any kind of war chariot. For protection German infantrymen held round shields of wood, sometimes covered with toughened leather. Some fighters could afford armor of small metal rings, but most went into battle wearing only trousers. The heads of families helped decide which battles would be fought, casting "yes" or "no" votes in assemblies called by their chiefs.

Around the chief, who was expected to lead the charge, was his *comitatus* of elite warriors pledged to defend him to their deaths. Ordinary soldiers fought in *hundreds,* similar to the Roman centuries. The hundred was comprised of kinfolk and local soldiers recruited to fight. The German forces plunged into battle in a wedge formation, hoping to break enemy lines, but if the leader was killed in this charge, confusion resulted. The German armies were strong on offense, but weak on defense. Soldiers' families followed the troops, in covered wagons where possible, but otherwise on foot, for every man was responsible for feeding himself and for providing whatever he needed on campaign.

During one spring festival the image of the fertility goddess Nerthus was drawn in a wagon from village to village, with her priests scourging themselves along the way. Slaves were ordered to wash her statue in the sea and were afterward killed in a ceremony meant to guarantee fertility. This festival was known as Easter, and its wintertime counterpart was called Jul.

When not called out to fight Romans, the Germanic people fought one another. Like the Celts, Germans placed the highest value on learning military skills. Their society was extremely patriarchal. To right any wrong, real or perceived, the leading male, father or grandfather, decided how the family honor was to be redeemed. This frequently resulted in interminable feuds.

German villages were built in forest clearings, where several log houses stood on raised platforms. The houses were rectangular, with poles serving as the framework and branches or twigs covered with clay making up the exterior. Some were built large enough to shelter both a family and its livestock. Between the village and the forest, men cut down the trees and brush to make sure the village would not be taken unawares. For greater security, a log palisade was constructed around some settlements. At a greater distance from the village, farmers laid out their fields and had pens for their cattle and pigs. Hunting wild animals, surprisingly, was so infrequent an activity that wild game made up less than two percent of the German family's diet.

German men wore long jackets, woolen or linen trousers, and soft boots. Women's costume was a long, sleeveless dress, and it was customary for them to wear their hair long and plaited. Men who could afford to practiced polygamy. Women's major tasks were to care for the young children, weave the family's clothes, and look after the brewing of beer, ale, and mead, the latter a drink made from fermented honey. Gallons of these drinks were consumed on festive occasions. In villages that were prosperous enough, one building was set aside for community affairs, distinct from the chieftain's residence.

German society had but few slaves, or thralls, who were either prisoners of war or were obtained through purchase. For a prisoner, becoming a thrall had the advantage of avoiding hanging from an oak tree as a sacrifice to the gods.

Because each village was relatively self-sufficient, there was only limited trade among the Germans. From the Mediterranean regions in time of peace came imports of bronze and silver vessels, glass, a variety of ornaments, and gold coins. The Germans exchanged amber, hides, and furs to pay for them

German gods and goddesses were many. They did not have temples, for their worship took place in sacred groves, and offerings were presented to them in streams, rivers, and bogs. Wodan was the god of the dead; Tiwaz was the sky-god and the one who brought victory in war; Thor or Donar caused thunder and was master of the storm; and Njord controlled the sea. Freyr and his twin sister Freyja, wife of Wodan, watched over love and marriage. Later, in Anglo-Saxon England, the four middle days of the week would be named for the German divinities. Artists were sparing in representing their gods and goddesses; an exception was made for Tiwaz, whose symbol, the sun, was put on all kinds of objects to bring good fortune. Roman authors who wrote about the Germans identified these deities with their own gods and goddesses.

During one spring festival the image of the fertility goddess Nerthus was drawn in a wagon from village to village, with her priests scourging themselves along the way. Slaves were ordered to wash her statue in the sea and were afterward killed in a ceremony meant to guarantee fertility. This festival was known as *Easter,* and its wintertime counterpart was called *Jul.* When warriors went into battle, they called on spirits, the valkyries, for assistance. If a soldier had fought well and died, he was ushered into a paradise, Valhalla, for his reward. Much of what is known about Germanic religion shows it to have had a very pessimistic tone. In the end, the Germans believed, everything would be destroyed, even the gods and goddesses, in a universal *Götterdämmerung.*

THE BALTS

First-century Baltic peoples lived along the Vistula River and the Gulf of Riga and extended into the interior of northwestern Russia. Their land was a flat countryside of sandy soil, pine forest, and cool temperatures year-round, an environment more conducive to raising cattle than to growing crops, though they did grow some cereal grains to supplement their diet. The Romans knew Balts as the Aestii and were interested in them only to the extent that their merchants supplied the Roman world with amber. Unfortunately, due to the Romans' lack of interest and the Balts' lack of writing, archaeologists have little information on the early Balts beyond their material culture. Today the Latvians and Lithuanians are their descendants. Once there was another Baltic nation, the Prussians, but during the Middle Ages they were so overwhelmed by German invaders that they ceased to exist, and their name now refers to the Germans.

FURTHER FACTS

Modern-day Estonia gets its name from the Roman name Aestii, which probably originated with the historian Tacitus and referred simply to the land's location east of Roman borders.

Little, too, is known of the Estonians and Finns, who lived to the north of the Balts. They occupied a land almost devoid of human life when they first arrived, a country of thousands of lakes and dense forests. Most likely they displaced the Lapps, who followed the wild reindeer on whom they depended to the north. Despite the challenges the climate presented, both the Finns and the Estonians were farmers. Both were also exceptions to the rest of the northern Europeans in terms of their languages. Finnish and Estonian belong to the Finno-Ugric linguistic family, closely related to languages spoken by Inner Asian peoples. Archaeologists estimate that the speakers of these tongues first moved from Asia to their present location sometime after 100 B.C., which means that their migration was likely in progress during Jesus' lifetime.

Little can be known of the Baltic peoples of the first century, for they were not in touch with literate societies, and building structures of wood in damp climates means that few remains of early times can now be discovered. One possible source that opens the past is within the folk songs that can be traced back several centuries, but hardly two thousand years ago to the time of Jesus.

SLAVIC PEOPLES

Today a plurality of Europeans speak Slavic languages, but almost nothing is known about the Slavs at the time of Jesus, making it a true puzzle to explain their ancient history and their phenomenal increase in population. Recent archaeological investigations in present-day Poland and the Czech Republic have identified early settlements in their countries, but were these of Slavic origin? The Romans wrote of a people living to the northeast of the Germans whom they called Venedi, but there is considerable doubt as to whom this name belongs. The Roman geographer Ptolemy, writing in the first century, calls the Carpathian Mountains "the mountains of the Venedi," and the Baltic "the sea of the Venedi," so a strong presumption must exist that he is speaking of Slavic peoples. Nevertheless, the first certain reference to the Slavs is not found in a narrative source until the sixth century A.D.

Historians who attempt to reconstruct the Slavic past on so little information argue that at the time of Jesus there was still but a single language spoken among them. Later, as the Slavs dispersed eastward into the Russian forests, west to the Elbe and beyond, and south into the Balkans, the Slavic languages developed the different grammars and vocabularies that now distinguish them from one another. The earliest archeological finds point to a people living in village hill forts, farmers and herders who, unlike the Celts and Germans, wanted nothing more than to be left alone, with no great urge to make conquests at the expense of their neighbors. Weapons are not nearly so numerous as those found on the sites of their neighbors. There are objects that had drifted their way from the Sarmatians (that is, the Iranians), then living on the steppes of southern Russia, and some authorities would argue that at least the upper class of Serbs and Croatians reflect Sarmatian origins.

Above all, the Slavic peoples centered their lives on farming. Using wooden plows, they tilled the soil to produce the grains and vegetables upon which they lived. Village chieftains must have existed, but medieval writers make a point of the fact that the Slavs had no kings or princes at that time.

Little enough is known about Slavic religion. As might be expected, there was a sky-god, Perun, who rode in a heavenly chariot and carried a hammer, much like the German Donar. His devotees sacrificed a variety of animals to persuade him of their need for protection. Svętovit was the god of war and watched over the fields, and people celebrated his festival at harvest time. Svaros was the patron of the sun and of fire, and Volos was the divinity called upon to safeguard livestock.

SARMATIANS

The area that is now southern Russia and Ukraine was during Jesus' lifetime inhabited by various peoples, all of whom followed a uniform economy based on herding livestock and fighting as cavalrymen. Predominant were the Sarmatians, speaking languages similar to modern Iranian, and divided into Alans, Aorsi, Roxolani, and Iazyges, to mention but a few of the more prominent nations. Some descendants of the Sarmatians are still living today, the Ossetians of the Caucasus Mountains.

The great invention of the Sarmatian people was the stirrup, which gave them a huge advantage over other steppe horsemen. The stirrup gave their warriors the stability they needed to shoot their arrows with much greater accuracy, and in this way they overwhelmed the Scythians, their predecessors on the steppes. From childhood, boys were taught the skills of horsemanship. In times of peace they used their weapons on the hunt; in times of war they clustered in close formation, charging against enemies with javelins drawn and bows and arrows at the ready. For protection they wore armor so heavy that a man knocked from his mount could not get up without help. Greek and Roman authors were surprised to see women dressed in trousers accompanying the men on the hunt and in war.

Sarmatian flocks included cattle, sheep, and, of course, herds of horses. Mare's milk was drunk in both fermented and unfermented forms in large quantities. Sarmatians based their lives around the changing seasons, leading their animals to pasture and making sure that water was available once the days grew longer. During the warm months, therefore, they lived in ox-drawn wagons. In winter, clans came together, forming small settlements of tents that sheltered them from the winter winds. Artists decorated their few possessions with the animal designs that they borrowed from the Scythians.

During the lifetime of Jesus, the steppe lands were full of people migrating to the west. The Turkic-speaking Huns had arrived on the scene, bringing the eastern grasslands under their rule, and none of the Sarmatians wanted them for neighbors. Their reputation as warriors had preceded them. A Roman historian noted that the Huns "eat, drink, sleep, and hold their conversations on their horses." Their culture was based on raiding weaker peoples. The result was a general push of the Sarmatian peoples westward. From A.D. 20 to 30, the Iazyges occupied the Pannonian Plain (modern Hungary and the lowlands of Slovakia), dispersing the Celts who were there before them. The Roxolani found new homes in western Ukraine, and the Aorsi held on to what territory remained up to the southern Ural Mountains.

The Crimea was one of the few regions in Europe with city life during Jesus' day, for several Greek colonies had been planted in the region of the Sea of Azov. At Panticapaeum, now Kertch, a wealthy kingdom was established that served as the great merchant city between the Mediterranean world and the steppes. Here there was a mixing of Greek and Sarmatian culture, as merchants of both peoples followed their occupations. The goldsmiths of Panticapaeum held a well-deserved reputation for their work in jewelry and ornaments and competed for orders with merchants, who shipped tons of grain to feed the population of Roman Greece.

Europe north of the Alps was a world of restlessness during the time of Jesus, in the midst of a period of movement seldom equaled in the history of the continent. Although reading the classical authors gives contemporary historians a few insights into the details of the migrations, the lack of written records from the peoples themselves prohibits any really thorough study.

Polytheism prevailed in the central and northern European religions. Priests and priestesses busied themselves pacifying the many unseen gods and spirits who, if it pleased them, might put off disaster and bring fertility and victory. In addition, war and religion were closely aligned; it was almost universal that prisoners of war were sacrificed to their captors' gods.

Thus it remains difficult to perceive Jesus' message of reconciliation receiving a warm welcome among the peoples of northern Europe during his lifetime. The Celts, Germans, and other Europeans lived in an environment where survival was the greatest concern of most families and where violence was expected to solve most problems, and these factors were reflected in their belief systems. Jesus' profession of love, nonviolence, and peace would have seemed preposterous to them. Furthermore, nomadic peoples would have been poor prospects for Christian conversion two millennia ago: for Jesus' message to take hold, a relatively settled society, in which at least the upper classes were literate, seems to have been a necessity.

Chapter Five

Africa South of the Sahara

The Sahara Desert very effectively cuts the southern part of Africa off from the north, forming a formidable barrier to communication and transportation between the Mediterranean and the African interior. Contact did continue in the Nile Valley between the Nubians and the Egyptians, but this was the only exception to the rule that Africa south of the Sahara went largely its own way. It was not until the Roman period in North Africa, possibly a century after the lifetime of Jesus, that regular patterns of communication were established with Africans living below the Sahara. At that time the introduction of the dromedary allowed the caravans of the Tuareg, one of the Berber peoples, to travel across the desert.

The region of sub-Saharan Africa is distinguished by a variety of climates and landforms. Near the equator, rain forest covers much of the country, and men and women who live in its perpetual shade must cope with high temperatures and constant rain throughout the year. In the north, between the desert and the forest, is a band of land called the *sahel*, a transition zone between a completely arid world and one that receives a little rain, though the amount fluctuates from year to year. On either side of the rain forest, the grasslands of the savannahs appear; in East Africa they are home to the largest collection of wild animals in the world. The tallest mountains and the Great Rift Valley, a depression that runs the length of the continent, are in East Africa. An ancient fault line in the African plateau explains the valley's origins. The large lakes of the Great Rift Valley contain much of the continent's fresh water, and it is here that the Nile has its origin.

There are several great river systems in central and southern Africa, but they are difficult to navigate from the ocean. Waterfalls and cataracts impede travelers seeking to journey into the interior. In addition, there are few good harbors along the coast, contributing to the isolation of this part of the African continent during ancient times. None of the African peoples developed commercial links with the outside world, for these depended on the ocean. In Jesus' lifetime, trading ships from India came to the east coast of Africa, following the monsoon winds that blew across the Indian Ocean, but the Africans were content to allow the Indians to do the sailing.

AFRICAN PEOPLES

Three major groups of people lived in Africa south of the Sahara in Jesus' time. One was the Mbuti, or Pygmies, known for their small stature. If modern Mbuti are a guide to their predecessors, the average man stood about four feet eight inches tall and weighed about ninety pounds. In the first century the Mbuti made their home in the rain forests, moving about in small bands. The men depended on the bow and arrow to bring down the game on which their families lived. Women and children supplemented their diet through gathering wild foods that the forest provided. They continue to live this way today. The present-day Mbuti are one of the world's few remaining hunting societies and probably follow the same traditions as their ancestors did two thousand years ago.

A second group was made up of those who spoke Khoisan languages, two peoples who are thought to be closely related because of the similarities in their languages. In addition to typical consonant and vowel sounds, speakers use "clicks" unknown in any other spoken tongue. The Khoi were limited to southern Africa, while the San ranged from Egypt south through East Africa's savannahs all the way to the tip of the continent, now called the Cape of Good Hope. These people were also hunters, using the bow and arrow to kill the large animals of the African savannahs.

In the first century, Negroes made up the third group of Africans in sub-Saharan Africa. They were the creators of the first African sculpture. Archaeologists have discovered the first certain remains of people known to be Negroes in two widely dispersed sites, the Lake Region and the Sudan, where people lived by fishing. About 1500 B.C., Negroes of the Niger River Valley began to practice farming at a time when rainfall was much more dependable than it is today. Their major crops were cereals: millet and sorghum, which could provide flour for making bread. Farmers also cultivated a species of cotton for cloth. These early Nigerians also discovered some local plants that could be domesticated, including a variety of yams, gourds, and the oil palm. By contrast, guinea fowl were the only indigenous animals that could be raised in captivity. In Ethiopia, farmers grew root crops and cowpeas, but no farming succeeded in the rain forest environment. Central and southern Africa's lack of large animals capable of domestication was a serious drawback to further agricultural development.

FURTHER FACTS

The tsetse fly feeds on the blood of humans and animals, in the process often transmitting the parasite that causes sleeping sickness. The disease's first symptoms are flu-like, but un-treated it attacks the nervous system, eventually resulting in coma and death.

This disadvantage was partially compensated for when cattle were introduced from Egypt into sub-Saharan Africa. Several nations who had been hunters and gatherers eagerly adapted the herding way of life, and cattle raising spread both westward and southward. Cattle became so important that their number was equated with wealth, and they became a medium of exchange. Unfortunately, the tsetse fly, which carries sleeping sickness, was fatal to cattle as well as to people; because of them, large areas of Africa were uninhabited at the time of Jesus.

About 500 B.C. ironwork first appeared in Africa south of the Sahara. The technology came from two directions: Egypt and Carthage. Prior to this, tools and weapons were made of wood, horn, or stone. The obvious advantage of replacing these objects with ones made of iron

Strabo on the land of Meroe.

Source: Strabo, Geography. *Trans. H.L. Jones.*

THEY LIVE ON MILLET AND BARLEY, FROM WHICH ALSO A BREAD IS PREPARED. THEY HAVE NO OIL, BUT USE BUTTER AND FAT INSTEAD. THERE ARE NO FRUITS, EXCEPT THE PRODUCE OF TREES AND THE ROYAL GARDENS. SOME FEED EVEN UPON GRASS, THE TENDER TWIGS OF TREES, THE LOTUS, OR THE ROOTS OF REEDS. THEY LIVE ALSO UPON THE FLESH AND BLOOD OF ANIMALS, MILK, AND CHEESE. THEY REVERENCE THEIR KINGS AS GODS, WHO ARE FOR THE MOST PART KEPT UP IN THEIR PALACES. :: THEIR LARGEST ROYAL SEAT IS THE CITY OF MEROE, OF THE SAME NAME AS THE ISLAND. THE SHAPE OF THE ISLAND IS SAID TO BE THAT OF A SHIELD. ITS SIZE IS PERHAPS EXAGGERATED. ITS LENGTH IS ABOUT 3000, AND ITS BREADTH 1000 STADIA. IT IS VERY MOUNTAINOUS, AND CONTAINS GREAT FORESTS. THE INHABITANTS ARE NOMADS, WHO ARE PARTLY HUNTERS AND PARTLY HUSBANDS. THERE ARE ALSO MINES OF COPPER, IRON, GOLD, AND VARIOUS KINDS OF PRECIOUS STONES. IT IS SURROUNDED ON THE SIDE OF LIBYA BY GREAT HILLS OF SAND, AND ON THAT OF ARABIA BY CONTINUOUS PRECIPICES. IN THE HIGHER PARTS ON THE SOUTH, IT IS BOUNDED BY THE CONFLUENT STREAMS OF THE RIVERS ASTABORAS, ASTAPUS, AND ASTASOBAS. ON THE NORTH IS THE CONTINUOUS COURSE OF THE NILE TO EGYPT, WITH ITS WINDINGS, OF WHICH WE HAVE SPOKEN BEFORE. :: THE HOUSES IN THE CITIES ARE FORMED BY INTERWEAVING SPLIT PIECES OF PALM WOOD OR OF BRICKS. THEY HAVE FOSSIL SALT, AS IN ARABIA. PALM, THE PERSEA (PEACH), EBONY, AND CAROB TREES ARE FOUND IN ABUNDANCE. THEY HUNT ELEPHANTS, LIONS, AND PANTHERS. THERE ARE ALSO SERPENTS, WHICH ENCOUNTER ELEPHANTS, AND THERE ARE MANY OTHER KINDS OF WILD ANIMALS, WHICH TAKE REFUGE FROM THE HOTTER AND PARCHED DISTRICTS IN WATERY AND MARSHY DISTRICTS.

was immediately grasped. Thus a class of smiths, who learned smelting techniques, developed in many African nations. Ironsmiths were honored in some societies, while in others they became a despised caste. By A.D. 1, iron making had reached the Congo basin.

During the lifetime of Jesus, a great migration of Negroes was in progress. The Bantu-speaking people were on the move from their homelands in Nigeria and Cameroon, where they had lived on the edge of the rain forest, southward and eastward. As they traveled, some took up agriculture and others herding. When people settled in villages, men and women began to accept the authority of chieftains, many of whom claimed descent from gods and goddesses. The role of ancestors remains an integral part of Bantu religious life into modern times.

The Bantu probably moved very slowly in small bands of related individuals, for the migration was still in progress when Europeans first came to southern Africa many centuries later. They assimilated the San who lay in their path, or sometimes pushed them into more remote areas. Today more than four hundred Bantu languages are spoken in Africa, demonstrating just how isolated and fragmented the Bantu migration was. It is tempting to link the spread of ironwork with the Bantu expansion, but archaeologists have thus far been unable to confirm this theory.

KUSH

Fifty miles south of the first cataract of the Nile, the border of Roman Egypt ended. Beyond it the Negroes of sub-Saharan Africa constructed the first kingdom on the banks of the White Nile in the region of Nubia (modern Sudan). It was known as Kush, and its capital was at Meroe. At the time of Jesus, its culture had reached its peak.

For many centuries, the people of Nubia had close connections with the Egyptians. Unlike Egypt, Nubia received sufficient rainfall for agriculture, and the land grew forests for wood. Close to the White Nile were plentiful grasslands for pasturing cattle, which were the mainstay of the early Kushite economy. About 1100 B.C. the Nubian people's dependence on Egypt ended when they developed a powerful Kushite

state. Several centuries later, in fact, the relationship between Kush and Egypt was reversed when the former's strongest monarch, Piy, led an army northward that made him supreme over the Egyptian people. Piy assumed the name of pharaoh for himself, and all subsequent Kushite rulers kept that title. While the Kushite occupation of Egypt was not long-lived, it counts as Egypt's Twenty-fifth Dynasty.

FURTHER FACTS

There were more pyramids built in Kush than in Egypt.

About 500 B.C., the Kushites learned to work with iron, a development which quickly made Meroe the center of African iron production. Laborers flocked into Meroe to find employment in manufacturing iron instruments and tools that were exported throughout eastern Africa. Ore was plentiful and charcoal, used in the smelting process, easy to obtain because of nearby forests. The site of ancient Meroe still is distinguished by hills of slag cast off during the smelting process.

At the time of Jesus, the pharaohs of Meroe were rich from the network of trade that radiated out from it. Caravans brought imports to the Kushite capital from as far away as India. The pharaohs were so wealthy that they could afford to keep a herd of elephants to grace royal processions. Palace scribes kept records of the rulers' possessions, but the Kushite script, of which little survives, is still not deciphered. Therefore, the details of Meroen history remain obscure. What does remain in quantity are the great pyramids that the pharaohs of Meroe put up for their tombs at a time when pyramid-building had gone out of fashion in Egypt itself. The Roman occupation of Egypt must surely have made the pharaohs of Meroe consider themselves the true heirs of ancient Egyptian traditions. The Romans seemed to acknowledge this, since Caesar Augustus welcomed Kushite ambassadors to Italy. Augustus also donated funds for a temple to their god, Mandulis, who during the time of Jesus was in competition with Isis for the veneration of the Kushites.

The pyramids of the Meroen kings and queens in modern-day Sudan were built between 300 B.C. and A.D. 400.

Archaeologists also have found evidence of Ethiopian kingdoms to the south of Nubia, but almost nothing is known about them. Sometime before the birth of Jesus, Semitic-speaking people crossed the Red Sea from Yemen and mixed with the native population, thus giving birth to a distinctive Ethiopian physical appearance. The great days of Ethiopia

The Nigerians of Jesus' day had a rich mythology to explain both the natural world and their own customs.

Source: Elphinstone Dayrell, Folk Stories from Southern Nigeria *(1910)*

WHY DEAD PEOPLE ARE BURIED

IN THE BEGINNING OF THE WORLD WHEN THE CREATOR HAD MADE MEN AND WOMEN AND THE ANIMALS, THEY ALL LIVED TOGETHER IN THE CREATION LAND. THE CREATOR WAS A BIG CHIEF, PAST ALL MEN, AND BEING VERY KINDHEARTED, WAS VERY SORRY WHENEVER ANYONE DIED. SO ONE DAY HE SENT FOR THE DOG, WHO WAS HIS HEAD MESSENGER, AND TOLD HIM TO GO OUT INTO THE WORLD AND GIVE HIS WORD TO ALL PEOPLE THAT FOR THE FUTURE WHENEVER ANYONE DIED THE BODY WAS TO BE PLACED IN THE COMPOUND, AND WOOD ASHES WERE TO BE THROWN OVER IT; THAT THE DEAD BODY WAS TO BE LEFT ON THE GROUND, AND IN TWENTY-FOUR HOURS IT WOULD BECOME ALIVE AGAIN. WHEN THE DOG HAD TRAVELED FOR HALF A DAY HE BEGAN TO GET TIRED; SO AS HE WAS NEAR AN OLD WOMAN'S HOUSE HE LOOKED IN, AND SEEING A BONE WITH SOME MEAT ON IT HE MADE A MEAL OFF IT, AND THEN WENT TO SLEEP, ENTIRELY FORGETTING THE MESSAGE WHICH HAD BEEN GIVEN HIM TO DELIVER. :: AFTER A TIME, WHEN THE DOG DID NOT RETURN, THE CREATOR CALLED FOR A SHEEP, AND SENT HIM OUT WITH THE SAME MESSAGE. BUT THE SHEEP WAS A VERY FOOLISH ONE, AND BEING HUNGRY, BEGAN EATING THE SWEET GRASSES BY THE WAYSIDE. AFTER A TIME, HOWEVER, HE REMEMBERED THAT HE HAD A MESSAGE TO DELIVER, BUT FORGOT WHAT IT WAS EXACTLY; SO AS HE WENT ABOUT AMONG THE PEOPLE HE TOLD THEM THAT THE MESSAGE THE CREATOR HAD GIVEN HIM TO TELL THE PEOPLE WAS THAT WHENEVER ANYONE DIED THEY SHOULD BE BURIED UNDERNEATH THE GROUND. :: A LITTLE TIME AFTERWARDS THE DOG REMEMBERED HIS MESSAGE, SO HE RAN INTO THE TOWN AND TOLD THE PEOPLE THAT THEY WERE TO PLACE WOOD ASHES ON THE DEAD BODIES AND LEAVE THEM IN THE COMPOUND, AND THAT THEY WOULD COME TO LIFE AGAIN AFTER

TWENTY-FOUR HOURS. BUT THE PEOPLE WOULD NOT BELIEVE HIM, AND SAID, "WE HAVE ALREADY RECEIVED WORD FROM THE CREATOR BY THE SHEEP THAT ALL DEAD BODIES SHOULD BE BURIED." IN CONSEQUENCE OF THIS THE DEAD BODIES ARE NOW ALWAYS BURIED, AND THE DOG IS MUCH DISLIKED AND NOT TRUSTED AS A MESSENGER, AS IF HE HAD NOT FOUND THE BONE IN THE OLD WOMAN'S HOUSE AND FORGOTTEN HIS MESSAGE, THE DEAD PEOPLE MIGHT STILL BE ALIVE.

The Negroes were the creators of the first African sculpture, of which this terra-cotta head discovered in Nigeria is an excellent example.

would come in the fourth century A.D., when its rulers at Axum would inherit the legacy of Meroe.

If, two thousand years ago, Jesus had lived in Africa south of the Sahara, his mission would never have become known outside a small group of disciples trained in oral traditions. Over time, it would probably have been pared down to a handful of myths that portrayed him as a man with supernatural healing powers — or have been forgotten altogether. Without writing to record the events of his life he would, like millions of Africans, have lived and died outside the notice of the rest of the world.

FURTHER FACTS

Women were accorded high status in Nubian culture. Kings traced their lineage through their mothers, and a king's successor would usually be the son of his sister. For this reason kings would often marry their sisters, ensuring that their own sons would succeed them.

Certainly religion was important in African society. Public worship, in which dance played an especially vital role, provided communities with festivals throughout the year, and personal religion was closely associated with the healing arts. Unfortunately, the Africans' concept of the gods had little in common with Jesus' teachings about a single, loving God. He did not consider rulers or ancestors to be more divine than anyone else, and this was an idea at the heart of many religions in sub-Saharan Africa.

Chapter Six

China

OF ALL THE WORLD'S early cultures, China's is the youngest, but it has also been the most enduring. Geographically remote from other ancient centers of civilization, it was able to develop free of outside influences. Despite its differences, though, it is easy for historians to study today, for it was a literate society long before the time of Jesus. In the first century, Chinese historians had already established a tradition of recording the events that shaped the country's development.

Chinese civilization began in the Yellow River Valley, where the soil was especially rich. Known as loess, the earth was made up of layers of the topsoil of Inner Asia that strong winds blew into northern China over thousands of years. Chinese farmers appreciated the fertility of the earth, but were constantly challenged by the unpredictability of the river. One year it would be too low, foreshadowing drought; another season would bring floods, drowning farms and rotting the seed the farmers had so carefully planted. The Chinese over the centuries built hundreds of dikes to control the course of the river, but with only limited success. Fortunately, the Yellow is not the only major waterway in China: a second great river valley exists thanks to the flow of the Yangtze in the southern part of the country. Unlike the Yellow, the Yangtze flows to the sea with quiet ease from the eastern Sichuan region to the Pacific.

The mountains of China run north to south in some parts of the country, and from east to west in others. As a result, ancient China was made up of isolated regions where people living in one location knew little of their neighbors, who also spoke Chinese, but in dialects that made it incomprehensible to them. Maintaining national unity has challenged every government that has ruled China from the distant past up to the present.

If a family neglected prayers and sacrifices for its ancestors, deceased family members were thought to go out of existence.

The Chinese climate is very diverse. In northern China, winters are severe, with strong, dry winds carrying clouds of dust; while in the extreme southern part of the country a subtropical climate exists. The north depends on summer rains, while in the south torrential monsoon rains sweep in from the Pacific.

Farmers in the Yellow River Valley grew wheat, barley, vegetables, and millet, and kept pigs, ducks, geese, and chickens for meat. In southern China, rice was the staple of people's diet. Farmers used iron plows, pulled by teams of oxen, to prepare their fields in the north, while in the south water buffalo and humans had to ready the rice paddies. Cultivating rice required intense labor during the planting season, for young rice plants must stand in water in order to grow. In the first century, southern China was only sparsely populated, and rice production just beginning to take hold.

ANCIENT CHINESE CULTURE

The Chinese measured time in dynasties rather than in centuries. Time, they thought, was cyclical, with one age following another in unchanging succession. They marked the beginning of history with the Xia dynasty and the emperor Yu the Great, who is credited with setting a pattern for all subsequent events in Chinese history. Yu's half-mythological reign is dated about 2200 B.C., and was followed by the historical Shang, Zhou,

Qin, and Han dynasties. The Han period had two divisions: the Western, or Early, and the Eastern, or Later, Han Dynasty. Wang Mang, the sole Xin emperor, held the imperial throne between these two dynasties and was the sovereign of China during the time of Jesus' youth.

DAILY LIFE

If Jesus had been reared in China, he would have received a very secular education whose goals were to instill a sense of moral sensitivity and duty toward people and the state. Interpersonal communication, social customs, and music would have been main elements of the curriculum.

By the first century B.C., China had already made significant progress in many areas of science and the arts. Probably the Chinese were already the world's most creative society. They were certainly among the most numerous. A census taken in A.D. 2 counted 58 million people.

Foremost among Chinese discoveries was writing. Pictograms — images of the objects or ideas that people wanted to record — made up the script, and were first used on oracle bones that shamans used to predict the future. Over the centuries, these pictures became more abstract and complex, eventually developing into a system of characters. Only scribes could master the script, for more than six thousand individual characters had to be memorized. In Jesus' time, there were probably more books written in Chinese than in any other script.

The Chinese were also masters of wooden architecture. In Anyang, the capital of the Shangs until 1050 B.C., architects designed a palace for the emperor, offices for members of his staff, and warehouses to hold the grain collected as taxes. Shang metalworkers learned how to cast bronze into such objects as animals, mirrors, and cauldrons, which were used in religious ceremonies. Other artisans specialized in lacquerware and ceramics.

Like nearly all other ancient peoples, the Chinese were animists. They thought of the universe in terms of both physical and immaterial beings. The spirit of the heavens was called Tien, and one of the major concerns of every emperor was to make sacrifices to Tien so that the kingdom should prosper. Many other celestial bodies were personalized and became the object of religious devotion, as did the forces of nature.

Every Chinese family was duty-bound to honor its ancestors, for ancestral spirits could intervene in the present world for better or for worse depending on how they were treated. If a family neglected prayers and sacrifices for its ancestors, deceased family members were thought to go out of existence.

Chinese religion never developed a sacred scripture or a priestly class, and it lacked any sense of divine revelation. When individuals needed aid or advice from the spiritual realm, they could call in a shaman to contact it. Shamans used music and chanting to reach an ecstatic state in which the spirits were thought to use them as mediums. Despite the presence of shamans, though, Chinese religion was essentially a family matter, and its emphasis was more on family values than on the spiritual world, making China the most secular society in the ancient world.

CHINESE SOCIETY

↓

The silk made by Chinese women was prized by aristocrats as far away as Rome. Though this painting dates from the eleventh century, it depicts a process that had changed little since Jesus' day.

The Shang emperors and their successors claimed to be Sons of Heaven. They considered themselves more than ordinary mortals, and believed that heaven itself had designated them to rule. They therefore held a responsibility to stand before the gods as representatives of their subjects. Through sacrifices and ceremonies, they sought to ensure that heaven would continue to look favorably on them. If, on the other hand, religious duties were neglected, they believed that heaven's mandate could be withdrawn, and another dynasty chosen to supplant the old one.

Ranking just below the imperial family — the emperor and his many wives and children — were court officials and the nobility who lived in the capital. In China, to be noble was to be a landowner. Whether they had their mansions in the city or were content to make their home in the countryside, for an aristocratic family the key to social status and economic well-being was the careful management of their estates. The work of peasant farmers sustained the lifestyles of the aristocrats. The nobility filled their days with hunting, horse racing, archery, and games, while the peasants spent all their waking hours at work in the fields. When the aristocrats felt bored, they made war on one another.

In every Chinese family, whether peasant or noble, the oldest male had decision-making power. He oversaw the property, found marriage partners for his children, and sought opportunities for the family's social advancement. The eldest female supervised all other women in her household. Wives of her sons came to live in her family, and she assigned them their work and made sure that their children learned obedience to their parents, considered to be the highest virtue in Chinese society. Women played no part in public life, and were taught unquestioning obedience to their husbands and, by extension, to their mothers-in-law.

One of the tasks assigned to women was the care of silkworm larvae. Several times each day the larvae had to be fed mulberry leaves. They also had to be kept at just the right temperature to ensure that they would move into the pupal stage of development. At this stage they began to weave cocoons, which, once finished, furnished the raw material for silk

Confucius's teachings stressed justice, order, and propriety.

Source: Confucius, Analects, *ch. 20. Trans. James Legge*

TSZE-CHANG SAID, "WHAT IS MEANT BY BEING BENEFICENT WITHOUT GREAT EXPENDITURE?" THE MASTER REPLIED, "WHEN THE PERSON IN AUTHORITY MAKES MORE BENEFICIAL TO THE PEOPLE THE THINGS FROM WHICH THEY NATURALLY DERIVE BENEFIT; — IS NOT THIS BEING BENEFICENT WITHOUT GREAT EXPENDITURE? WHEN HE CHOOSES THE LABORS WHICH ARE PROPER, AND MAKES THEM LABOR ON THEM, WHO WILL REPINE? WHEN HIS DESIRES ARE SET ON BENEVOLENT GOVERNMENT, AND HE SECURES IT, WHO WILL ACCUSE HIM OF COVETOUSNESS? WHETHER HE HAS TO DO WITH MANY PEOPLE OR FEW, OR WITH THINGS GREAT OR SMALL, HE DOES NOT DARE TO INDICATE ANY DISRESPECT; — IS NOT THIS TO MAINTAIN A DIGNIFIED EASE WITHOUT ANY PRIDE? HE ADJUSTS HIS CLOTHES AND CAP, AND THROWS A DIGNITY INTO HIS LOOKS, SO THAT, THUS DIGNIFIED, HE IS LOOKED AT WITH AWE; — IS NOT THIS TO BE MAJESTIC WITHOUT BEING FIERCE?" :: TSZE-CHANG THEN ASKED, "WHAT ARE MEANT BY THE FOUR BAD THINGS?" THE MASTER SAID, "TO PUT THE PEOPLE TO DEATH WITHOUT HAVING INSTRUCTED THEM; — THIS IS CALLED CRUELTY. TO REQUIRE FROM THEM, SUDDENLY, THE FULL TALE OF WORK, WITHOUT HAVING GIVEN THEM WARNING; — THIS IS CALLED OPPRESSION. TO ISSUE ORDERS AS IF WITHOUT URGENCY, AT FIRST, AND, WHEN THE TIME COMES, TO INSIST ON THEM WITH SEVERITY; — THIS IS CALLED INJURY. AND, GENERALLY, IN THE GIVING PAY OR REWARDS TO MEN, TO DO IT IN A STINGY WAY; — THIS IS CALLED ACTING THE PART OF A MERE OFFICIAL." :: THE MASTER SAID, "WITHOUT RECOGNIZING THE ORDINANCES OF HEAVEN, IT IS IMPOSSIBLE TO BE A SUPERIOR MAN. :: "WITHOUT AN ACQUAINTANCE WITH THE RULES OF PROPRIETY, IT IS IMPOSSIBLE FOR THE CHARACTER TO BE ESTABLISHED. :: "WITHOUT KNOWING THE FORCE OF WORDS, IT IS IMPOSSIBLE TO KNOW MEN."

thread. Because this process was so time-consuming and labor-intensive, the cost of silk was extremely high. To wear it was an immediate sign that a man or woman should be treated with deference. This, of course, created a huge demand for silk garments in the imperial court and among its courtiers. Aristocrats as far away as the Roman Mediterranean wanted to imitate the Chinese upper classes in wearing silken attire.

China was probably the world's wealthiest civilization at the time of Jesus. Thanks to the country's rich soil and favorable climate, there were surpluses of food even as the population grew. But this wealth was not an unmixed blessing, leading often to frequent wars among regional leaders over land, prestige, and position.

CONFUCIUS

It was during one of these periods of warfare that the most renowned philosopher of ancient China came upon the scene. This was Kongfuzi, whom Westerners call Confucius. Until the twentieth century his teachings were second only to Jesus' in their influence on subsequent history.

Born about 550 B.C., Confucius was a member of the Chinese lower nobility. He once tried to obtain a position at court, but failed and took up the life of a teacher instead. His goal was to diminish the violence that permeated the Chinese upper class, and therefore his teachings were centered around the pursuit of harmony. He insisted that the way to find this harmony was to be content with one's position in life: "Let the ruler be a ruler, and the subject a subject. Let the father be a father and the son a son." If pride and ambition were to be abolished, as he felt they should be, then men and women had to accept where they were in life, and be willing to serve an emperor, even an evil one, because of his position. Of course, Confucius pointed out, the ruler especially should be devoted to truth and justice, and he should act as the father of his people, promoting honesty and justice among his officials.

Like Jesus, Confucius did not write anything himself, but left others to remember what he had said and to put it into books. Much of the literature ascribed to Confucius was not written until long after his

These excerpts from the *Dao-de Qing* typify its emphasis on simplicity and adaptability.

Source: Tao-te Ching. *Trans. James Legge (1891).*

29 IF ANYONE SHOULD WISH TO GET THE KINGDOM FOR HIMSELF, AND TO EFFECT THIS BY WHAT HE DOES, I SEE THAT HE WILL NOT SUCCEED. THE KINGDOM IS A SPIRIT-LIKE THING, AND CANNOT BE GOT BY ACTIVE DOING. HE WHO WOULD SO WIN IT DESTROYS IT; HE WHO WOULD HOLD IT IN HIS GRASP LOSES IT.

THE COURSE AND NATURE OF THINGS IS SUCH THAT
WHAT WAS IN FRONT IS NOW BEHIND;
WHAT WARMED ANON WE FREEZING FIND.
STRENGTH IS OF WEAKNESS OFT THE SPOIL;
THE STORE IN RUINS MOCKS OUR TOIL.

HENCE THE SAGE PUTS AWAY EXCESSIVE EFFORT, EXTRAVAGANCE, AND EASY INDULGENCE.

81 SINCERE WORDS ARE NOT FINE; FINE WORDS ARE NOT SINCERE. THOSE WHO ARE SKILLED (IN THE DAO) DO NOT DISPUTE; THE DISPUTATIOUS ARE NOT SKILLED IN IT. THOSE WHO KNOW (THE DAO) ARE NOT EXTENSIVELY LEARNED; THE EXTENSIVELY LEARNED DO NOT KNOW IT.

THE SAGE DOES NOT ACCUMULATE. THE MORE THAT HE EXPENDS FOR OTHERS, THE MORE DOES HE POSSESS OF HIS OWN; THE MORE THAT HE GIVES TO OTHERS, THE MORE DOES HE HAVE HIMSELF.

WITH ALL THE SHARPNESS OF THE WAY OF HEAVEN, IT INJURES NOT; WITH ALL THE DOING IN THE WAY OF THE SAGE HE DOES NOT STRIVE.

This painting, *Seeking the Dao in the Autumn Mountains,* is an excellent example of the serene landscape paintings inspired by the teachings of Laozi.

death, and this makes it difficult to sort out. How much of Confucian writing can really be attributed to Confucius, and how much should be ascribed to his followers? The principal book of Confucian wisdom is found in the *Analects.*

Quite in contrast to Jesus, Confucius had little interest in religion. He claimed no revelation from God and was unconcerned with matters pertaining to life after death. His message was meant for this world, not the next.

DAOISM

Although Confucian values were preeminent in China in Jesus' day, Confucius was not alone in shaping Chinese ethics. Other sages arose to challenge or modify his doctrine. The most striking alternative was that offered by Daoism, whose adherents followed "the way." The founder of Daoism, Laozi, is difficult to pinpoint in history. In fact, he may not have existed at all, but a book, the *Dao-de Qing,* whose title can be loosely translated as "The Way of Power," "The Way of Life," or "The Classic of the Way of Virtue," is attributed to his authorship. Daoism departed from Confucius's teachings in several ways. Most significantly, it rejected his way of achieving harmony, finding it too formal, too static, and too unwilling to consider the role played by emotion in people's lives.

The Daoist message urged people to imitate nature. It was in adapting to life the way nature adapted to circumstance that men and women could best live their lives. Chinese landscape painting, with its serene views of mountains, lakes, and forests, best represents the strong influence Daoism had on the Chinese consciousness.

Yin and yang were concepts significant to both Confucianism and Daoism at the time of Jesus, meant to explain why opposites exist: good and evil, hot and cold, light and darkness, male and female, earth and sky. Every object, the Chinese believed, was dominated either by yin or by yang, yet there was also a bit of yin in yang, and a bit of yang in yin. Thus nothing could ever be truly stable in life, for there were opposing forces at work in everything. Along with the values of Confucianism, the idea of yin and yang fostered a sense of fatalism in the Chinese mind-set, and served to confirm the view that history was cyclical.

THE QIN DYNASTY

In 221 B.C., the Mandate of Heaven was withdrawn from the Zhou emperors, who had succeeded the Shang. A new dynasty, the Qin, inherited it. For the first time in history a single emperor, Qin Shi Huangdi, ruled with a firm hand from Qangan (six miles northwest of modern Xian in Shaanxi Province) over both northern and southern China. Shi Huangdi means First Emperor, and the Qin ruler thought of himself as the first effective ruler of his land. Hungry for power, his attitude toward Confucianism was predictable: he buried many of its teachers alive, and burned every one of its books he could find. Fortunately, scholars who got wind of these massacres hid many of Confucius's books, and these are the ones extant today. Qin Shi Huangdi believed essentially that might made right, and China, "the Middle Kingdom," had a duty to conquer its weaker neighbors. His armies plunged south into Vietnam and north into Korea, bringing both under his sovereignty.

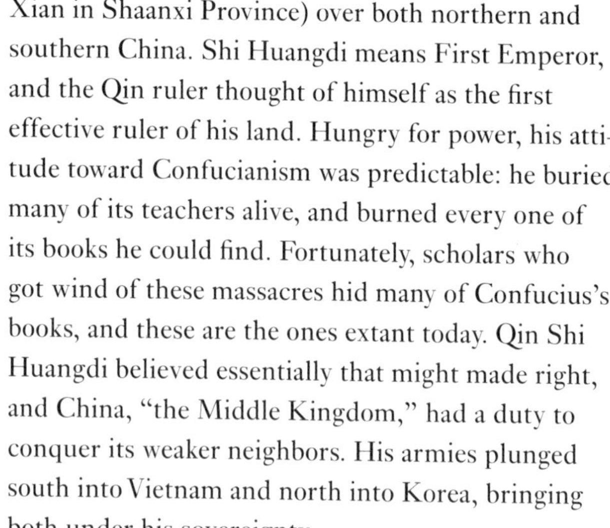

Qin Shi Huangdi is remembered for ordering the construction of two great monuments: the Great Wall

FURTHER FACTS

Despite his extravagant tomb, Qin Shi Huangdi was ill at ease regarding death. He spent his last years commissioning alchemists to find or create a potion that would make him immortal, drank mercury believing it would increase his longevity, and died due to an illness contracted on a voyage to Japan in search of the elixir of life.

and his own tomb. In order to hold back raids by the nomadic horsemen to the north of the country, earlier emperors had built walls to protect themselves. Qin Shi Huangdi sought to connect these walls into a single edifice that would run the length of the border. His government conscripted thousands of workers from all over the nation to work on this project.

For his tomb Qin Shi Huangdi ordered a mountain close by Qangan excavated. For thirty years laborers worked on this project. Then, to assure that he would not be bereft of an army in the afterlife, he commissioned 7,500 life-sized soldiers, each one different, to be made out of clay and buried with him. (Only in 1974, after having been lost for centuries, was the tomb discovered and its contents brought to light.) Most Chinese regarded Qin Shi Huangdi's centralization of the government, his conscription of labor, and the grueling tax burden he placed on the populace to be in direct contrast to their own values. Not surprisingly, only four years after his death rebels overthrew his second son and put in his place a more moderate regime, the Han dynasty.

HAN CHINA

Liu Bang, an officer in the army, became the agent for the Qin dynasty's demise. In 202 B.C., he ascended the imperial throne to become the first of the Han emperors. His descendants, the Western Hans, would rule China up to the time of Jesus. These rulers, particularly the Gao Zu Emperor, spent much of their wealth beautifying Qangan to be a fitting capital, full of palaces, parks, and wide avenues, and surrounded by a packed earth wall pierced with twelve gates. A center lane in all the major streets was reserved for the emperor's carriage. In addition to the palaces an armory, temples, and nine markets were located inside the city walls.

The Han appointed landowners to handle governmental affairs on the local level. They had little interference from Qangan so long as taxes were dispatched to the capital. Peasants paid a poll tax and were subject to a certain number of days of free labor on public works, and young men had to serve in the local militia. In comparison to the Qin rulers, the

To assure he would not be bereft of an army in the afterlife, Qin Shi Huangdi commissioned 7,500 lifesized soldiers, each one different, to be made out of clay and buried with him.

In Jesus' time there were probably more books written in Chinese than in any other script. The above scroll is "The Eulogy of Ni Kuan," a classic Confucian text.

Han emperors lightened the burdens of the peasantry. Little was done, however, to keep them from falling into debt to the nobles whose land they worked. This was a problem that never found an adequate solution, but was addressed in Jesus' time.

About 124 B.C., one of the Han emperors, seeking to avoid dependence on officeholders from the nobility, inaugurated a system of examinations for candidates seeking employment in the imperial civil service. In theory, any person who could pass, no matter what his class, would be granted an official position. This, naturally, demanded years of study, especially of the Chinese classics, with works attributed to Confucius at the core. The examination system, unique to China, meant that the governing officials of the country were remarkably similar in background and outlook, for most had passed through the same cultural and educational experience. The Chinese ideal was the gentleman-scholar, a man of refined taste and impeccable courtesy, and a far cry from the leaders of other societies of the time, in which a military career provided the easiest entrance into political life.

A major event in Chinese history occurred during the century before Jesus' birth: the inauguration of the Great Silk Road. The Mediterranean world for several centuries had provided a market for Chinese prestige goods, especially silk. However, it was not until the first century that Chinese merchants, with the encouragement of the emperor, organized the silk trade in an efficient manner. About 52 B.C. they first outfitted camel caravans that set out from northern China, then passed into Inner Asia, where local people at oases offered a bit of relaxation before the caravan proceeded. There were several routes, but all ended where Parthian or Persian merchants became the middlemen who brought the precious cargo to ports in Syria and Egypt. The aristocrats of Rome paid for the silk in gold coins, for the Chinese found nothing they wanted to import from Europe. The Great Silk Road, the first major international trade link between East Asia and Europe, traded only in one direction.

THE RISE OF WANG MANG

The Han ruler governing from Qangan a few years before the actual time of Jesus' birth was the Aidi Emperor, who began his rule in 7 B.C. His brother, the Chengdi Emperor, had governed China for the previous twenty-six years, from 33 to 7 B.C. During both of their reigns their mother, Wang, dictated much of their policy. The Aidi emperor's first minister was his cousin, Wang Mang, who had already built his reputation as a devoted Confucian scholar. Although he was a Wang, his father had never received a court position, so Wang Mang had been forced to rely on his own talents. At the age of twenty-four he was named Gentleman of the Golden Gate, his first court appointment. From there, he ascended the bureaucratic ladder until attaining the highest office of state, War Minister, in the Aidi Emperor's administration. He ordered the construction of a sacred hall and a new palace to please the emperor. To curry favor with Confucian scholars he brought the most famous of them, Liu Xin, to the capital and appointed him archivist of the imperial library. His deportment stood in great contrast to the other ministers at court, who spent their days in hunting, banqueting, and visiting their concubines.

FURTHER FACTS

In China today, Wang Mang is not remembered for his attempted reforms, but rather as "The Usurper."

Wang Mang felt it urgent to do something to better the economic condition of China's millions of peasants. After the farmers paid their taxes to the government and their rent to the landlords, they had practically nothing left. Men and women in China were close to despair. In 3 B.C., a terrible drought struck the Shandong region. Refugees poured out of the area to march on the capital, where they had been told they should make sacrifices to a goddess who would bring them food and make them immortal. Several years later, in A.D. 11, the dikes on the Yellow River broke, inundating thousands of acres of farmland. In crises like these, to demonstrate his solidarity with people in distress, Wang Mang would fast, eating only sparse meals of vegetables.

After several years of allowing Wang Mang to oversee his empire, the Aidi Emperor began to feel threatened by his power. He ousted him and appointed another aide, Dong Xian, to take his place. However, the Aidi Emperor did not have long to live. His health was failing, and on August 15 of the year 1 B.C. he died.

The Dowager Empress Wang now intervened. At seventy years of age she still maintained an interest in politics and wanted to be sure the succession passed into the right hands. She hurried to the imperial palace, where she took the seals of state into her possession and then summoned the Council of Three, who were the power brokers of Qangan, to select the next emperor. The choice fell on her grandnephew, Liu Qidzu, a child of eight years, then holding the title of prince in an outlying province. He was brought to Qangan for his coronation.

On October 15, Liu was crowned as the Pingdi Emperor. For his regents, he had the Dowager Empress and Wang Mang recalled to active service. This meant that family relatives were to become prominent in the capital once more. Dong Xian and his wife committed suicide, paving the way for Wang Mang to once again hold uncontested authority in Qangan. To ensure this, all of the Aidi Emperor's relatives were sent into exile, as was his first wife, the Empress Fu, who later also killed herself.

It was predictable that Wang Mang should return to power, thanks to his previous position at court and the patronage of his aunt. Like Jesus, Wang Mang apparently had an honest desire to better the life of the poor. His attitude angered his fellow courtiers, who had little regard for those beneath them. His unpopularity among the officials at court had made it easy for the Aidi Emperor to dismiss him.

Now, as regent, he returned to office knowing full well that he had a major task before him in changing how the court dealt with domestic affairs. More titles came his way: Chief of the Palace Guards and Grand Imperial Secretary. In the latter position, no petition could reach the

→

A Chinese bronze mirror from the Han Dynasty.

emperor without passing through his hands. More honors followed. He assumed the role of Commander-in-Chief of the army and Duke Protector of the Han. To solidify his position even further, he arranged a marriage of his daughter to the Pingdi Emperor and at the same time ordered all the rest of the Han relatives to leave Qangan.

With all power finally concentrated in his hands, Wang Mang began his reforms. He placed the governors of the country under scrutiny and dismissed those who were especially incompetent. Then he set up warehouses for distributing food to the needy, a move meant to curb landowners' speculation on grain prices. He added wine to the list of government monopolies — a list that already included salt, iron, and metals extracted from mining. To rein in the high cost of borrowing money for funerals, which often bankrupted peasant families, Wang Mang offered government loans at no interest for a certain number of days. Agricultural loans carried interest at three percent a month or ten percent annually.

Wang Mang was ruthless in his efforts to get rid of corruption and disloyalty. Learning that his elder son was planning to smear the gate of his house with blood as a sign that the gods were angry with his father, Wang Mang ordered him jailed for treachery. The son committed suicide and his pregnant wife was killed after her baby was delivered.

Wang Mang ordered new schools and libraries constructed, and filled them with copies of China's literary classics. His former humble life vanished and a large entourage of guards and aides began to accompany his every public appearance.

FURTHER FACTS

The Han government established the first "newspaper" in China—wooden slips or bamboo strips inscribed with official news and circulated to anyone who wished to read them. Later, Wang Mang used this method extensively to publish news of his reforms and to curry favor with his subjects.

Then, in February of A.D. 5, the Pingdi Emperor died after a short illness. Many people suspected that his death was not from natural causes, although no one could prove that Wang Mang had had a hand in the young man's death. Now in a position to name the new king, Wang Mang chose a two-year-old, Liu Ying, to be the Han ruler. Liu Ying was the great great grandson of the Han Emperor Xuan, and his appointment left Wang Mang in a stronger position than ever.

WANG MANG AS EMPEROR

Throughout China a number of Han relatives revolted, and in Tibet a rebel army formed. Wang Mang disposed of them all within the next few years. Convinced that his enemies had been dealt with, Wang Mang in January of A.D. 9 donned the imperial robes and presented himself at the temple of Gao Zu, the legendary emperor of the Han past. Here the ministers handed him the royal crown and a document placed in a golden casket, giving him the commission to rule China. Back at the Weiyang Palace, Wang Mang announced that the Mandate of Heaven had passed to him and that henceforward he would begin a new calendar as the first emperor of the Xin dynasty. The coup was complete. Nothing more was heard from Liu Ying.

The new emperor had plans to restore the Confucian values that had fallen into disuse, little aware that a young carpenter on the other side of the Asian continent was offering an alternate set of standards. But despite his efforts, the upper classes of China resisted Wang Mang's tampering with their privileges. Some he exiled; others lost their position. On one occasion, Wang Mang issued a decree that the Qangan wealthy were to bring their gold to the palace. Here clerks would take it into the imperial treasury; in return the dispossessed nobles would receive bronze coins in the shape of a knife as compensation. The reason for the confiscation, according to palace spokesmen, was that the gold was needed for the poor. However, no one knew if that was the case, and no one knew whether the poor actually benefited. Wang Mang changed the value of imperial coins several times during his rule, making hoarding useless.

The emperor had little respect for businessmen because Confucius had taught that their occupation was unworthy of a gentleman. He irked them when he sought to impose a new system of weights and measurements, and he angered them when he imposed a law forcing them to pay a double poll tax, but their displeasure was a matter of indifference to him.

Wang Mang then went after the landowners in the countryside. He forbade the purchase or sale of any private property and announced that land was to be radically redistributed. Every household of five people became eligible for four and a half acres to grow their food. While the program seemed wonderful to the long-suffering Chinese peasantry, its implementation proved impossible. No one could be sure how to redistribute the land equitably, and clever landowners found several ways to impede the program. After two years, the land reform came to a halt.

Although they made up only perhaps one percent of China's population, Wang Mang also sought to better the lives of slaves. Most were domestic servants in the private homes of the rich. He abolished all slavery and trade in slaves, but again the failure of the civil service to implement the imperial policies meant that little happened. In A.D. 17, forced to abandon his plan because of resistance from the wealthy, he was content to levy a heavy tax on all slaveholders. Throughout China the rich felt threatened by Wang Mang and passively resisted change. To tamper with tradition was a dangerous thing, and they waited eagerly for the day when their emperor would fall from power.

To compound his problems, the Shandong Peninsula once more experienced a terrible flood along the Yellow River that turned peasant farmers into bandits desperate to feed their families. The imperial army could not control the thousands of starving peasants pouring into the south, and orderly government there simply disappeared.

In A.D. 22, resistance to Wang Mang coalesced into an organized movement of peasant rebels with the colorful name of the Brotherhood of the Red Eyebrows, so named because members dyed their eyebrows in order to recognize one another. In the Nanyang region, a Han general, Liu Xiu, took to the field, and the Xiong-nu of Mongolia joined the coalition. In order to meet these threats, the emperor had no choice but to draft thousands of peasants into his armies. Where once he was acclaimed their benefactor, Wang Mang now appeared a tyrant. People noticed strange omens in Qangan, such as a shadow on the sun, which the city's astrologers interpreted as a mandate for a return to Han rule. Wang Mang's days were numbered. On October 4 of A.D. 23, the Han army entered Qangan, and two days later Wang Mang was killed in the fighting.

THE LATER HAN

Two years later, in Luoyang in eastern China (located eight miles east of the present city in Hunan Province), Liu Xiu gathered his Han relatives together, urging them to reclaim their inheritance. They chose him to become the new ruler; he assumed the name of the Guang Wudi Emperor and took Luoyang as his capital. Now the Red Eyebrows, who occupied Qangan and had promoted one of their leaders to become emperor, were his problem, and for the next thirteen years war ensued. The site of numerous battles, Qangan was reduced to ruins.

Despite the cost of the conflict, the Guang Wudi Emperor laid the foundation of a new building known as the North Palace, whose grounds covered much of the area in the capital. He also oversaw the construction of the imperial academy, the Tai Xue, between A.D. 29 and 32. Eventually thirty thousand students enrolled to prepare for the civil service examinations. Ordinary citizens had to live outside the walls of the city, which, like Qangan, had twelve gates. The emperor canceled Wang Mang's reforms, restoring to the aristocrats, many of them his relatives, their estates and private militias. Central control of China had proven too difficult to sustain. Peasants were once again oppressed, and in the first century A.D. thousands of them migrated to the south of the country in order to escape the vagaries of the Yellow River plain.

The Guang Wudi emperor was in power at the time of Jesus' public ministry and death. He was the first ruler of the Later or Eastern Han dynasty, which was to continue for the next two hundred years.

FURTHER FACTS

Although most of The History of the Early Han *was written by Pan Ku, it was completed after his death by his sister, Pan Chao, one of the few women who became a respected scholar in ancient China.*

Information on the emperors who ruled during the time of Jesus comes from the work of Pan Ku, an historian who wrote *The History of the Early Han.* His work begins with events occurring in 206 B.C. and ends with the fall of Wang Mang in A.D. 23. He followed the tradition of the earlier author Sima Qian, who set the standard for historical writing in China. Pan Ku's father, Pan Piao, born in A.D. 3, was also an author and may very well have started the *History,* but he fell afoul of the emperor and was imprisoned, leaving his son to complete the work. Pan Ku did not like Wang Mang and considered him a usurper whose goal from the beginning was simply to win power.

It is impossible two millennia later to accurately assess the personality of Wang Mang. Was he simply a shrewd schemer, or was his concern for China's poor sincere? If the latter supposition is true, then his life has a certain similarity with that of Jesus. Of course, Jesus was never in a position of political power and denied every attempt to have it thrust upon him. Wang Mang, on the other hand, sought to rule without any constraints on his authority. Apparently he believed he could use power, and violence if necessary, to bring a better life to the people of China. Jesus did not seek a "kingdom of this world," but appealed for individual conversion to goodness. We can only imagine that to Wang Mang, Jesus would have appeared a hopeless idealist, while to Jesus, Wang Mang would have seemed a ruthless politician. Still, each ultimately died because his life posed a threat to those in power, suggesting that though far apart in distance and in method, they were possibly very close in aspiration.

We can certainly make comparisons between Jesus, Confucius, and Laozi, the sages who did so much to influence Chinese culture. The main difference between them lay in their approach to eschatology. Jesus believed that his incarnation was the beginning of a messianic age that would be the forerunner of God's kingdom on earth. He prophesied that at the end of time he would return in power and glory to initiate the final chapter in world history. For him and his disciples, time was linear and proceeding toward a goal: the kingdom of God realized in a redeemed world.

These concepts were far removed from the decidedly secular views of Confucius and Laozi. They were intent on instructing men and women on how to find harmony in this life, not in any life to come. History was always repeating itself as periods of Yin followed those of Yang; their teachings were designed to help people make the best of it. There was little talk of God in either of their work, and certainly no emphasis on a cosmic goal for humanity, both of which were cornerstones of Jesus' message.

Chapter Seven

Korea and Japan

DURING JESUS' LIFETIME, Korean and Japanese cultures were similar in a number of ways. Linguistically, they were among the world's few speakers of languages belonging to the Tungus family; geographically, rugged mountains forced farmers to treasure every bit of arable land; and economically, they relied on the sea to sustain them. Despite these similarities, though, they were isolated politically: each valley of Korea and Japan was ruled by its own chieftain, and geography and tradition effectively thwarted every effort to centralize government.

The Korean peninsula juts into the sea from the Asian continent, 600 miles in length and between 125 and 150 miles in width. Its first inhabitants were Manchurians or Siberians who arrived during the Old Stone Age; the chipped tools that they made testify to their presence. By 3000 B.C., they had developed a unique kind of pottery decorated with comblike incisions, and they lived in pit houses with central fireplaces. Huge mounds of shellfish remains attest to their centrality in the coastal diet.

The introduction of bronze to Korea in 900 B.C. spearheaded an age of progress. Bronze replaced stone in manufacturing weapons, and bronze weapons became symbols of status among the aristocracy. In death, the status of the aristocracy was marked by burial under dolmens — enormous slabs of stone resting on smaller stones. This way of life remained unchanged until 300 B.C., when Old Chosôn, the first true political entity in Korea, appeared on the peninsula. Even today, little is known about its origins or its government. Archaeology has revealed that the farmers living there used iron plows and sickles to harvest the rice that was the mainstay of their diet, but nearly all other aspects of life in Old Chosôn remain unknown.

KOREA UNDER HAN RULE

In 108 B.C., the Wu Di Emperor of China led an army into Korea, scattering the resistance of Chosôn and the remaining chiefdoms of Korea. Worried that Chinese culture might not take root in Korea's fragmented society, Wu Di established four Chinese colonies in Korea. These colonies later developed into the three kingdoms of Jesus' day, all formed in the fifty years before his birth. Koguryô, the largest, was located in the north; Paekche, in the southwest; and Silla, in the southeast. Because each of the kingdoms sought to expand at its neighbors' expense, warfare was constant. On the positive side, however, Chinese culture offered

In death, the status of the aristocracy was marked by burial under dolmens such as this one — enormous slabs of stone resting on smaller stones.

much of value to the Koreans, and after many decades of development, the Korean rulers assimilated the state institutions of China. Despite Chinese efforts, though, they tenaciously clung to their own language.

ANCIENT JAPAN

The Japanese people at the time of Jesus inhabited the same islands that they live on today. Demographers estimate their population at six hundred thousand in Jesus' day, spread thinly over the mountainous countryside and concentrated on the four largest islands: Honshu, Kyushu, Shikoku, and Hokkaido. As in Korea, the vast majority of the Japanese were rice farmers.

FURTHER FACTS

The Ainu were one of the few ancient peoples to believe that humans could legitimately argue with the gods, and even deprive a god of its status if it caused humans undue harm for no apparent reason.

The earliest people to come to Japan arrived from the Asian continent perhaps as early as a hundred thousand years ago, when a land bridge still linked Japan and Korea. It was only twenty thousand years ago that the ocean's rise separated the Japanese islands from the East Asian continent, and by that time another migration had probably brought the Ainu to the islands. The Ainu were hunters, gatherers, and fishermen, attracted to the islands by the gentle climate, where summer monsoons delivered ample rain, and bountiful game flourished in the great forests covering the mountains. Like their counterparts in Korea, they used stone hammers and knives, hunted with bows and arrows, and, of course, learned the dietary benefits of living near the sea. About 8500 B.C. the early people of Japan became the first known potters to commonly use a rope pattern in their craft, and anthropologists have named their culture Jomōn, after the site where the first Japanese pottery was found. Presumably they used wood to make tools, but these artifacts have not survived Japan's damp climate.

About 2000 B.C., ancestors of the modern Japanese began a migration onto the islands. They were quite different physically from the Ainu, who, after living in Japan for thousands of years, were either assimilated or forced to flee northward. Like their predecessors, the newcomers came by

Jesus in Japan?

According to local legend in the northern Japanese village of Shingo, Jesus escaped his death sentence at the last minute and traveled through Siberia to Japan. There he settled down, married, had three daughters, and died at the ripe old age of 106. Some of the town's residents call it Kirisuto no Sato, "Hometown of Christ," and claim they know the spot where Jesus is buried. It is unknown who, if anyone, is buried in the tomb they claim is Jesus', but some speculate it may be an Ainu leader or wise man.

Shinto temples such as this one, built in the eleventh century and destroyed by fire in 2000, were designed to reflect the simplicity and harmony with nature the religion emphasized.

way of Korea and spoke an Altaic language, similar to that of Korea and other parts of Inner Asia. About 300 B.C., yet another migration of people from the mainland brought a new variety of rice seed with them, and the improved nutritional value of this rice caused a population explosion. People began living longer, and stronger mothers began giving birth to healthier babies. This new wave of immigrants also enriched their new culture technologically. They knew how to fashion iron agricultural implements, such as hoes and rakes, as well as how to forge bronze weapons, which quickly replaced their stone predecessors. Bronze was also used to make great bells, which became status symbols in the homes of the wealthy. They used the potter's wheel and were familiar with the techniques of textile weaving. The arrival of these immigrants made possible the establishment of permanent, self-sufficient villages of wooden houses, some of which were raised on stilts. They established the first trading patterns among the islands. Their culture became known as the Yayoi, and it remained the dominant Japanese culture during the time of Jesus. Despite their other achievements, the Yayoi developed no written language, so it was not until Chinese travelers included descriptions of Japan several hundred years later that any narrative histories of the period came into existence.

These Japanese farmers kept their surplus food in large storage jars placed close by their houses. In addition to growing rice, they imported wheat and barley, since neither grain was native to Japan. Trade increased, especially in weapons, for the times appear to have been very turbulent, with valley chieftains constantly seeking to increase their territory and water rights.

Japanese expeditions began to set sail for China, returning with bronze mirrors, which soon also became coveted signs of prestige among the wealthy. Indeed, some aristocrats insisted that their mirrors as well as their weapons be buried with them. A preferred burial practice was to place the bones of the deceased into jars that were then buried in a grave circle. The splendor of some graves in contrast to the poverty of others demonstrates the extreme class differences that existed during this period of Japanese history.

In ancient times, the Japanese religion became known as Shinto, "the way of the gods." Followers of Shinto believed that all of nature is good, and that the spirits that lived in the world, the *kami,* expected people to reverence them and to offer prayers and sacrifices. Men and women worshiped in small wooden temples with thatched roofs, demonstrating the simplicity of the religion, which had no concept of either divine revelation or sacred scriptures. We can imagine that Jesus would have sympathized with the concern of Shinto to appreciate and cultivate the beauty of nature, even though he did not share the Shinto belief in countless spirits inhabiting the world. He would also surely have found the simplicity of the Japanese and Korean ways of life attractive. But since they lacked a written language and the urban centers where scribes could have copied down his teachings, it is difficult to imagine him preaching his message here. Eventually both Korea and Japan would come under the influence of Chinese character writing, each adapting it to their own needs, but this development was centuries away at the time of Jesus.

Yayoi culture was extremely stratified; lower-ranking men and women who met a superior on the road were expected to step aside and bow as the superior passed. This and similar practices continued in Japan into the nineteenth century.

Chapter Eight

Inner Asia

ASIA IS HOME TO A number of the world's most striking geographical features: the dense forests of Siberia, the soaring Himalayan mountains, the historic plains of Manchuria, and the Caspian Sea, the largest lake in the world. The region between these is known as Inner Asia. A vast, featureless expanse of high plateaus, it extends two thousand miles in width and seven thousand in length. Its plateaus are known to geographers as steppes, and their openness has always facilitated the movements of people and armies across Inner Asia.

Because of its landlocked position, Inner Asia's climate is one of extremes. Winters are marked by fierce cold and biting winds; summers are sweltering. While only six months of the year are frost-free, rain is sparse, requiring a constant search for water late in the summer. Only springtime compensates for these extremes; temperatures are mild and lush green grass, nurtured by winter rain, carpets the land. This grass covers much of the steppes, sustaining both wild and domesticated animals.

Human settlement in Inner Asia, by contrast, has typically been along the few rivers that wind across the plateaus, or near a number of oases on the periphery of the plains. Because of their fertility, several valleys, especially the Ferghana west of the Tien Shan Mountains, have also been home to dense populations. Deserts and mountains make much of the rest of the Inner Asia inhospitable; over eighty-five percent of modern Turkmenistan, for example, is dominated by the Kara Kum Desert, and Tibet is home to the Himalayas, the highest mountains in the world. The challenges presented by Inner Asia's cold, arid climate, monotonous topography, and limited resources have historically restricted the number of people the land could support. Few large cities have ever developed here. In Jesus' day, despite its relative geographic proximity, Inner Asia was far distant from the densely populated world he knew.

The first people to settle around the steppe oases were hunters who spoke an Indo-European tongue — possibly, anthropologists suggest, the originators of that language family. They were, according to linguistic evidence, related to modern Iranians and to the ancient Hittites, who made their home in Anatolia. Other settlers arrived later, speakers of Turkic, Mongol, Tibetan, and Tungusic languages, the ancestors of the modern peoples of Inner Asia. Today, most Inner Asians speak Turkic languages, the only major exception being the Tajiks. Their use of an Iranian speech, as well as their cultural preference for farming rather than herding, lends credibility to their claim to be the oldest of the steppe peoples.

Steppe chieftains demanded burials in great kurgans to memorialize their importance in this life and to ensure it for the next one.

It is entirely from Chinese, Persian, and Greek records that the story of Inner Asian history can be followed, for the steppe people remained illiterate until the eighth century A.D. Various peoples were constantly migrating into the steppe lands, so that the population became very diverse while the economy remained unchanged for ages.

THE CULTURE OF THE STEPPES

Since their domestication around 3200 B.C., horses have been integral to life on the steppes. They were first trained to pull carts and chariots, and it was not for another 1500 years after this that anyone attempted to ride them. Inner Asian horses were small and stocky, with large heads and shaggy coats, remarkably different from today's thoroughbreds. Yet their endurance was tremendous, and their resistance to the cold unsurpassed. They used their hooves to dig through the snow and reach food other animals could not. They were invaluable to herders, who used them to round up the sheep, goats, and cattle they kept. Though perhaps indirectly, they also impacted the world of fashion: along with riding came the invention of trousers, worn by both men and women in Inner Asia at a time when the rest of the world still wore robes, skins, kilts, or nothing at all.

Though perhaps indirectly, steppe horses impacted the world of fashion: along with riding, and the practical need to be able to straddle a horse, came the invention of trousers, worn by both men and women in Inner Asia at a time when the rest of the world still wore robes, skins, kilts, or nothing at all.

In war, which was almost constant on the grasslands, horses served as mounts. Cavalry revolutionized steppe warfare, providing unsurpassed mobility and allowing relatively small numbers of soldiers to dominate much larger sedentary populations. It replaced long-drawn-out battles with swift, unexpected charges, often allowing soldiers to avoid contests on foot. In case of setbacks, horsemen were also able to retreat swiftly, thus avoiding total disaster.

Horses were nowhere to be found in Tibet, however, where some villagers lived above sixteen thousand feet. Yaks replaced them, sustaining human populations by providing meat, milk, and transportation. Sheep, too, were kept in high altitudes, but cereal agriculture proved impossible above twelve thousand feet. Beyond these sparse details, unfortunately, next to nothing is known about life in first-century Tibet.

For the rest of Inner Asia, summer was a time of migration, with herders in a constant search for pasture and water. Families traveled together, the women driving wagons hitched to oxen, while the men, on horseback, kept the herds under control. To ensure mobility, they carried little with them: what few possessions they had were tools of leather, wood, or metal. When winter encroached, families returned to camp in tent villages and occupied themselves with carpet weaving, which to this day remains a highly prized skill. Each family belonged to a clan; each clan claimed descent from a real or mythical ancestor.

Two inventions in particular were responsible for improving the quality of life on the steppes. One, the horse bridle, was developed around 600 B.C. and gave riders infinitely more control over their animals. The other, ironwork, appeared on the steppes about two hundred years later, allowing people to replace their copper and bronze weapons and tools with stronger, more durable ones.

With the advent of these technologies, strong chieftains became hungry for even more power. Warfare spread like wildfire across the grasslands. Chieftains who made successful raids on their neighbors' herds became heroes to their people. Conquest of land was not their goal; rather, they sought to rob one another of livestock, or to take prisoners for ransom or tribute.

When not at war, looting horsemen often preyed upon the handful of farmers who grew their crops near oases. A bit more fortunate were townspeople who lived on the edge of the steppes. Their communities were protected by stone walls, but even they had to resign themselves to the fact that paying tribute was the only sure way to stave off nomadic plundering.

Like most first-century rulers, steppe chieftains demanded burials that would memorialize their importance in this life and ensure it for the next. To this end they developed kurgans — large mounds of earth or stone, fortified by walls or great stone slabs. Inside each kurgan was a log chamber, lined with thick carpets. In each chamber was the chieftain's sarcophagus, along with rich grave gifts for use in the afterlife: daggers, knives, battle-axes, bows, and arrows. Chieftains' wives were also interred in kurgans, and with them their jewelry, pottery, mirrors, and knives. For the most powerful chieftains, a horse was included among the grave gifts, saddled, bridled, and sacrificed. A few even demanded that each clan donate two animals: a horse and another of the chieftain's choosing.

Inner Asia was home to some of the ancient world's finest artisans. Woodworkers carved and smiths forged intricately detailed images of animals: bulls, sheep, ibexes, horses, and other creatures indigenous to the steppes, some fighting and others at rest. Women, while typically not trained in these crafts, wove cloth embellished with gold and beautiful repeating patterns.

Little is known about the Inner Asians' religion. It is likely they were animists, sensing in nature the presence of spirits whose worship might bring good fortune and avert disaster. Perhaps, like so many animistic societies, they employed shamans to contact these spirits and thus heal the sick and predict the future. One thing, though, is certain: the hundreds of kurgans that still dot the steppes of Siberia testify to their belief in an afterlife. For if death were the end, why would a chieftain need his horse and a wife her jewelry?

THE SCYTHIANS

The expansion of the Scythians produced the first major empire on the steppes. Likely the descendants of early Iranian-speaking peoples, the Scythians began to occupy southwestern Asia in about 700 B.C. Around this time, they forged an alliance through marriage with the Assyrians, but the alliance did not last; in 674 B.C. they aided in the destruction of the Assyrian Empire. They kept to themselves after this, until in 514 B.C. Darius, king of the Persians, led a number of inconclusive battles against them in an attempt to limit their raids on his land. The Greek historian Herodotus visited them around this time, and devoted a whole chapter of

The Greek historian Herodotus was amazed at the savagery of the Scythians of his day.

Source: Herodotus, Histories. *Trans. George Rawlinson (1858).*

THE SKULLS OF THEIR ENEMIES, NOT INDEED OF ALL, BUT OF THOSE WHOM THEY MOST DETEST, THEY TREAT AS FOLLOWS. HAVING SAWN OFF THE PORTION BELOW THE EYEBROWS, AND CLEANED OUT THE INSIDE, THEY COVER THE OUTSIDE WITH LEATHER. WHEN A MAN IS POOR, THIS IS ALL THAT HE DOES; BUT IF HE IS RICH, HE ALSO LINES THE INSIDE WITH GOLD: IN EITHER CASE THE SKULL IS USED AS A DRINKING-CUP. THEY DO THE SAME WITH THE SKULLS OF THEIR OWN KITH AND KIN IF THEY HAVE BEEN AT FEUD WITH THEM, AND HAVE VANQUISHED THEM IN THE PRESENCE OF THE KING. WHEN STRANGERS WHOM THEY DEEM OF ANY ACCOUNT COME TO VISIT THEM, THESE SKULLS ARE HANDED ROUND, AND THE HOST TELLS HOW THAT THESE WERE HIS RELATIONS WHO MADE WAR UPON HIM, AND HOW THAT HE GOT THE BETTER OF THEM; ALL THIS BEING LOOKED UPON AS PROOF OF BRAVERY.

his *Histories* to the Scythians. They were, he advised his readers, a hard-drinking, wine-guzzling, hemp-smoking people who venerated countless gods and goddesses. They were also fierce warriors who were known to use the gold-plated, leather-lined skulls of their dead enemies for cups.

In Jesus' time, however, their best days were behind them. Another steppe people, the Sarmatians, had come to power, and driven most of the Scythians into exile in Moldova, the Ukraine, and the Caucasus. The Sarmatians' secret weapon was the stirrup, which allowed their cavalry to maintain balance while firing volleys of arrows. All that remained of the Scythians was their name: thanks to Herodotus, the Greeks gave that name to all nomadic peoples they encountered for centuries to come.

THE YUEH-ZHI AND XIONG-NU

↘

The Chinese were dismayed to learn that, to the Xiong-nu, the Great Wall was more a sieve than a barrier. It slowed their entry into China, but did not prevent it.

One advantage of the Great Wall of China — particularly from a Chinese perspective — was that it established a border between the Chinese and the nomadic peoples of northern Inner Asia. These were a mixed group, but two rose to prominence while Jesus walked the earth: the Yueh-zhi and the Xiong-nu. The former were Indo-Europeans who lived north

of present-day Afghanistan. The latter were their longtime enemies, and had over the years gradually forced the Yueh-zhi westward. Eventually their territory began to encroach on Chinese lands — including, to Chinese alarm, parts of the Great Silk Road. Thus the Chinese sought to make them allies.

In Jesus' time, the Yueh-zhi were enjoying a period of stability and prosperity under their sovereign, Kujula Kadphises, who began his rule in A.D. 25. Kujula had, early in his reign, united all the Yueh-zhi under his control, and was now welcoming trade with merchants from India and as far away as the Mediterranean. His relations with the Sogdians, who inhabited the wealthy trade cities of Bukhara and Samarkand, were also strong, thus strengthening even further the Yueh-zhi economy. Kujula minted coins, similar to the Greek currency of Bactria, that pictured an image of the Buddha and the inscription "Steadfast in the Faith," reflecting both his own religious devotion and the Yueh-zhi skill at metallurgy. Although some of the Yueh-zhi remained nomads, his reforms encouraged more and more to settle in one place. Gradually they expanded as far as India, where they were known as Kushans.

In the first century the strongest nation north of the Great Wall were the Xiong-nu, a people who were either Turkic, Mongol, or, more likely, a mixture of the two. They dominated the grasslands from 209 B.C. to A.D. 155. The leader held the title *shan-yu,* and his influence was such that even the Chinese emperor had to treat him, reluctantly, as an equal despite the great disparity in the number of their subjects: an estimated 67 million Chinese to one million Xiong-nu. Unlike nearly all its other neighbors, the Xiong-nu were indifferent to Chinese culture, concerned only with the transfer of its wealth to themselves. The Chinese, on the other hand, were not indifferent to this indifference: historian Sima Qian complained, "The Xiong-nu people act against the Heavenly Way. Their business is robbing and stealing." Another writer pointed out that Xiong-nu noses were too large and their bodies much too hairy, easily qualifying them as barbarians.

The homeland of the Xiong-nu was the Ordos Valley of Inner Mongolia. Here they lived for centuries outside the light of history, but developing the skills that made life on the steppes possible. Hunting made them experts at archery, a skill, they discovered, as useful in war as in the hunt. After a raid, the Xiong-nu always melted back into the vast steppe interior, where detection proved impossible.

The Xiong-nu lived in round houses known as yurts. These were made of layers of felt stretched over a framework of poles, easily dismantled when the summer migrations came. In winter, clans that claimed a common ancestor camped together, their yurts covered with additional thick blankets of felt to keep the cold at bay. Early on, the Xiong-nu recognized that the environment in which they lived was far more suitable for herding than for farming. They obtained what grain and vegetables they needed from their neighbors, either by trading or by raiding.

THE CHINESE AND THE XIONG-NU

In the second century B.C., the armies of the Shi Huangdi Emperor launched an expedition into the Ordos region of Inner Mongolia, seeking to expand Chinese rule there. The Xiong-nu, preferring exile to Chinese domination, left their homeland until 207 B.C., after the Qin dynasty fell. During their self-imposed exile, the chieftains rallied around a charismatic leader, Motun, who became the founder of the Xiong-nu Empire. In addition to the usual chieftain's duties of settling disputes and leading his people in war, Motun established the precedent that only the shan-yu should deal with the Chinese. His own dealings with them were remarkably fruitful: in just one year's time, he prevailed upon the Chinese to send him gold, grain, silk, and a princess for his harem. The year after this, his horsemen crashed over the Great Wall to take whatever they wanted by force.

Two advisors aided the shan-yu: the Wise King of the Right and the Wise King of the Left. The latter, usually a son or brother of the shan-yu, was in a particularly enviable position, for he was first in line to succeed the shan-yu. Twenty-four subordinate chieftains, along with the heads of conquered peoples living inside the empire, led the army of archers. At its height, the Xiong-nu Empire extended from southern Manchuria to the Pamir Mountains of modern Tajikistan.

↑

Bronze appliqués such as these discovered in Mongolia — each of which depicts a tiger standing over a stag he has caught — were used as decorations on clothing.

The strategy of the shan-yus, constantly shifting back and forth between war and peace, kept the Chinese in a dilemma: should they try to deal with the Xiong-nu peacefully? Or should they send an army against them? Because the cost of outfitting a military force was so great, the usual response of the Chinese rulers was to send the shan-yu on an annual basis whatever he demanded. The shan-yu, in turn, distributed much of this booty among his captains in an attempt to guarantee their loyalty. On several occasions the frustrated Chinese were able to push back the Xiong-nu from their borders, but they soon learned that the Great Wall was more a sieve than a barrier. Perhaps even more frustrating was the fact that the Chinese were dependent on the Xiong-nu for horses; their own land, despite its size, offered sufficient pasture for comparatively few animals. Their traders had to make their way to the markets of the Xiong-nu and carry enough gold and silk with them to strike a deal.

After the Chinese opened the Great Silk Road to trade with the West, the emperors in Qangan became obsessed with protecting it. The road opened during a time of civil war among the Xiong-nu, who were divided in their support for two rival heirs to the shan-yu. One of these factions eventually retreated to the north, leaving the remnant weakened and disorganized. The Chinese saw this as an opportunity to subdue their longtime antagonists, and dictated that henceforward the shan-yu was to visit periodically the royal court in Qangan to pay the emperor his respects and to acknowledge his authority. In return, the shan-yu would receive many of the gifts that his predecessors obtained by force in earlier times.

At the time of Jesus' birth the shan-yu was Wa-zhu-liu-ruo-ti, a man renowned for his cleverness. In 1 B.C., he announced to the Chinese court that he was coming to Qangan to pay homage to the Pingdi Emperor, but what he really had in mind was to return home with as much of the wealth of China as possible, a task in which he proved successful. The Pingdi Emperor was happy to be rid of him, for the Wa-zhu had brought his astrologers with him, and the Chinese were convinced that they could cast a spell on the court if they were displeased.

Wang Mang, then serving as regent and the real power behind the imperial throne, was not at all pleased by the arrangement between the Chinese and the Xiong-nu. Although he continued to send the usual gifts to the shan-yu's court, Wang Mang included with them a seal and a sash to wear. These adornments marked Wa-zhu as a Chinese official rather than an independent sovereign. He also suggested that the shan-yu rid himself of his barbarian name and choose a Chinese one. None of these actions sat well with the shan-yu, and in A.D. 5, he had an opportunity to assert his authority. At that time, Wa-zhu offered asylum to a group of Chinese rebels. Wang Mang demanded that they be given up, and Wa-zhu agreed to do so, but returned them to China with a request that they be pardoned. Wang Mang ignored this plea and ordered them beheaded.

Only four years later, when Wang Mang had taken the imperial title for himself, a similar incident occurred. A number of Chinese fleeing the wrath of Qangan sought refuge among the Xiong-nu, and once more relations were strained. The Xiong-nu on the border began raiding China to convey to Wang Mang their displeasure at his attempts to dominate affairs in their country. Wang Mang retaliated by announcing that China would recognize fifteen captains of archers of the Xiong-nu empire as shan-yus, providing each of them with a generous amount of gold. Only a few defected to the Chinese, so a single shan-yu remained in control of the Xiong-nu territories. Wang Mang also prepared a force to invade the Xiong-nu lands, but once it reached the Great Wall, it stayed there.

In A.D. 23, the Xiong-nu were among the military forces that infested Qangan and overthrew Wang Mang. Once the Han were restored to power, the new emperor was quick to establish the old equilibrium with the Xiong-nu. In A.D. 25, the Guang Wudi Emperor sent envoys to Shan-yu Hu-tu-erh-shi, professing a desire to revive the friendship between their two peoples. Guang Wudi promised that the Xiong-nu would have complete autonomy over Inner Mongolia. Hu-tu-erh-shi accepted the gifts of the Guang Wudi emperor. But, to no one's surprise, in A.D. 30, the probable year of Jesus' death, the Xiong-nu began to raid China once more. In Qangan, the Chinese emperor's advisors recommended sending an army against them, but the emperor, well aware of the difficulties of mounting a campaign, preferred not to seek a military solution.

Had Jesus been a member of an Inner Asian culture in the first century, his impact on the world would likely have been limited to a handful of relatives and friends. Of course, he could have preached his message about the Kingdom of God, but blank stares would surely have greeted him, for the steppe peoples had religious sensibilities but would have had no preparation for the gospel that Jesus preached. Even had he won over disciples to carry his message abroad, lasting conversions would have been few. The Christian message has always had difficulty reaching herding peoples; historically it has depended on city cultures. And these, of course, were very rare in Inner Asia apart from the handful of towns along the Great Silk Road. It would not be until the sixth century that followers of Jesus would successfully establish churches from Iran to China in these oases.

Chapter Nine

India

THE FIRST CENTURY was a time of transition in India. One great empire, the Mauryan, had fallen, and a second, the Gupta, had not yet risen from its ashes. During the lifetime of Jesus, there was but one strong kingdom in the entire land: the branch of the Yueh-zhi known as the Kushans. They had formed a nation in the northwestern part of the land that extended beyond the Indian borders into Afghanistan and the oasis cities along the Great Silk Road. Their rulers followed the teachings of the Buddha, which they had learned from their Chinese neighbors in the second century B.C.

Much of the rest of India was divided into hundreds of small principalities. Each of these had its own ruler, the raja, who often governed under the guidance of a council of nobles. A great cultural gap sliced the land in two: the north was home to the Aryan peoples, and the south to the Dravidian ones. Dozens of smaller ethnic groups peppered the Indian landscape, unattached to anyone except their own kin and local chieftains. Curious stories purport that Jesus lived for a time in India, either as a teenager or later in life, but absolutely no hard evidence exists to lend credibility to such tales.

Unfortunately, few written records come from this period of Indian history. While a comparatively large number of Indians could read, the

Nicholas Notovitch, a Russian doctor, traveled extensively in the Indian subcontinent during the 19th century. He recorded this legend of Jesus' teenage years from Buddhist monks living there.

Source: Nicholas Notovitch, The Life of Saint Issa *(1894).*

IN THE COURSE OF HIS FOURTEENTH YEAR, THE YOUNG ISSA [JESUS], BLESSED OF GOD, CAME ON THIS SIDE OF SIND AND ESTABLISHED HIMSELF AMONG THE ARYAS IN THE LAND BELOVED OF GOD. FAME SPREAD THE REPUTATION OF THIS MARVELOUS CHILD THROUGHOUT THE LENGTH OF NORTHERN SIND, AND WHN HE CROSSED THE COUNTRY OF THE FIVE RIVERS AND THE RAJPUTANA, THE DEVOTEES OF THE GOD JAINE PRAYED HIM TO DWELL AMONG THEM. BUT HE LEFT THE ERRING WORSHIPPERS OF JAINE AND WENT TO JUGGERNAUT IN THE COUNTRY OF ORISSA, WHERE REPOSE THE MORTAL REMAINS OF VYASA-KRISHNA AND WHERE THE WHITE PRIESTS OF BRAHMA MADE HIM A JOYOUS WELCOME. THEY TAUGHT HIM TO READ AND UNDERSTAND THE VEDAS, TO CURE BY AID OF PRAYER, TO TEACH, TO EXPLAIN THE HOLY SCRIPTURES TO THE PEOPLE, AND TO DRIVE OUT EVIL SPIRITS FROM THE BODIES OF MEN, RESTORING UNTO THEM THEIR SANITY. HE PASSED SIX YEARS AT JUGGERNAUT, AT RAJAGRIHA, AT BENARES, AND IN THE OTHER HOLY CITIES. EVERYONE LOVED HIM, FOR ISSA LIVED IN PEACE WITH THE VAISYAS AND THE SUDRAS, WHOM HE INSTRUCTED IN THE HOLY SCRIPTURES.

cost of employing scribes was prohibitive to most village rajas, and archaeology, therefore, must tell us most of what we know about first-century India. To compensate for this dearth, a wealth of religious literature is extant from the centuries before Jesus' birth, detailing the beliefs of the Indian people who were his contemporaries.

The Indian subcontinent juts like a triangle into the Indian Ocean. Along with Pakistan, Bangladesh, the island of Sri Lanka, and the mountain kingdoms of Nepal and Bhutan, it is part of what geographers call South Asia. Great mountain chains in the north — the Himalayas, the Karakoram, and the Hindu Kush — separate India from the rest of Asia. Passage through these ranges is difficult, but not impossible; enough mountain passes penetrate them to allow travelers and invading armies to go in either direction.

The great rivers of India arise in these mountains: the Indus, the Ganges, and the Brahmaputra. For millennia these rivers have carried silt to the large, fertile plains where most Indians make their homes. The Deccan, a vast, arid region in the center of the country, is far more sparsely populated; its inhabitants are mostly herdsmen. Tropical forests cover much of the southern coastlands, thanks to high temperatures and more than ample rainfall. Heat in India is persistent, but its climate is ultimately governed by monsoons. When these winds blow in from Inner Asia, the days are bright and pleasant. And so they remain until mid-June, when the wind reverses direction and sweeps across the Indian Ocean, bringing torrential rains. In the first century, India's climate led to myths that it was a fabulously wealthy, exotic land, where strange plants and animals flourished and famine was unknown.

ANCIENT INDIA

India's first inhabitants arrived during the Stone Ages, pursuing the game that then filled the land's vast forests. Learning to domesticate a handful of these animals allowed them to settle in permanent villages. As early as 3000 B.C., the population of the Indus and Sarasvati river valleys, today divided between Pakistan and India, had grown large enough to establish cities. The largest of these were Ganweriwala, Harappa, and Mohenjo-Daro. Remarkably, these were planned towns, with streets laid out in a grid pattern. Houses, made of mud brick, had several rooms; many included bathrooms with the world's first indoor plumbing. Huge walls surrounded towns, and each town had its own citadel, which served as the center of both religious and public life.

Harappa was perhaps the most important of these early urban centers. Its economy depended on a complex irrigation system, which allowed farmers to divert river water into their fields. These were planted with wheat, rice, various vegetables, and cotton, and were sometimes used to graze cattle. The Harappans were a literate society — they first developed a script around 2800 B.C. — but to this day linguists have been unable to completely decode their writings.

About 1900 B.C., the Indus Valley cities slipped into an inexplicable decline. Possibly they failed to weather a change in climate; perhaps an unforeseen drought decimated their numbers. One historian has suggested that the silting of the mouth of the Indus, brought about by

↓

Mohenjo-Daro, whose ruins are shown here, had indoor plumbing long before Jesus' day. Each house had a bathroom floor with a brick drainpipe that flowed into an ingenious municipal sewage system. Pipes on the roofs of houses carried rainwater down to the sewage pipes as well. Manholes dug in the street allowed for periodic cleaning and maintenance of the system.

volcanic action, caused the river to back up and drown the farmers' fields. Whatever the case, the Harappans abandoned their cities and apparently scattered throughout other parts of India, where eventually local populations assimilated them. For the next millennium India had no more cities, only villages.

THE ARYAN MIGRATION

About 2000 B.C., a people known as the Aryans migrated to northern India, and about six hundred years later a second wave followed them. Migrations of this sort were common in ancient Asia, and the newcomers, who spoke an Indo-European language called Sanskrit, were content to settle among the indigenous peoples of India, spreading out over the Indus and Ganges Valleys and the hill country below the northern mountains.

The Aryans were a frontier people and preferred herding to farming. Cattle and sheep provided them with meat, milk, transportation, and hides, which they used to make tents for shelter. Though families measured their wealth in terms of the number of cattle they possessed, horses rivaled them in importance, for they provided mounts for Aryan warriors, who delighted, as most frontier horsemen did, in raiding one another's herds. Warriors renowned for their prowess in battle were always able to recruit followers, who were eager to share in the fame of successful campaigns.

Not surprisingly, given their warlike ideals, the Aryans' culture was extremely patriarchal. Life in all their villages was similar: men spent their time hunting, raiding, and gambling, while women tended to the demands of home and family. Apart from music and making the instruments needed to play it, artistic expression was unknown among them.

A centralized Aryan state was finally created in response to foreign invasion. In 326 B.C., Alexander the Great appeared with his Macedonian and Greek army in the Indus Valley. The Aryan leader of the state of Magadha, Chandragupta Maurya, rallied the rajas of the Ganges Valley to accept his authority and resist the European intruders, inaugurating an empire that lasted until 184 B.C. The Mauryan Empire's capital, Pataliputra, outside modern Patna, became the largest and wealthiest city in India, full of palaces, gardens, and markets for the merchants who came from all over India to trade there. But when the empire eventually disintegrated, India fell back into the old rhythms of small competing principalities and myriad local rajas.

NEW INVADERS

In the third century B.C., remnants of Alexander the Great's expedition into India remained in a state called Bactria. Here, descendants of Macedonian generals had ruled independently since about 250 B.C., when they broke away from the Hellenistic kingdom of the Seleucids of Syria. One hundred years later their king, Menander, adopted the teachings of Buddhism, effectively erasing all traces of Hellenism in Bactria. Over time, the nation came to serve as a bridge between the West and India, blending the arts and sciences of each. The gold coinage of Bactria is some of the most remarkable of the ancient world. The kingdom flourished until about 50 B.C., when the last Bactrian king died fending off new invaders, the Scythians and Parthians, who had arrived off the steppes of Inner Asia.

The Scythians and Parthians each formed their own territories in northwestern India. The former became known as the Sakas; the latter the Pahlavas. For a time, the two states were partners, ruling an area known as the Punjab. One Pahlava ruler, Vonones, who began his rule in 30 B.C., styled himself with the Persian title "King of Kings," but so little is known of his activities that it is difficult to imagine that he lived up to the title. In fact, nearly all the Pahlava and Saka rulers are remembered today as little more than names.

The next invaders of India were the Kushans, who, as noted above, were the dominant people of northwest India during Jesus' lifetime. They had defeated the Pahlavas and pushed the Sakas deeper into the Indian interior, where the remnants of both peoples were eventually absorbed into Aryan society.

***The Periplus of the Erythraean Sea* describes the voyages of traders in the Indian Ocean around the time of Jesus.**

Source: The Periplus of the Erythraean Sea, *trans. W. H. Schoff (1912).*

62. ABOUT THESE PLACES IS THE REGION OF MASALIA STRETCHING A GREAT WAY ALONG THE COAST BEFORE THE INLAND COUNTRY; A GREAT QUANTITY OF MUSLINS IS MADE THERE. BEYOND THIS REGION, SAILING TOWARD THE COAST AND CROSSING THE ADJACENT BAY, THERE IS THE REGION OF DOSARENE, YIELDING THE IVORY KNOWN AS DOSARENIC. BEYOND THIS, THE COURSE TRENDING TOWARD THE NORTH, THERE ARE MANY BARBAROUS TRIBES, AMONG WHOM ARE THE CIRRHADAE, A RACE OF MEN WITH FLATTENED NOSES, VERY SAVAGE; ANOTHER TRIBE, THE BARGYSI; AND THE HORSE-FACES AND THE LONG-FACES, WHO ARE SAID TO BE CANNIBALS.

63. AFTER THESE, THE COURSE TURNS TOWARD THE EAST AGAIN, AND SAILING WITH THE OCEAN TO THE RIGHT AND THE SHORE REMAINING BEYOND TO THE LEFT, GANGES COMES INTO VIEW, AND NEAR IT THE VERY LAST LAND TOWARD THE EAST, CHRYSE. THERE IS A RIVER NEAR IT CALLED THE GANGES, AND IT RISES AND FALLS IN THE SAME WAY AS THE NILE. ON ITS BANK IS A MARKET-TOWN WHICH HAS THE SAME NAME AS THE RIVER, GANGES. THROUGH THIS PLACE ARE BROUGHT MALABATHRUM AND GANGETIC SPIKENARD AND PEARLS, AND MUSLINS OF THE FINEST SORTS, WHICH ARE CALLED GANGETIC. IT IS SAID THAT THERE ARE GOLD-MINES NEAR THESE PLACES, AND THERE IS A GOLD COIN WHICH IS CALLED CALTIS. AND JUST OPPOSITE THIS RIVER THERE IS AN ISLAND IN THE OCEAN, THE LAST PART OF THE INHABITED WORLD TOWARD THE EAST, UNDER THE RISING SUN ITSELF; IT IS CALLED CHRYSE; AND IT HAS THE BEST TORTOISE-SHELL OF ALL THE PLACES ON THE ERYTHRAEAN SEA.

Three Dravidian kingdoms were in place in southern India in the first century: Kerala, Chola, and Pandya. People here spoke Tamil rather than Sanskrit, and, though they borrowed the caste system from Aryan culture, had their own literature and customs. Warfare among them was constant, with armies of infantry and corps of soldiers riding elephants. Fortified with gallons of rice wine before going into battle, these fierce beasts terrorized opposing forces. In fact, the chaos they inspired is perhaps an apt metaphor for the turbulent political situation in India while Jesus walked the earth.

INDIAN SOCIETY

India's hundreds of villages were made up of peasant farmers who tilled the soil day after day to support an economy that prevented them from ever rising above their poverty. Women lived their lives entirely dependent on decisions made by husbands, fathers, or brothers. Most were married off to older men at sixteen, and compelled to accept obligations set down by mothers-in-law. As in China, farm families often fell into hopeless debts, which tied them to their land.

DAILY LIFE

Education, like everything else in India in Jesus' day, was centered on religion. When a boy was between eight and twelve years old he would have been sent to study with several others at the home of a teacher, who would have taught him the Vedas and the rules and rituals of Brahmanism.

In Dravidian India, south of the Vindhya Mountains, prosperity came from cultivating pepper and other spices and from the mining of minerals. Spices were in great demand in all the countries of the Indian Ocean coastline, and were gradually even introduced to the Roman world. In A.D. 21, while Jesus was practicing carpentry in Galilee, an Indian delegation visited Rome, bringing with it a menagerie of animals from their country. For the first time, Romans were treated to the sight of a tiger.

By Jesus' time, the Indian Ocean had already become a highway for the exchange of goods from Indonesia to East Africa, Southeast Asia, and the Persian Gulf. Unfortunately, records of this period are few and far between, but archaeologists have evidence of a huge trading network, which flourished as a result of the predictability of the Indian Ocean monsoons. One narrative, entitled *The Periplus of the Erythraean Sea,* is dated about A.D. 50.

THE BRAHMAN RELIGION

While the political history of early India remains somewhat obscure, its cultural life can be painted in vivid detail, thanks largely to its religious literature. This is contained in the Vedas, four collections of hymns and other sacred writings, and in two great epic poems, the Mahabharata and the Ramayana, which remain to this day the most treasured works in the Indian literary canon. From ancient times, when they were transmitted orally, they have been as significant to their followers as the Hebrew and Christian scriptures were to their adherents.

The authors of the poems were Brahmans, the priests of the Aryan religion, who performed the sacrifices and prayers their worship required. The Aryans venerated a pantheon of deities, including Indra, the classic warrior; Agni, the fire-god; Varuna, keeper of cosmic order; and Soma, who was memorialized in an intoxicating drink that the Brahmans used in offerings for the well-being of the people. In later centuries, popular devotion shifted to Vishnu, who was believed to have become incarnate nine times, sometimes in human form and sometimes animal, to come to the aid of humanity, and Siva, who was acclaimed the "Lord of the Beasts" and, much later, in southern India, the "Cosmic Dancer." Brahma, from whom the Brahmans took their name, was believed to be the creator of the universe, though he was actually a lesser deity as far as popular devotion was concerned.

The Brahmans' religion, not called Hinduism until a seventh-century Arabic invasion, taught that at the moment of creation, four classes of human beings appeared. First came the priestly class of Brahmans; second, the ruling class of rajas and warriors; third, the merchants, artisans, and farmers who sustained the Indian economy; and finally the peasants and servants who performed manual labor. Men and women in the first three groups comprised the upper and middle classes, and they alone had access to the sacred recitations of the Vedas. Even the peasants, though, were

In this extract from the Bhagavad Gita, Arjuna is taught not to fear death, for it is part of the cycle of reincarnation.

Source: Bhagavad Gita, *Chapter II. Trans. Edwin Arnold (1885)*

LIFE CANNOT SLAY. LIFE IS NOT SLAIN!
NEVER THE SPIRIT WAS BORN; THE SPIRIT SHALL CEASE TO BE NEVER;
NEVER WAS TIME IT WAS NOT; END AND BEGINNING ARE DREAMS!
BIRTHLESS AND DEATHLESS AND CHANGELESS REMAINETH THE SPIRIT FOREVER;
DEATH HATH NOT TOUCHED IT AT ALL, DEAD THOUGH THE HOUSE OF IT SEEMS!
WHO KNOWETH IT EXHAUSTLESS, SELF-SUSTAINED,
IMMORTAL, INDESTRUCTIBLE, — SHALL SUCH
SAY, "I HAVE KILLED A MAN, OR CAUSED TO KILL?"

NAY, BUT AS WHEN ONE LAYETH
HIS WORN-OUT ROBES AWAY,
AND, TAKING NEW ONES, SAYETH,
"THESE WILL I WEAR TO-DAY!"
SO PUTTETH BY THE SPIRIT
LIGHTLY ITS GARB OF FLESH,
AND PASSETH TO INHERIT
A RESIDENCE AFRESH.

I SAY TO THEE WEAPONS REACH NOT THE LIFE;
FLAME BURNS IT NOT, WATERS CANNOT O'ERWHELM,
NOR DRY WINDS WITHER IT. IMPENETRABLE,

UNENTERED, UNASSAILED, UNHARMED, UNTOUCHED,
IMMORTAL, ALL-ARRIVING, STABLE, SURE,
INVISIBLE, INEFFABLE, BY WORD
AND THOUGHT UNCOMPASSED, EVER ALL ITSELF,
THUS IS THE SOUL DECLARED! HOW WILT THOU, THEN, —
KNOWING IT SO, — GRIEVE WHEN THOU SHOULDST NOT GRIEVE?
HOW, IF THOU HEAREST THAT THE MAN NEW-DEAD
IS, LIKE THE MAN NEW-BORN, STILL LIVING MAN —
ONE SAME, EXISTENT SPIRIT — WILT THOU WEEP?
THE END OF BIRTH IS DEATH; THE END OF DEATH
IS BIRTH: THIS IS ORDAINED! AND MOURNEST THOU,
CHIEF OF THE STALWART ARM! FOR WHAT BEFALLS
WHICH COULD NOT OTHERWISE BEFALL? THE BIRTH
OF LIVING THINGS COMES UNPERCEIVED; THE DEATH
COMES UNPERCEIVED; BETWEEN THEM, BEINGS PERCEIVE:
WHAT IS THERE SORROWFUL HEREIN, DEAR PRINCE?

This stone bas-relief sculpture, known as "Arjuna's Penance," is the largest in the world, 27 meters long and 9 meters high. It dates from the 7th century A.D. and depicts scenes from the Mahabharata, one of the great epic poems of the Brahman religion.

considered to be above those born outside the Brahman religion. Each class had hundreds of subdivisions called *jatis,* which later became known to Europeans as castes. The caste system placed everyone into a category, effectively determining a person's social status, residence, occupation, marriage partner, even whom one might eat with, for contact with the lowest castes often required ritual purification afterward. No one could escape his or her caste in a single lifetime.

The name "Upanishads" comes from a word meaning "to sit next to," or "to sit at the feet of," describing the relationship that developed between the gurus and their followers.

Caste was determined by karma, the balance of good and evil from individuals' past lives weighed against each other. A major tenet of Brahmanism came to be taught in the story known as the Bhagavad Gita, the Lord's Song, a poem in the form of a conversation between a soldier, Arjuna, and his charioteer just before a battle. The charioteer is, in fact, Lord Krishna, one of Vishnu's incarnations. Arjuna knows that he has family in the opposing army; he is saddened by the thought that he must try to kill them and that they, in turn, must seek to take his life. Lord Krishna explains to Arjuna that the physical body is simply one part of a person. Although a soldier may die in battle, the spiritual self will live on and be reborn into a higher existence.

In the period between 700 and 500 B.C., a number of critics of orthodox religion arose in India, intent upon dispelling a number of false teachings that had become part of the faith. They were known as gurus, and they were held in highest esteem by their disciples. After many years of development, their ideas were written down and placed in collections called Upanishads, from a word meaning "to sit next to," or "to sit at the feet of," and describing the relationship that developed between the gurus and their followers.

The gurus, though some of their teachings differed from one another, were unanimous in professing that everything in the universe is but a single reality, and underneath all material objects is one and the same substance, *atman,* which forms the incorruptible essence of all things.

This concept is expressed in one of the most famous of the Upanishads in the form of a dialogue between a father and his son. The father speaks first:

"Bring me a fruit from the sacred fig tree."
"Here is one, sir."
"Break it open.
"What do you see there?"
"Small seeds, sir."
"Now, break open a seed.
"What do you see now?"
"Nothing, sir."
"My son, that hidden essence that you cannot see,
of that very essence the great sacred fig exists."

The authors of the Upanishads taught that death brings bodily existence to an end, but the human *atman,* imperishable, will then inform another body and begin life anew. Depending on the karma gained in previous lives, a person will be born into a higher or lower caste or even, if the karma is particularly bad, into the body of an animal. Among some, this fostered the belief that people in lower castes were themselves to blame for their oppressed positions in life. Gurus taught that the principal goal of life was to free oneself from any attachment and to be rid of karma, thus escaping the cycle of death and rebirth. With this escape, souls were thought to attain *moksha,* a condition that released the self from individual existence and commenced a state of higher experience.

DAILY LIFE

In India in Jesus' day, doctors performed a wide variety of surgeries: removal of tumors, stitching of wounds, extraction of foreign objects, amputations, and caesarean sections. Alcohol was used as a narcotic, and hot oils and tar were used to stop bleeding. Surgical instruments were made of various kinds of metals.

JAINS AND BUDDHISTS

As the gurus were teaching the Upanishads, a new insight into religious experience bloomed in the doctrine of a teacher, Vardhamana, who became known as Mahavira, the Great Hero. His followers in Jesus' day, as today, were known as Jains, "Conquerors," for they regarded the Mahavira as pointing the way to gain complete control over one's appetites. According to Jain teaching, the Mahavira was twenty-fourth in a line of prophets that extended back millions of years.

The most devout of the "sky-clad" Jains rejected wearing clothing — even when appearing in public.

The Mahavira, according to Jain tradition, was born about 595 B.C. into a wealthy family, and could have looked forward to a life of indolent luxury. Rejecting this, he set off on a journey to discover the meaning of life, particularly why evil was so much a part of human existence. After many years of seeking, he gained the insight that the desire for wealth and material possessions was the root of human discontent. Therefore he rid himself of all belongings in an attempt to be free of desire and to find true freedom through renunciation.

The Mahavira also came to understand the intrinsic value of all life, and he made it an essential part of his teaching that no animals should ever intentionally be killed. His followers were strict vegetarians, and because farmers had no choice but to kill insects and other small forms of life while preparing their fields, Jains were forbidden that occupation. This turned the Jains of Jesus' day into a community of merchants.

After their leader's death, Jain missionaries carried the Mahavira's message throughout India. Thousands accepted his teaching as the truth, though many adapted it to fit their own lifestyles. Those who refused any compromise, the "sky-clad," rejected all material possessions and pushed small brooms ahead of them to avoid inadvertently stepping on insects. Obviously, Jainism flew in the face of some of the major tenets of Brahmanism: it forbade animal sacrifices, ignored the rituals of the Brahmans, and rejected the caste system. Still, its high regard for life and for nonviolence worked its way into the mainstream of Indian thought, where it still has a place today.

A second prophetic voice also arose in India around this time. This was Siddhartha Gautama, whom the world now knows as the Buddha, the Enlightened One. While the rigorous demands of Jainism limited its growth, already by Jesus' day the followers of the Buddha numbered in the millions, and were probably the largest, or at least the second largest, religious community on earth in the first century. Possibly Brahmanism had more adherents, but it is impossible to know the relationship between the two. India's population in the first century is estimated at 140 million, easily more than any other society at the time.

The life of Siddhartha has many similarities with that of the Mahavira. He is thought to have been born about 563 B.C. in a small village in what is now Nepal. Tradition holds that his father was a prince of the Sakyas, a people of the Himalaya hill country, who wanted to protect his son from seeing or hearing anything that would cause him pain. But the day came when Siddhartha left the sanctuary of his father's estate and came across an old man bent with age, a sick person, a dead body, and a starving beggar. This experience shattered his insular world. Like the Mahavira, he abandoned his family and wealth, determined to find the reason for evil in the world and how best to deal with it. At first he sought the wisdom of the Brahman wise men and took up the study of the Vedas, but they left him unsatisfied. Next he adopted a strict, ascetic lifestyle, but this also disappointed him. Frustrated with his years of searching, he resolved to sit under a banyan tree until the meaning of human existence came to him. And come to him it finally did.

The Buddha taught that the human condition could be explained in terms of the Four Noble Truths. First among these was the reality that suffering was a part of every human life. Secondly, suffering and unhappiness were the result of ignorance, and of the desire for power and wealth. This led to the third truth: that to be rid of suffering, men and women had to purge themselves of desire. The final truth was that following the Eightfold Path would lead individuals to enlightenment. This journey required an ascent through correct understanding, desire, speech, conduct, employment, striving, benevolence, and meditation. Once a

person had completed the path, he or she would reach nirvana, a state of existence in which the self is no longer conscious of existence, for it has merged with the *atman* of the universe.

The Buddhist nirvana was very similar to the Brahman moksha, for each freed souls from the cycle of rebirths and karma that always entailed suffering and unhappiness. And like the Jains, the Buddha taught that the pursuit of peace and respect for all life were necessary for human fulfillment.

By the time of Jesus the Buddha already had thousands of followers. This bust was made in northern India about three centuries after Jesus' death.

After the Buddha's death around 483 B.C., his disciples converted thousands to his way of thinking. Because Buddhism was unconcerned with caste, it appealed to men and women of the lower classes. Then as now, however, its adherents differed on whether the Buddha intended to found a religion or simply an ethical system that emphasized a correct approach to the good life. The congenial spirit associated with Buddhism has permitted both views to exist peacefully for over two millennia.

According to tradition, the Buddha rejected all attempts to draw him out on questions about God. To such he responded that an exploration of the human condition was quite enough. Despite this disclaimer, his disciples developed a doctrine of an afterlife in which the good were rewarded and the bad punished. Therefore, they told their followers, it was best to attain nirvana by joining a *sangha,* a body of like-minded people similar to a monastic community, in which distractions were kept to a minimum. Joining a sangha required that a person take vows of chastity, poverty, and nonviolence. Buddhist monks and nuns wore simple saffron robes, went barefoot, and each morning left their monasteries with empty rice bowls to beg for their day's food.

Buddhist missionaries in the third century B.C. were so persuasive that they succeeded in winning over Emperor Ashoka at the very peak of Mauryan power. Formerly renowned for his bloody conquests, Ashoka astonished his court at Pataliputra when he announced there would be no more military campaigns and, in a rare demonstration of courage for a political leader, apologized for all the suffering his wars had caused. Throughout his territories, he had tall stone pillars erected and engraved with inscriptions promoting Buddhist values, and he ordered that a large stone monument be placed over the Buddha's grave.

Even more importantly for the future of Buddhism, Ashoka financed the travels of missionaries, who spread the Buddha's message throughout southern Asia, Burma, Sri Lanka, and the Himalayan mountain states. Thousands of people converted. But Buddhism was to enjoy its greatest success in China, which its missionaries reached in the twenty years following Jesus' death.

The period after Ashoka's death in 232 B.C. was a time of turbulence for Indian Buddhism. Arguments over the interpretation of Buddhist scriptures divided the sangha leaders. Some argued that authentic Buddhism demanded a life of asceticism; others contended that ordinary people living ordinary lives were no less likely than ascetics to attain nirvana in a single lifetime.

In the Buddhist tradition, exceptionally good men and women were held up for admiration as bodhisattvas. Even though their lives on earth fitted them for entrance to nirvana, bodhisattvas generously remained on earth to help others. Their role in Buddhism has many parallels to that of the saints in Christian tradition.

Despite such significant challengers, Brahmanism ultimately remained the dominant Indian religion, for it had a remarkable ability to absorb each new religious and ethnic group that appeared. The Brahmans simply assigned it a caste and treated its members accordingly. In their estimation, the Buddha was simply an incarnation of Vishnu.

SRI LANKA

Sri Lankan history was not recorded until long after Jesus' lifetime. All archaeology reveals is that the first settlers, the Sinhalese, appeared in the sixth century B.C. Ashoka's missionaries brought them into the Buddhist fold, where they demonstrated their devotion by building hundreds of stone monuments called stupas. Centuries later, Tamils from South India crossed onto the island, holding fast to their connections to their homeland and its Brahman religion.

CHRISTIANITY AND INDIAN RELIGIONS

It is a fascinating question to ask what Jesus' message would have sounded like had it been nurtured in India. The story of his life could certainly have been recorded, since India had long been a literate society. It is safe to surmise that Jesus would have had much more in common with the Mahavira and the Buddha than with the Brahmans, for he was born into a working-class family, one that had no pretensions to status or power. Neither the Mahavira nor the Buddha embraced the caste system, which forced countless people into lives of hardship, and reserved lives of privilege for only a few. Jesus would have followed suit. He intended his message to be for all people, regardless of rank or social standing. In fact, it may be argued that Jesus was even more inclusive than they were, for he was not afraid to take in women as his disciples. Women were

Hundreds of stupas, such as this one, were built as Buddhist shrines. This one was commissioned by Ashoka in the 3rd century B.C.

allowed only a marginal role in the Brahman and Jain traditions, and even the Buddha had to be persuaded that women could join sanghas.

Jesus' message, of course, spoke nothing of reincarnation, a concept that played a pivotal role in both Brahman and Buddhist thought. Rather, he taught that individuals would have to give an account of their lives to God after a single lifetime. And while asceticism was later embraced in some Christian traditions, Jesus' life demonstrated a respect for matter. Indeed, his incarnation, for Christians, implied the sanctity of matter as well as spirit. They believed that at the end of time the body would rise again to be united with the soul.

Heaven, Jesus taught, was a state of personal, conscious union with God, not the impersonal absorption into the cosmic spirit that the gurus and Brahmans taught. Not only would people there be united with God, they would also be reunited with the friends and family they had known and loved on earth. And while Brahmanism spoke of a pantheon of deities, and the Buddha professed little interest in the divine, Jesus encouraged his followers to cultivate a relationship with a single God of three persons.

Jesus' role as savior was not entirely unlike that of Vishnu, and the biblical accounts of his resurrection would not have unsettled any Indian of the first century. The Mahavira would have applauded his teachings on nonviolence, and it would have pleased the Buddha to see monasticism flourish among Christians, as it did as the religion grew and spread. In the end, it is perhaps impossible to say what Christianity would look like today had it been nurtured in India. For Jesus and his message have many parallels to his counterparts there, but their significant differences cannot be overlooked.

Chapter Ten

Southeast Asia

SOUTHEAST ASIA EXTENDS from Burma in the west to the Philippine Islands in the east. Part of the monsoon zone of Asia, it is a warm, humid region isolated from China and India, its nearest neighbors, by rugged, almost impassable mountains. Within its own borders, the Indian Ocean breaks it up even further: while one part, the Malay Peninsula, clings to the Asian mainland, the rest is divided into thousands of islands. In the first century, as today, Southeast Asia was a transitional region, pulled by Chinese culture in the north and by Indian civilization in the south, but surprisingly isolated from both. Knowledge of its early history is extremely fragmentary, with what little we know today coming from the Chinese and Indians, who had not begun to write about the region until centuries after Jesus' lifetime.

PEOPLES OF SOUTHEAST ASIA

Archaeology indicates that the first inhabitants of Southeast Asia arrived there about forty thousand years ago. Some of these were Negritos, so called because of their dark skin and short stature. Their descendants today are the Semang of Malaysia and the Aetas of the Philippines.

Relatives of the Australian Aborigines also still live in the region, in the hill country of Malaysia. All of these peoples originated as hunters and gatherers, makers of stone tools and a unique kind of pottery decorated with cord impressions. It is believed that they supplemented their diet of game and wild plants with dry-rice farming. They were alone in the region until a succession of migrations between 2500 and 1500 B.C. brought newcomers speaking Austronesian languages. The new arrivals, originally from China and Tibet, pushed into Southeast Asia as far as the Philippines, forcing their predecessors into the mountains and other remote places. Ancestors of the present-day Malays, they signify the dawn of the New Stone Age in the region.

FURTHER FACTS

The Southeast Asians of Jesus' day must have been expert sailors; their goods, many of their musical instruments, including kettledrums and xylophones, have been found as far away as Africa.

The Austronesians left behind two kinds of adzes, both made of ground, polished stone. One was used for carving small wooden items, and the other for hollowing out logs to make canoes. They were also expert potters, and on Java the demand for earthenware grew so great that an industry sprung up for the manufacture of the flake and blade stone tools needed to make it. Over time, the Austronesians were forced to share their land with others; further migrations brought the Chams into central and southern Vietnam, the Khmers into the Mekong Valley, and the Mons into Burma. The Pyus settled the Irrawaddy and Sittaung valleys, and one branch of the Malays remained in the continent's southern peninsula. The people who gave their name to Thailand and Burma, the Thais and Burmese, were latecomers, not arriving in the region until long after the time of Jesus.

This head of Brahma, found in Cambodia and dating from the ninth century A.D., suggests that Brahmanism as well as Buddhism had its share of followers in ancient Southeast Asia.

The countryside of Southeast Asia was filled with villages of 35 to 50 houses. Farmers grew millet, rice, yams, and taro, and kept dogs, chickens, and pigs as livestock. Indian merchants landed on the shores of Southeast Asia after 500 B.C., seeking gold ore, while the Austronesians sailed in the other direction at about the same time in search of Indian goods. The seasonal change of direction in the monsoon winds facilitated traffic between the two. Some archeologists date the introduction of the water buffalo and wet rice cultivation into Southeast Asia at this time.

About 300 B.C., the Southeast Asian peoples began to import bronze

This oath attributed to Trung Trac is well known in Vietnamese legend.

I SWEAR, FIRST, TO AVENGE THE NATION;

SECOND, TO RESTORE THE HUNGS' FORMER POSITION;

THIRD, TO HAVE REVENGE FOR MY HUSBAND;

FOURTH, TO CARRY THROUGH TO THE END OUR COMMON TASK!

and iron from China. From bronze they fashioned adzes, knives, and plates of armor, all objects that quickly became signs of wealth and prestige. Smiths fashioned agricultural tools, especially plows, from the less-precious iron. Many of these artifacts were first unearthed in the Vietnamese village of Dong-son, and so the culture bears its name.

Archaeology suggests that the Dong-son people were flourishing around the time of Jesus. Like most cultures, they had their own style of pottery, and their potters also made earthenware urns, in which the cremated remains of their dead were placed. Some of their artists were sculptors; others erected large stone megaliths and carved images on them, probably to honor their ancestors. Remnants of their jewelry betray a fascination with glass beads, some of which appear to be imported from as far away as the Mediterranean. They built houses of wood or bamboo, many raised on stilts to protect them from floods.

Contact between India and Southeast Asia increased, as the former's desire for gold was apparently insatiable. The Indians, in fact, gave the name *suvarkabhumi,* "the land of gold," to the Cambodian and Malaysian ports they visited. Ashoka, the Indian emperor who converted to Buddhism, sent missionaries to Burma, and some archaeologists hold that at this time Indian colonists settled in Southeast Asia. Soon after Jesus' lifetime, the kingdom of Funan, which became a major power in the early Middle Ages, was founded in Cambodia. According to a Chinese chronicle, it was ruled by an Indian general, Kaudinya.

The religion of the Dong-son people combined ancestor worship with the veneration of fertility gods. In addition, they believed a life force pervaded all living beings, and that it had to be placated in order to ensure good fortune. Shrines were erected in holy places for rituals that included the playing of brass kettledrums, many of which survive to this day. In Java, the gamelan band, comprised of percussion instruments such as drums, gongs, and xylophones, accompanied religious ceremonies. A rich mythology accompanied worship, recounting cosmic battles between water and land spirits.

FURTHER FACTS

To make just one brass kettledrum required the smelting of between one and seven tons of copper ore and the use of up to ten large crucibles at one time.

THE VIETNAMESE

In the second century B.C., a people from southern China migrated into Southeast Asia and settled among the indigenous population, thus forming the nucleus of the Vietnamese people. This led to the development of ties with China that paralleled those that the rest of Southeast Asia had made with Indian culture. The Chinese called the region Nam Viet. At one point a local chieftain, An Duong, attempted to establish a state there. But the Qin Emperor, Shi Huangdi, sent an army into the region to discourage such nationalistic sentiments, and, after the overthrow of the Qin, the Vietnamese became loosely attached to a breakaway southern Chinese state whose capital was at Guangzhou.

VIETNAM UNDER THE CHINESE

During the reign of the Wu Di Emperor, China once again began to feel constrained by its borders. In 111 B.C., the emperor sent five armies into Vietnam, and the Lacs, a family of aristocrats, determined that resistance

→

This bronze statuette of a warrior is typical of the sculpture of the Dong-son.

would be futile. They bargained with the Chinese army generals to allow them to serve as their lieutenants in Vietnam, in which position they served until A.D. 43. The Lacs were given the seal and sash, symbols of authority granted them by the emperor, but there was little question that decision-making took place in Qangan, the imperial capital.

The Chinese divided the country into three provinces ruled by a single governor who represented the emperor. As far as the Chinese were concerned, the Vietnamese were barbarians, fit for paying taxes and little else. These taxes were paid in the form of goods and crops, and Chinese soldiers garrisoned in the land ensured that collection went smoothly. In A.D. 2, when Jesus was a young child, the Chinese took a census of their Vietnamese subjects, counting 981,755 in the three provinces that they controlled. The Chinese governor at this time was Xi Kuang, and his goal was to introduce Chinese culture into Vietnam. For the first time in Southeast Asian history, a true urban society formed. Xi Kuang opened schools for the teaching of Confucianism and Chinese script, required Chinese ritual at wedding ceremonies, ordered the wearing of Chinese hats and sandals, and instituted an administrative system modeled on the Chinese bureaucracy.

When Wang Mang became emperor, he appointed one of his supporters, Jan Yen, as governor; Jan Yen made it his goal to further the policies of his predecessors. He recognized that it would be to the advantage of the Chinese to establish a stable, patriarchal society in Vietnam, but he was far from popular among his subjects. By A.D. 29, while Jesus was about his public ministry and after civil war had engulfed China upon the overthrow of Wang Mang's regime, the Lacs, who had remained co-rulers with the Chinese, were fed up with their presence in Vietnam. Trung Trac, the wife of one of the Lac lords, and her sister, Nhi, organized the resistance. Under Trung Trac's leadership, soldiers from across Vietnam joined in the struggle to rout the Chinese. They were overwhelmingly successful. The people proclaimed the Trung sisters queens, and sixty towns recognized their authority.

A decade after the death of Jesus, the Chinese returned with a large, disciplined army and Trung Trac's forces suffered a major defeat. Facing capture and execution, the sisters drowned themselves, and not long after their death direct Chinese rule was imposed on northern Vietnam for another thousand years. The example of the Trung sisters, however, was never forgotten; their spirits lived on in near-constant rebellions against the Chinese until, centuries later, they were finally driven from Vietnam.

Little can be said about events taking place off the mainland of Southeast Asia at the time of Jesus. Each community went its own way. There was no one to record tales of success or of failure, for the people of Indonesia and the Philippines were still too far removed from the literate nations of India and China. They were lands of small villages, in which life revolved around the tasks of hunting, gathering, and growing enough food to eat. So pressing were these tasks that religion was stripped down to bare necessities, providing the sparest of mythologies to explain nature's mysteries.

Since his teachings blossomed largely out of the framework of the Jewish tradition in which he was reared, it is difficult to imagine how Jesus' message would have sounded in Southeast Asia, where religion was at its least organized. And even had literacy been known, written records would have had little chance of surviving millennia in Southeast Asia's hot, humid climate. While Jesus emphasized the fact that his message was for all people, the environment of Southeast Asia was far removed from both the spiritual and material structure that allowed his earthly ministry to flourish.

Chapter Eleven

The Pacific Islands and Australia

As is the case with Southeast Asia, painting a picture of life in first-century Australia and the Pacific Islands is no easy task. Once more we are dealing with illiterate societies, and once more we are faced with a land that has only recently felt the touch of the archaeologist's spade. Even what findings we have can tell us comparatively little, for countless sites have yet to be excavated, and their discoveries pieced together.

The Pacific Ocean covers nearly a third of the earth. Scattered over its surface are perhaps twenty-five thousand islands, about a thousand of which are inhabited. Most of these are very small; indeed, land represents less than one percent of the total Pacific area. Some are the product of volcanic eruptions, while others are the result of a buildup of coral, resting on the skeletons of billions upon billions of these tiny creatures. Often the two exist side by side, islands of coral forming atolls around extinct volcanic cones.

While they are often thought of as a kind of tropical paradise, the Pacific Islands have not always been kind to their inhabitants. They are plagued by typhoons, which often strike without warning and result in immense damage. Thin soil and lack of fresh water are problems now just as they were two thousand years ago.

Traditionally, anthropologists have divided the peoples of the Pacific into three major categories: Melanesians, Micronesians, and Polynesians. More recently, a system has been developed which speaks of the region in terms of Inner and Outer Islands, classifying them according to how recently they were settled. The Inner Islands, close to the Asian continent, were home to some of the very first human populations; the Outer Islands, on the other hand, along the rim of the western Pacific, remained uninhabited until centuries after the birth of Jesus. It was not until about A.D. 300, for example, that settlers first landed on the Hawaiian islands, and not for six hundred years thereafter that they reached New Zealand. Today, most of the island populations are the result of multiple waves of settlers, ultimately resisting any system of classification. Indeed, the fact that they are home to nearly a thousand different languages testifies to their isolation even from one another. Yet all of these languages are very similar, belonging to only two families: the Papuan, spoken only in parts of New Guinea, and the Austronesian, spread throughout the Pacific.

Headhunting had spiritual significance. By displaying a victim's head in public and performing certain purification rituals, the Melanesians believed that the dead enemy's soul could be converted into an ally in the afterlife.

THE MELANESIANS

The Melanesians were the first to arrive in the islands, emigrating from Southeast Asia as early as 40,000 B.C. and settling in New Guinea. At that time, there was still a land bridge connecting the two, making the crossing relatively easy. Later Southeast Asian emigrants spread farther out, populating the Bismarck and Solomon Archipelagos, Vanuatu, New Caledonia, and Fiji. All these islands shared a warm, humid climate, though the fertility of the soil varied significantly from one to another.

New Guinea, the largest Melanesian island, was populated, as it is today, by hundreds of tiny societies that fiercely maintained their independence from one another. Agriculture was their livelihood, and had been for centuries; archaeologists estimate that farming was discovered there as early as 8000 B.C. and techniques for irrigation five thousand years later. Staple crops included yams and taro, and later sugar cane and tree crops such as coconuts, breadfruit, and bananas. Pigs were the most important livestock.

While the earliest inhabitants of New Guinea spoke Papuan languages, the second wave of colonists to arrive spoke Austronesian tongues. These may have introduced the distinctive pottery that archaeologists call Lapita ware. Tracing the spread of Lapita pottery from New Guinea suggests that the new arrivals reached the Bismarck Archipelago around 2000 B.C., and Fiji a thousand years later. Other traces of human habitation in Melanesia include tools and decorations made of shells, bones, and polished stones.

Hereditary chieftains were the political leaders in Melanesian society. They settled disputes among their subjects and, more often than not, made war against their neighbors. Headhunting often sparked and perpetuated these wars, for warriors' prowess was measured by the number of trophies they acquired. Men in Melanesian cultures often belonged to secret societies, which granted entry only to initiates; women, too, had their own societies and rituals, and were allowed to sell the handicrafts they made. Their religion was a mixture of ancestor worship, totemism, and magic, and placed special emphasis on the human body, which was therefore a popular subject for artists and sculptors.

FURTHER FACTS

Worship in Melanesia was so secretive that, when Christian missionaries first brought news of Jesus there several centuries after his death, village elders were alarmed that children were talking and singing about him aloud on the street. They believed that if he was God's son his name must be uttered only during worship.

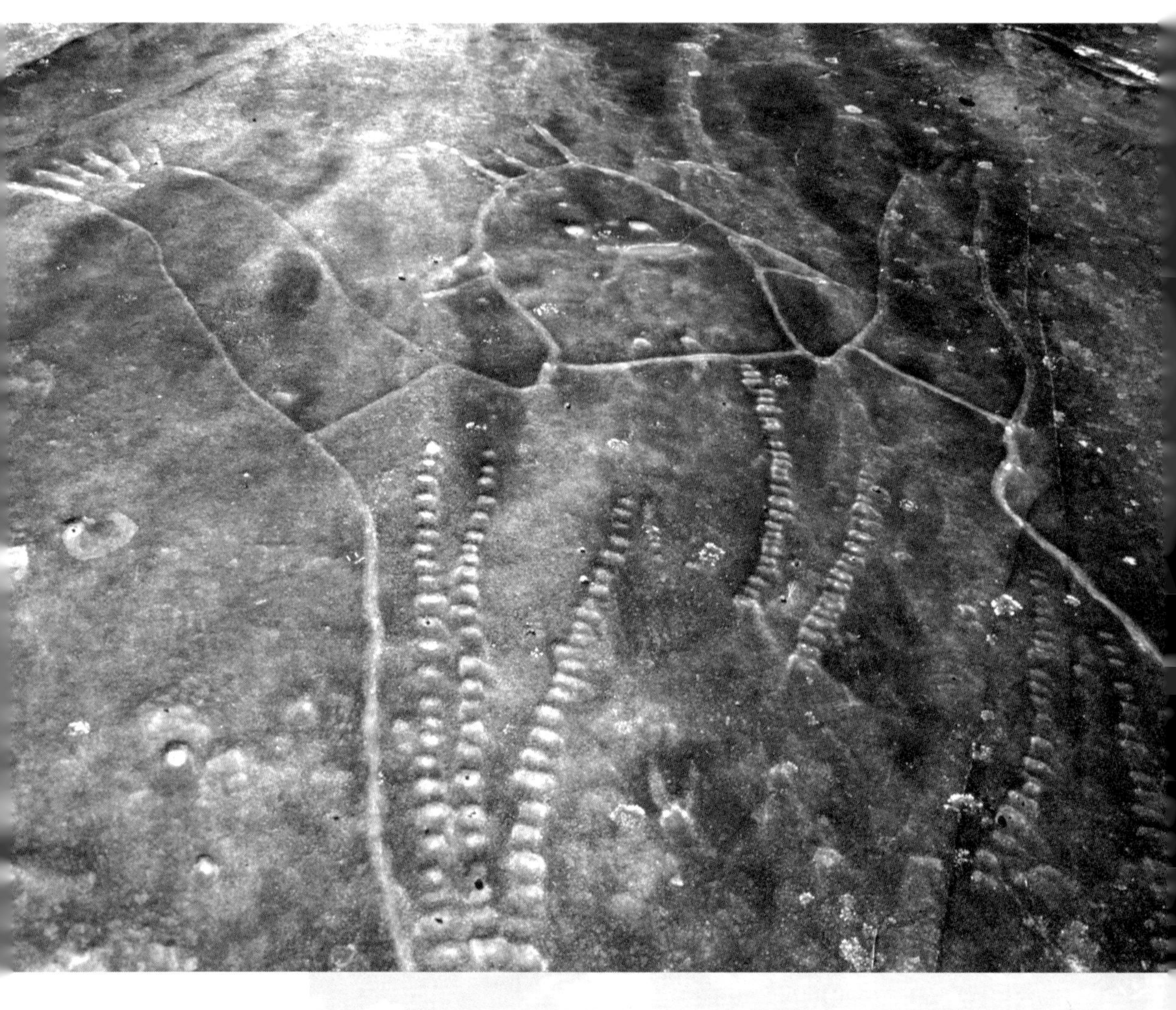

MICRONESIANS

Micronesians — the people of Palau and Kiribati and the Marianas, Caroline, and Marshall Islands — weathered environments far more hostile than New Guinea. They settled in villages along the ocean shoreline, depending on the sea for their livelihood. Archaeologists trace their settlements back to 3500 B.C., and identify ten major linguistic groups. Some islands were very heavily populated in Jesus' day, sparking constant conflict over property rights. Like the Melanesians, they carved art and instruments from shells and bones, but their religion lacked the high ceremonial elaboration of the Melanesians, emphasizing instead informal worship in family groups.

←

Petroglyphs were incised in rocks at aboriginal sacred sites. Their creation was attributed to clan ancestral beings who formed the landscape during the Dreamtime.

POLYNESIANS

The Polynesians comprised the last wave of emigrants to the South Pacific. Eventually they inhabited a great triangle of islands extending from Hawaii in the north to Easter Island in the east and New Zealand in the south. Archaeologists believe that Samoa and Tonga were the two major centers of Polynesian culture in 2000 B.C. and that from there it spread to New Zealand by A.D. 900. They brought with them more than 100 different languages, indicating that, like the Micronesians and Melanesians, they settled their islands in waves over many centuries. They also adopted the Lapita pottery of the Melanesians, enabling archaeologists to trace their early migrations.

At the time of Jesus, the western Polynesians were about to begin the expeditions that would eventually take them all over the Pacific. By 200 B.C. they had landed in the Marquesas and the Cook Islands, but had yet to reach the outermost islands of the Pacific.

Polynesian culture was characterized by marked class differences. Chiefs claimed that their authority came from divine ancestors, and they insisted that their subjects venerate them during religious ceremonies. In addition to this, prayers and sacrifices had to be offered to a number of deities: Tangara, Tine, Tiki, and Mauir. The gods and goddesses, they

A Polynesian creation myth

Source: Sir George Gray, Polynesian Mythology and Ancient Traditional History of the New Zealanders *(1854).*

MEN HAD BUT ONE PAIR OF PRIMITIVE ANCESTORS; THEY SPRANG FROM THE VAST HEAVEN THAT EXISTS ABOVE US, AND FROM THE EARTH WHICH LIES BENEATH US. ACCORDING TO THE TRADITIONS OF OUR RACE, RANGI AND PAPA, OR HEAVEN AND EARTH, WERE THE SOURCE FROM WHICH, IN THE BEGINNING, ALL THINGS ORIGINATE. DARKNESS THEN RESTED UPON THE HEAVEN AND UPON THE EARTH, AND THEY STILL BOTH CLAVE TOGETHER, FOR THEY HAD NOT YET BEEN RENT APART; AND THE CHILDREN THEY HAD BEGOTTEN WERE EVER THINKING AMONGST THEMSELVES WHAT MIGHT BE THE DIFFERENCE BETWEEN DARKNESS AND LIGHT; THEY KNEW THAT BEINGS HAD MULTIPLIED AND INCREASED, AND YET LIGHT HAD NEVER BROKEN UPON THEM, BUT IT EVER CONTINUED DARK. HENCE THESE SAYINGS ARE FOUND IN OUR ANCIENT RELIGIOUS SERVICES: "THERE WAS DARKNESS FROM THE FIRST DIVISION OF TIME, UNTO THE TENTH, TO THE HUNDREDTH, TO THE THOUSANDTH," THAT IS, FOR A VAST SPACE OF TIME; AND THESE DIVISIONS OF TIMES WERE CONSIDERED AS BEINGS, AND WERE EACH TERMED "A PO"; AND ON THEIR ACCOUNT THERE WAS AS YET NO WORLD WITH ITS BRIGHT LIGHT, BUT DARKNESS ONLY FOR THE BEINGS WHICH EXISTED. :: AT LAST THE BEINGS WHO HAD BEEN BEGOTTEN BY HEAVEN AND EARTH, WORN OUT BY THE CONTINUED DARKNESS, CONSULTED AMONGST THEMSELVES, SAYING: "LET US NOW DETERMINE WHAT WE SHOULD DO WITH RANGI AND PAPA, WHETHER IT WOULD BE BETTER TO SLAY THEM OR TO REND THEM APART." THEN SPOKE TUMATAUENGA, THE FIERCEST OF THE CHILDREN OF HEAVEN AND EARTH: "IT IS WELL, LET US SLAY THEM." :: THEN SPOKE TANE-MAHUTA, THE FATHER OF FORESTS AND OF ALL THINGS THAT INHABIT THEM, OR THAT ARE CONSTRUCTED FROM TREES: "NAY, NOT SO. IT IS BETTER TO REND THEM APART, AND TO LET THE HEAVEN STAND FAR ABOVE US, AND THE EARTH LIE UNDER OUR FEET. LET THE SKY BECOME AS A STRANGER TO US, BUT THE EARTH REMAIN CLOSE TO US AS OUR NURSING MOTHER."

believed, possessed large amounts of *mana,* power, and could punish those who performed actions that were *tapu,* forbidden. Dance, to the accompaniment of drums, was an important part of worship.

Scholars of Polynesian history are still awed by the seamanship of the islanders. In double-hulled canoes that could carry 100 individuals, they set out on the ocean, always having faith that they would find land. In addition to their human cargo, the canoes also had to have room for the plants and animals that would sustain them in their new homes: dogs, chickens, pigs, and, unwittingly, rats. Provisions had to be sufficient to last a month at sea, and navigators skillful enough to make numerous return trips between their old and new homes. Many canoes and their passengers were surely lost, but enough survived to colonize the eastern Pacific.

FURTHER FACTS

The following actions were all tapu *to Polynesians, and could invoke the anger of the spirits: eating too much rich food before approaching them; engaging in sexual relations in the forests where they dwelled; urinating or defecating in their realms; making excessive noise in their presence; or destroying a tree or other object in their realm.*

AUSTRALIAN ABORIGINES

The recent discovery of a stone monument of extreme antiquity in Australia suggests that it may have been inhabited long before archaeologists once surmised-perhaps as many as seventy thousand years ago. European Australians have given the name Aborigines to these people. The Aborigines came in several waves to Australia from Southeast Asia at a time when the ocean was low enough for there to be a land bridge between the two. What they discovered was a continent that measured 2,000 miles north to south and 2,400 miles east to west. For the most part, it was an uninterrupted expanse of arid plains and plateaus, in which finding water would be a constant concern. In ancient times, about two hundred Aborigine languages were spoken, about eighty-five percent of which were closely related to one another. By the time the first Europeans reached Australia, anthropologists estimate the native population at about three hundred thousand. It was surely much less in the first century.

The Aborigines depended entirely on hunting and gathering for sur-

Nearly every feature of Ayers Rock in northern Australia had some kind of religious significance to the Aborigines.

vival. Only one animal, the dingo, was half-domesticated, and even that was for companionship more than for livestock. Often hunters used fire to stampede the wild animals that they hunted, and some scholars claim that the overuse of this tactic led to the extinction of Australia's large animals and the destruction of their habitats. Smaller creatures, such as kangaroos and opossums, survived, and these furnished the Aborigines with meat and hides.

Family was the center of Aboriginal culture, essential both for survival and for all social interaction. Men served as hunters, and women and children as foragers. Marriages were arranged between clans when children, particularly girls, were still very young. Many families formed bands of twenty to thirty people, traveling together within loosely defined areas. Sometimes they built houses of bark or brush, but these were never intended to be permanent homes. Spears, spear throwers, harpoons, boomerangs, fishing hooks, and a handful of wood and stone tools were the extent of their technology. Women searched for edible plants with a digging stick and used nets and baskets to bring home what they found. Textiles were unknown, so people went unclothed most of the time, adorned only with bone and shell jewelry. When temperatures sank, men and women wrapped themselves in cloaks of opossum or kangaroo skins.

In contrast to their material austerity, the Aborigines had an extraordinarily rich supply of myths and religious ceremonies. According to their tradition, the creation of the world happened at a time known as the Dreamtime. During the Dreamtime, powerful spirits, including the All-Father, the All-Mother, and the Rainbow Serpent, shaped the physical features of the world and created men and women. When their work was finished, the spirits remained on earth, inhabiting trees, springs, and especially stones. Of particular import among these was Ayers Rock, a breathtaking natural monolith in northern Australia whose every feature had some kind of religious significance. Rocks and trees were often painted or carved as religious gestures, and each individual had a special totemic relationship to an animal and venerated it in dance and song. Men participated in secret societies and women had their own rituals; both men and women participated in fertility and initiation rites. Among some bands, young boys were subjected to an ordeal that required the

A 20th century aboriginal painting on eucalyptus bark, depicting an iguana. From earliest times animals had religious significance to the Aborigines and were the subject of countless paintings and carvings on rocks and trees.

extraction of a tooth. Occasionally many clans convened for what was known as a corroboree, a tumultuous celebration involving days and nights of dancing, theater, and religious ceremony.

The Aborigines did not consider death to be a natural event, but rather the result of sorcery. When a member of a clan died, therefore, it befell its leaders to root out the guilty party and assign an appropriate punishment. But while death could kill the body, they believed, it did not touch the soul. All the dead lived on as spirits, continuing to influence the lives of those who survived them.

Tasmanian Aborigines, now an extinct people, lived on the island south of Australia that carries the name of the Dutch explorer Abel Tasman, who discovered it in 1642. Their lives, though similar, were even simpler than those of their mainland counterparts, incorporating only the most basic of stone and wooden tools.

It is evident that Jesus, had he been either a Pacific Islander or an Australian or Tasmanian Aborigine, would never have left a trace of his existence. Life on the islands was a matter of survival in a harsh environment, where warfare, although fairly benign, was constant. There was little opportunity for philosophical speculation or doctrinal statements. The people who lived there during his lifetime were centuries away from developing systems of reading and writing; whatever their wise men and women taught had to be transmitted orally.

And while their world was full of supernatural beings and that mysterious element known as mana, they were not looking for revelation from a single transcendent deity. The God of whom Jesus taught would have been perceived as just one among countless powerful spirits. Despite these significant differences, though, a few commonalities remain: while so many first-century religions believed that the grave was the end, both the Aborigines and the early Christians believed in a life after death, and that our deeds in this life would have no little impact on the one to come.

Chapter Twelve

The Arctic

FEW REGIONS IN THE WORLD are less hospitable to human inhabitants than the North American Arctic. Yet it teems with wildlife, whose presence tempted Siberian hunters to begin settling there thousands of years ago. At that time, glaciers may have offered a land bridge between the two continents, making passage relatively simple. During the first century small bands of people, descendants of these early immigrants, were spread thinly across Alaska and Canada, a few even reaching the remote shores of Greenland.

The Arctic can be divided into two regions. The extreme north is a polar climate, covered with snow and ice year-round. Among these are the northernmost parts of Alaska, Canada, and Greenland. Since the Arctic Ocean never freezes over completely, ice floes sixty to one hundred feet thick jostle each other as they slowly drift along the surface of the sea.

Despite its perpetual cover of snow, the polar region receives little precipitation, averaging no more than eleven inches each year. Were it not for the surface snow, the far north would be a desert, for dry, still air hovers over the land day after day during the dark winter months. To its inhabitants, the scene is beautiful in its isolation and quiet.

Inland from the polar region is the tundra, a flat, treeless plain that gradually emerged when the last ice cap began to retreat eleven thousand years ago. In contrast to the polar region, the tundra enjoys moderate temperatures for two or three summer months. Since the sun never sets during these months, plant life flourishes: mosses, heath, grasses, and lichen. Ponds and lakes melt, but since the ground below is still frozen — a condition known as permafrost — the excess water has nowhere to drain, creating swampy conditions. Swarms of mosquitoes hatch and fill the air, providing food for native birds. But by late August, summer ends and the sun retreats. In early December, it dips below the horizon, commencing an Arctic night that envelops the land for six to eight weeks.

Alaska has a varied topography, dominated by two mountain ranges, the Alaskan and the Aleutian. The latter continues into the sea, forming islands whose temperatures, tempered by the ocean, are far milder than those on the mainland. Volcanoes, mostly dormant but always dangerous, dot the Alaskan peninsula, and along some parts of the ocean coast, ice freezes to a depth of three feet.

ARCTIC LIFE

Polar and tundra wildlife sustained human existence in the Arctic. Caribou, musk oxen, polar bears, Arctic foxes, and snow hares, not to mention an extensive bird population, provided Arctic men and women with food and with the hides they used to make clothing and tents. Hunters followed caribou on their yearly migrations: north for the summer and south for the winter.

At the time of Jesus, two peoples dwelled along the Alaskan coast: the Inuits, or Eskimos, and the Aleuts. Anthropologists believe that these two once formed a single people, the last to cross from Siberia to Alaska, but that over centuries they drifted apart, gradually forming distinctly separate cultures. It is uncertain when their ancestors arrived in North America, but evidence points to about 6000 B.C. The Aleuts settled in southwestern Alaska, and on the islands that bear their name; they so isolated themselves from the Inuits that their languages became mutually incomprehensible.

The Inuits became the only people to live year-round in the Arctic. Since neither they nor the Aleuts developed systems of writing, what can be known of their civilizations in Jesus' time must be gleaned from archaeological sites. These are fairly numerous, but due to their subjects' nomadic way of life, they are neither easy to find nor to interpret.

THE ANCIENT ARCTIC

Remains of the earliest Arctic peoples were first unearthed on Cape Denbigh in Alaska, and their civilization has since become known to archaeologists as the Denbigh Flint Complex. Originating around 3000 B.C., the patterns it set for Arctic life endured for several thousand years. Particularly distinguishing among its artifacts are numerous microliths: tiny stone blades that were attached to spears and used for hunting caribou and other game. Because they were dependent on the life cycles of these animals for their own survival, it was impossible for these cultures to live too long in any one place. They studied the migration patterns of their prey, and learned to move accordingly. The Inuits of the Arctic Small Tool Tradition, another northern culture, followed their quarry further and further east, and eventually became the first human beings to reach Greenland. This migration, which started as early as 1000 B.C., was in progress while Jesus was alive.

THE ARCTIC ECONOMY

While the Aleuts based their economy almost entirely on what the sea provided, the Inuits could look both landward and seaward for their livelihood. The usual Aleut method of hunting was for two men, a navigator and a harpooner, to put to sea in a kayak to hunt sea lions. The Inuits took to the sea, too, in search of whales and other sea mammals to feed their families, but since their kayaks were designed for just one occupant, they also used canoes. Inland, when the salmon began their annual migration upstream in the Alaskan rivers, Inuit fishermen awaited them.

↑

This model umiak contains a helmsman with members of his family manning the oars. All are dressed in waterproof seal intestine parkas.

Possibly the Inuits who were contemporaries of Jesus invented the umiak, a skin boat large enough for hunters to stand in as they harpooned their quarry. Inflated sealskins were attached to these harpoons so that, once dead, the animals would not sink to the bottom of the sea and be lost to them.

In the Arctic cold, surplus food needed neither smoking nor drying to be preserved. The oil rendered from whales and other prey provided people with cooking fuel, as well as lighting in carefully crafted stone lamps.

Inuit settlements were always near the seacoast. They constructed semisubterranean tent houses, sometimes round, sometimes square, whose foundations were approximately twenty inches under the ground. Animal skins provided the superstructure, and poles of driftwood and rocks or lumps of sod lent stability. In the Aleutian Islands, homes were built even deeper into the ground; men and women often entered their houses through the roof. Some Inuits in the Canadian Arctic built igloos, but their use was not widespread. All Arctic homes kept a hearth with a fire for warmth and cooking.

INUIT CULTURES

There were no chiefs among the Arctic people. Men famed for their hunting prowess enjoyed a certain preeminence, but individual families were expected to be self-sufficient. Age and sex determined the roles of men, women, and children. Women cared for the children, devoting special attention to girls, who had to learn the skills required to cook and make clothing. Fathers, in turn, taught their sons to hunt and fish.

In some Inuit communities, a large community house complemented the smaller dwellings of individual families. These, apparently, were used for religious ceremonies in which shamans, the religious leaders of the group, petitioned the spirits for a bountiful hunt or for the sick to be healed. If modern Inuit life may serve as a guide, the shamans of Jesus' day, accompanied by a drummer, would dance, taking the role of the animal to be hunted, so that through sympathetic magic, the upcoming hunt might be a success.

↓

The precise function of this tiny Dorset mask, only four centimeters high and dating from about 500 B.C., is unknown; it was most likely used by a shaman in his rituals or as a storyteller's prop.

At the time of Jesus, there were three different Inuit cultures. The Dorset, who were part of the Arctic Small Tool Tradition, inhabited Canada, Greenland, and the islands north of the Hudson Bay. Possibly, too, they had outposts in Labrador and in Newfoundland. Dorset settlements are identified by the distinctive shapes of their tools and utensils. Among these are stone blades for projectiles, carved slate knives, stone lamps, and polished burins, which were used for scraping hides. Dorset Inuits hunted caribou with spears and kept a handful of sled dogs for transporting the carcasses back to their homes. They were also the first to use ice creepers, which were made of ivory and strapped to hunters' legs, enabling them to walk on ice when on seal hunts. Dorset women used needles of bone and ivory to tailor the family's clothing.

A second Inuit tradition developed on Kodiak Island and the adjacent mainland. This culture was characterized by specially decorated stone lamps, polished slate tools and utensils, bone instruments, darts, and harpoon heads with toggles. These toggles made it difficult for harpoons to come loose from animals that had been struck.

Inuits on the Alaskan coast and inland had another distinct way of life, which archaeologists now call the Norton culture. This culture was about a thousand years old in Jesus' day, though new communities were still being established. One major settlement, Ipiutak, would have been just in its infancy about A.D. 1. Located at Point Hope on the coast of the Arctic Ocean, it is the site of the remains of over six hundred houses, whose inhabitants were primarily hunters of seal and walrus in the summer and caribou in the winter. They buried their dead with wooden masks and ivory chains. The Norton people were very skilled in carving wood, antler, and sometimes bone, but their greatest skill was with ivory. Animals were their preferred subjects, hardly a surprise given their reliance on hunting.

The Norton people were the first among the Inuits to develop pottery. Artisans made a kind of paddle out of ivory to shape the clay, which they then stamped with linear designs. Today, archaeologists use these lines to identify Norton settlements. Other remnants of their culture include adze blades, large projectile points, stone lamps, and harpoons, some of them large enough for whale hunting.

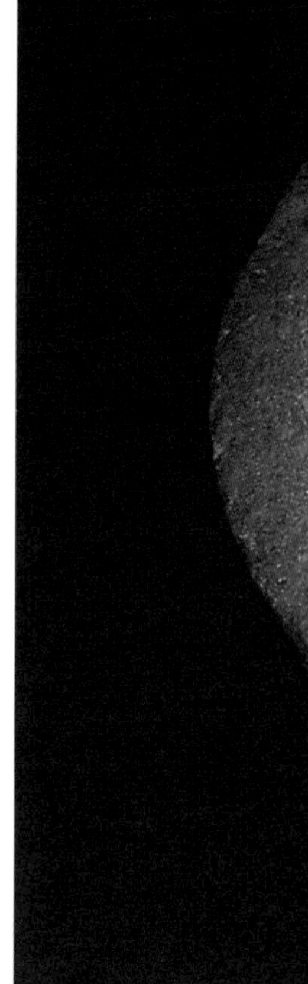

SIBERIAN PEOPLES

Siberia, the Arctic region of Asia, is a bit warmer than the American Arctic, with snow cover lasting only six months of the year. Some vegetation may be found along the coast, which inland opens into magnificent evergreen forests. Rivers run northward through the trees, emptying into the Arctic Ocean. These are of little value for transportation, choked with silt in summer and frozen solid in winter. When the spring thaw comes, they overflow their banks, creating swampland and shallow lakes that swarm with mosquitoes in uncounted billions.

Despite its inhospitable climate, Siberia was not uninhabited during the first century. These were the ancestors of the western Siberians — the Samoyeds, Zybrians, and Ostyaks — and of the eastern Siberians —

A seal is carved into the bowl of this Inuit seal-oil lamp. Lamps such as this one were lit with a wick of moss that was placed in a groove in the rim.

the Yakuts, Yukaghirs, Chuckchi, and Even. At the time of Jesus, some Inuits still lived along the Pacific coast of the Arctic, but most had already immigrated to Alaska, their abandoned hunting grounds taken over by Chuckchi and Koryaks from the Kamchatka Peninsula to the south.

Each of these Siberian peoples had its own language and culture, but the environment dictated a similar way of life both on the tundra and in the forest. In the first century, all depended on either hunting or fishing to sustain them. Hunters sought out wild reindeer, which spent winters in the shelter of the forests and summers on the open tundra. Although related to North American caribou, the Siberian reindeer are a bit smaller, and anthropologists believe that they were first domesticated around the time of Jesus. Gradually, this allowed herding to replace or supplement hunting among the Chuckchi and Yakuts. Domesticated reindeer provided hides for tents, milk and meat for food, and, when saddled, transportation to riders.

The Roman historian Tacitus was amazed at the lifestyle of the Lapps of Jesus' day.

Tacitus's Germania, *trans. Thomas Gordon (18th century).*

"IN WONDERFUL SAVAGENESS LIVE THE NATION OF THE FENNIANS, AND IN BEASTLY POVERTY, DESTITUTE OF ARMS, OF HORSES, AND OF HOMES; THEIR FOOD, THE COMMON HERBS; THEIR APPAREL, SKINS; THEIR BED, THE EARTH; THEIR ONLY HOPE IN THEIR ARROWS, WHICH FOR WANT OF IRON THEY POINT WITH BONES. THEIR COMMON SUPPORT THEY HAVE FROM THE CHASE, WOMEN AS WELL AS MEN; FOR WITH THESE THE FORMER WANDER UP AND DOWN, AND CRAVE A PORTION OF THE PREY. NOR OTHER SHELTER HAVE THEY EVEN FOR THEIR BABES, AGAINST THE VIOLENCE OF TEMPESTS AND RAVENING BEASTS, THAN TO COVER THEM WITH THE BRANCHES OF TREES TWISTING TOGETHER; THIS A RECEPTION FOR THE OLD MEN, AND HITHER RESORT THE YOUNG. SUCH A CONDITION THEY JUDGE MORE HAPPY THAN THE PAINFUL OCCUPATION OF CULTIVATING THE GROUND, THAN THE LABOUR OF REARING HOUSES, THAN THE AGITATIONS OF HOPE AND FEAR ATTENDING THE DEFENCE OF THEIR OWN PROPERTY OR THE SEIZING THAT OF OTHERS. SECURE AGAINST THE DESIGNS OF MEN, SECURE AGAINST THE MALIGNITY OF THE GODS, THEY HAVE ACCOMPLISHED A THING OF INFINITE DIFFICULTY; THAT TO THEM NOTHING REMAINS EVEN TO BE WISHED."

THE LAPPS

The people of the European Arctic are known as Lapps. As they did at the time of Jesus, the Lapps make their home north of the Arctic Circle in the northern reaches of Norway, Sweden, Finland, and the Kola Peninsula of Russia. They call themselves *Sami,* and anthropologists consider them to be the last remnant of those who populated the continent during the last European Ice Age. Linguists believe that the Lapps of two millennia ago most likely had their own language, but that over the centuries they abandoned it in favor of Finnish.

The first narrative to mention the Lapps was the Roman author Tacitus's *Germania,* composed about sixty years after the death of Jesus. Tacitus called them Fenni, speaking of them as people living in Europe's extreme north. Materially, he said, they were unbelievably poor: they dwelled in tents, subsisted mainly on herbs, dressed in furs, and lacked permanent homes, weapons, even beds. Women, he noted, were considered equal to men, even joining them on the hunt. All of this information would have shocked first-century Romans.

FURTHER FACTS

Storytelling was a far more developed art in Arctic cultures than elsewhere in North America — for the very practical reason that it helped to pass the endless winter nights.

Most anthropologists believe that Tacitus's report was accurate. What he described was a people who continued to live through hunting when most cultures no longer did so. But it was, in fact, hunting wild reindeer that made the Lapps' survival possible. Their methods were unique: rather than pursuing their quarry in a typical hunt, the Lapps herded the animals into enclosures where they were trapped and then slaughtered. A handful of reindeer were tamed; these came to be used as decoys to lure the wild animals.

The Lapps' religion was polytheistic. They believed that the world was created by a female deity, and was ruled by such gods as the sun and the Man of the Winds. As in other Arctic religions, the rituals of the shamans provided a link between humankind and the spirit world.

Since we lack all but the tiniest clues to the spiritual dimension of life in the Arctic — Tacitus's few observations and the relics of archaeology — it is difficult to draw conclusions about what Jesus' life and work would have been like there. It would be fascinating to know in some detail how the Inuits and Aleuts, the Siberians and the Lapps, worshiped. How did they relate their own experiences to the spiritual world? What were their ways of worship? Did they think of a spiritual world beyond shamanic rituals? Such questions cannot be answered with any certainty, but with what little we know it is not difficult to imagine how far they were removed from the world that Jesus knew in Galilee.

One ancient Lapp word has made it into several of the world's major languages: tundra.

Would his message have survived in the Arctic? It is unlikely. The region's small, decentralized, illiterate population would not have been conducive to the spreading of his teachings, and the hostile climate would have ensured that few traces of his life survived. As with so much of ancient Arctic life, his life, death, and teachings would today be virtually unknown, pieced tentatively together from tiny bits of archaeological evidence.

Chapter Thirteen

North America

At the time of Jesus, America north of the Rio Grande was sparsely populated, but certainly less so than the Arctic. Its inhabitants lived by hunting and gathering, a way of life they had been practicing for thousands of years. While small agricultural communities did exist in the American Southwest and in the Mississippi Valley, elsewhere they were very rare.

Because no written materials exist from Native American societies contemporaneous with the life of Jesus, we must look to the work of anthropologists and archaeologists to tell us about their cultures. Often gaps exist in the research, and as a result many questions remain unresolved. Nevertheless, enough agreement exists on most major issues to paint a fairly accurate picture of the Native Americans in the first century. Additionally, since American Indian culture was so very conservative, it is probably safe to say that most customs described by Europeans in the sixteenth century, when contacts between the two cultures were first made, were similar to images of life there many centuries earlier.

Anthropologists speak of eight geographical divisions in this part of the world. Farthest north was the Subarctic region of Canada. Shared between modern Canada and the present United States were the Eastern Woodlands, the Great Plains, and the Pacific Northwest. Areas now entirely within the present borders of the United States include the Great Basin — centered in Utah, Wyoming, northern New Mexico, and Arizona — the Southeast, the Southwest, and California. These eight diverse regions of the North American continent were already well defined in the first century.

THE FIRST AMERICANS

All Native Americans shared similar physical characteristics. These included straight black hair; high cheekbones with little or no facial hair; and in some groups an eye fold similar to that of people living in East Asia. These features suggest an emigration of people from Siberia in a past so distant that, by the first century, Native American men and women had little in common with their counterparts in Asia. Less obvious but more significant is the fact that almost all American Indians share type O blood and none have type A. This points to a single migration of a small band of people in the remote past, before the mixing of blood types that eventually took place among all other world populations.

There is no consensus regarding when humans first arrived in the Americas. Anthropologists look for a time when glaciation kept the waters of the Arctic Ocean frozen, forging a land bridge between Siberia and the eastern Aleutian Islands. This has happened several times over the past million years, most recently perhaps thirty-six thousand years ago, but recent theories argue that the original migration may have occurred much earlier than that. About seventy thousand years ago, the Bering Sea was three hundred feet below its present level; this would have left a mere fifty miles of ocean to separate North America from Asia.

Whenever they arrived, it is likely that the first Americans were a small band of families from northern China who set off in pursuit of new hunting grounds. There is little doubt that they were first attracted to North America because of its abundant wildlife, particularly its caribou. We know that they brought fire with them, the skills to make tent shelters, and stone tools and weapons. Women also had to know how to sew the fur garments needed to survive in Arctic climates.

The spearheads of these first Americans were simply made by chipping and flaking. We do not know whether hunters threw their spears or jabbed them into the animals they hunted, only that they eventually developed the atlatl, or spear thrower, which enabled them to propel their weapons with unsurpassed accuracy and force. The atlatl was a piece of wood or bone with a hook at the end, which, when a spear was cushioned in it, extended the force of the arm. It allowed hunters to kill grizzly bears and other animals far larger than themselves. Women and children supplemented the family diet by gathering wild seeds, fruits, and eggs; particularly in northern cultures, fishing, too, was an important source of food.

FURTHER FACTS

One method of hunting bison, the drive, required extensive planning and cooperation. Cairns were constructed out of stone and used to drive the animals into a bottleneck and off a cliff where, injured, they were easy prey for hunters waiting below.

After hundreds, perhaps even thousands of years spent in the Arctic or Subarctic, some bands of Native Americans began following the caribou migrations southward, possibly through the valley of Canada's Mackenzie River. As they went they found new game: the woolly mammoth, its cousin the mastodon, and herds of wild horses. Since none of these animals had ever before encountered human predators, hunting must have been extremely easy.

It is generally agreed that by 18000 B.C. the American Indians had spread out as far as the Rio Grande in the south and the Atlantic in the east; not surprisingly, the land was only sparsely occupied. People traveled in nomadic bands of closely related kin who were so isolated from one another that many mutually incomprehensible languages developed. In some places, such as California, people speaking completely different languages lived right next to each other, but never interacted.

About twelve thousand years ago, the Native Americans in the Southwest learned to produce a new kind of projectile. This was the Clovis point, named after the site where it was found in New Mexico. The Clovis point was widely distributed — as far north as the Great Plains and as far south as Mexico. Artisans, with extreme care, chipped the five-

↑

A toad is depicted in this Hopewell ceremonial stone pipe, which dates from Jesus' time.

inch-long blade symmetrically on both sides, and ground the base of the point to make it easier to attach to a wooden shaft.

About six centuries after its invention, the Clovis tradition disappeared, possibly because of a change in climate that caused many Great Plains animals to die out. Winters turned warmer very suddenly, perhaps over a span of just fifty years, and of all the prey that the Clovis people once hunted only the bison, or buffalo, survived. Hunters were forced to develop new skills, for in the warmer and drier climate only smaller game flourished: foxes, rabbits, and wild sheep and goats.

One more dramatic change in the Native American way of life appeared with the introduction of agriculture north of the Rio Grande. Only gradually did farming become a significant way of life, for few American Indians thought it worth the effort to spend their days cultivating crops rather than enjoying the adventure of the hunt. The earliest farmers in the Mississippi Valley planted gourds for containers and pumpkins and beans for food.

The invention of the bow and arrow sometime after 1000 B.C. caught on much more quickly than did farming. Armed with this new and much more efficient weapon, hunters were more successful than ever before. It confirmed most societies in their belief that hunting was a superior as a way of life to the mundane task of cultivating crops. As a result, at the time of Jesus' birth, the vast majority of peoples north of the Rio Grande were hunters living nomadic lives.

MOUND BUILDERS

Of all the many cultures in the present United States during the first century, the most advanced was found in the Eastern Woodlands. Anthropologists have named it Hopewell, after the Ohio farmer upon whose land abundant evidence of the culture was found. We do not know what the Hopewell people called themselves.

Mound building was the distinctive characteristic of the Hopewell. Approximately ten thousand of their mounds are scattered over much of the Eastern Woodland region and as far south as the Gulf of Mexico.

The most spectacular of these were built along the Scioto River near modern Chillicothe, Ohio, where thirty-eight mounds are still to be seen, averaging thirty feet in height and one hundred feet in diameter. These had to have been built by human hands, since the Hopewell had no large domesticated animals. Basket by basket, day after day, workers must have hauled earth up the mound and stamped it down with their feet until their project was finished. Their zeal for mounds may have been sparked by the Adena culture, which preceded them in the Ohio River Valley. The Adena not only constructed mounds, but also sculpted great earthen animals. The most famous of these, the Great Serpent, is four to five feet high and stretches more than twelve hundred feet.

FURTHER FACTS

The Hopewell mounds are, in total, estimated to contain three million cubic feet of dirt.

The Hopewell constructed mounds primarily to provide fitting burial sites for their chiefs and aristocrats. The dead were put into log chambers with their grave gifts, and the logs were set on fire. Mounds were then built over the ashes and regarded as sacred because the spirit of the deceased still hovered over them. A wide assortment of grave gifts have been unearthed: copper breastplates and earplugs, stone knives and axes, mica figurines of animals and humans, silver and copper bracelets, and necklaces of freshwater pearls and bears' teeth. More intriguing are the artificial copper noses that must have served as special ornaments for the Hopewell upper class. This copper was not smelted but hammered, and must have been imported from the Lake Superior region. Archaeologists believe that the common Hopewell were cremated as well, but with little or no ceremony attached.

A few mounds appear to have had religious significance, for they were large enough to have temples built on them. Others may have served as foundations for the homes of chiefs. Still others must have been fortresses, built as walls to protect Hopewell villages.

A few statuettes remain to depict the Hopewell people, cast in clay and then baked. Women are shown in the midst of everyday tasks, such as caring for their babies. Men are portrayed in various poses. Some of these figures are physically deformed; this may suggest that the disabled were treated with respect in Hopewell culture. Many are carved on ceremonial

Hopewell pottery was engraved rather than painted. The bones and severed hands on this piece connect it with death — perhaps the urn was a grave gift, or used in funeral ceremonies.

stone pipes, which have been found in ancient Indian villages as far away as New York. What did the Hopewell people smoke? Possibly a local plant, or perhaps tobacco imported from the Southeast.

The Hopewell preferred to settle in villages on bluffs overlooking rivers. Because their lifestyle was one of hunting and gathering, the population of each village could not exceed a few hundred. The forests provided deer, rabbit, raccoons, birds, beaver, and bears; rivers abounded with fish and freshwater mussels. Women and children harvested seeds from wild sunflowers and goosefoot, which in turn were used to make soup. Remarkably, hickory nuts were also a staple of their diet, despite the inordinate effort required to break the hard shell surrounding the kernel.

The Hopewell were the first American businessmen, trading throughout much of the present United States. Lacking coinage, their transactions had to be carried out by barter, and probably using sign language.

The rivers and lakes of the Midwest served them as avenues of traffic for both exports and imports, and trees were cut down to make dugout or birch bark canoes. The largest of these required six oarsmen.

Hopewell exports included ceremonial pipes, ornaments, flint, and obsidian tools and weapons. Near the Scioto is a place known as Flint Ridge, which offered excellent raw materials for manufacturing these objects. Other Native American aristocrats welcomed trade with the Hopewell, for it gave them access to exotic prestige goods. In exchange for these, the Hopewell merchants took copper nuggets, baskets, nets, ornaments, and, from the South, alligator teeth and possibly tobacco. Hopewell traders also carried locally made pottery that was decorated with engravings and different textures rather than with paint. Their culture lasted three hundred years after the death of Jesus before disappearing, suffering serious decline before its demise.

INDIANS OF CANADA AND ALASKA

Other Native American cultures of the first century varied according to their environments. Indians of Canada and Alaska were still able to hunt the caribou, deer, moose, and elk that survived in the colder subarctic climates. For those who lived near the coast, the sea provided fish and aquatic mammals in abundance. The short summer months were ones of migration, for enough food had to be gathered and stored away to sustain them through the winter. Apparently this way of life was very healthy, for no evidence exists among these peoples of the epidemics that plagued other societies of the world. The Hudson Bay divided speakers of Athabascan from speakers of Algonquian — the former in the west, the latter in the east. Both groups had little contact with the Inuits, whom they regarded as enemies.

FURTHER FACTS

Potlatches not only lasted for several days, but at their most extravagant required years of planning.

CULTURE OF THE NORTHWEST

The American Indians of the Northwest enjoyed a standard of living second only to that of the Hopewell. Their territory extended from northern California to southern Alaska, a region whose natural resources seemed endless. Chiefs of one tribe, the Tlingit, had wealth in such abundance that they were known to squander it in enormous celebrations known as potlatches. Months of preparation preceded these events, which involved days and days of feasting and dancing, and the awarding of lavish gifts and property to deserving guests. The more sumptuous the event, the more the prestige of the host was enhanced; this, of course, was the real purpose of the potlatch. When the guests departed, it was with the expectation that they would plan a feast even more extravagant than the one they had just attended. In Jesus' day, potlatches were probably less frequent than they were in centuries to come, owing to the time and effort involved in preparing them.

FURTHER FACTS

At a potlatch, consumption became a competition. Huge bowls, or sometimes even boats, were filled with berries, salmon roe, or other delicacies, and a group of guests would be challenged to eat all of it or face dishonor.

The Tlingits and other Athabascan-speaking peoples of the Northwest lived in log plank houses grouped together in villages of several hundred people. Chiefs wielded huge amounts of power, and were revered by their subjects. Society was highly structured, from the potlatch-giving chiefs to the class of slaves at the bottom. The latter were sometimes put to death when their chief died; they were buried under his house to ensure he would have servants in his next life.

Prosperity in the Northwest depended on two things: the salmon that spawned in the region's rivers, and the forests that surrounded the villages. Each year, chiefs announced the time when the salmon nets should be lowered, and when the fish were first spotted, they were welcomed with speeches prepared for the occasion. Northwest Indians regarded the salmon as supernatural creatures that were willing to sacrifice themselves for the sake of humans. When they were caught, their spirits were reincarnated in eggs, beginning the cycle again. Smoked salmon provided enough food to last throughout the year.

Forests provided the Native Americans with countless other resources.

Northwest Indians regarded the salmon as supernatural creatures that were willing to sacrifice themselves for the sake of humans. It is no surprise, then, that this shaman's rattle has been carved to look like a salmon.

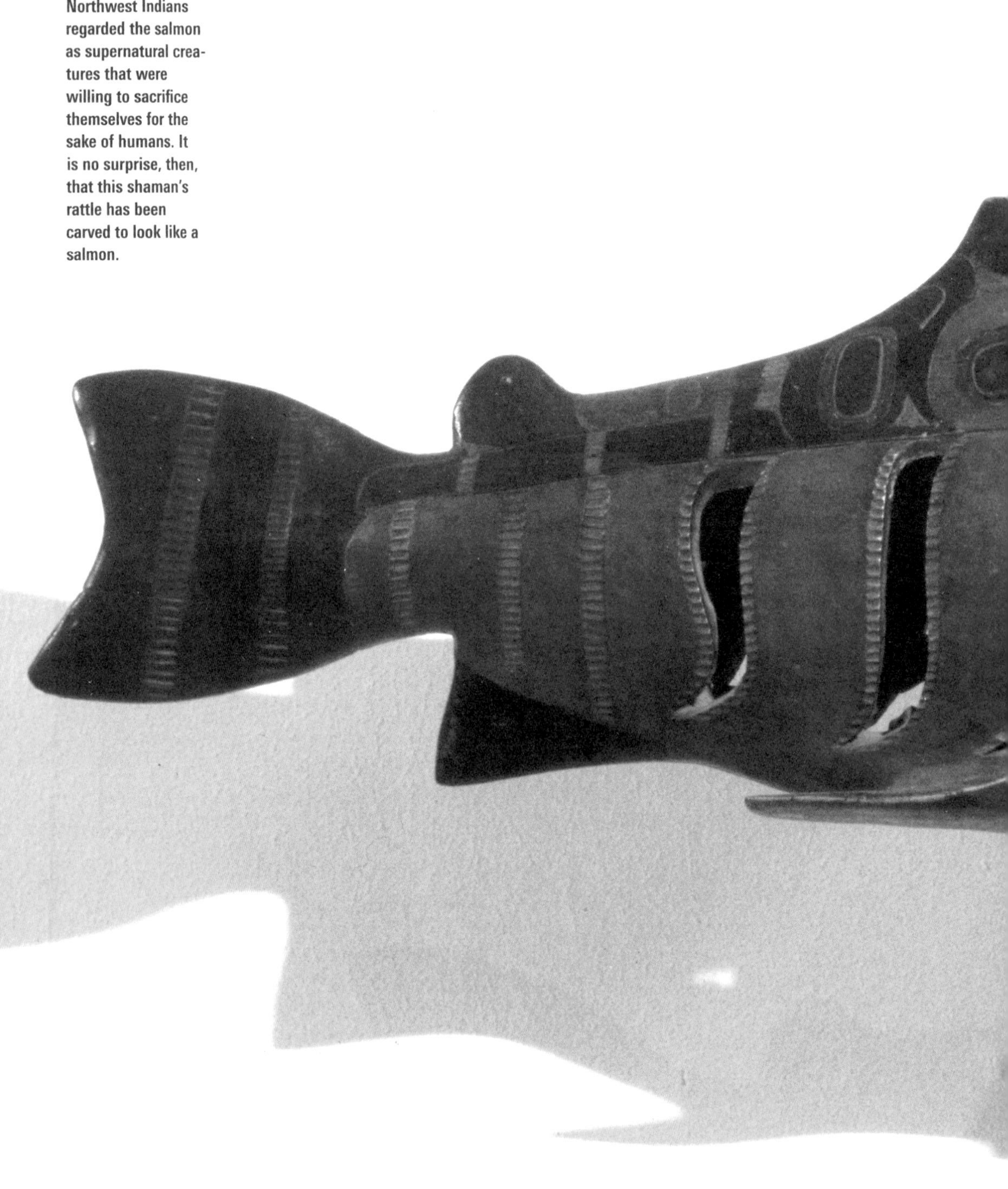

Its plants and small animals supplemented salmon in their diet, and its trees offered lumber for houses and boats. Most logs were cut into planks by craftsmen with stone axes; a select few were reserved by chiefs to be carved into totem poles, which depicted the animals that were the chiefs' special patrons.

Clearly the spirit world played a major role in the lives of the Northwest Indians, consisting not only of animal spirits but also of ancestors, who employed their powers for better or worse. Angering an ancestor could have disastrous consequences; whenever a person died, therefore, pallbearers made an opening in the wall of the house to remove the corpse, lest the spirit of the deceased should come back through the door.

PEOPLES OF THE GREAT PLAINS AND THE SOUTHWEST

While the Northwest was a land of abundance, the Great Plains compelled their inhabitants to live very simply. Their aridity severely limited the growth of plants and animals and, as a result, people had to be constantly on the move to seek out enough to eat. Settlements were often erected along rivers or lakes that attracted animals, but they were always temporary. Families sustained themselves and lived isolated from one another: the men hunted and the women wove blankets and baskets and prepared animal skins for clothing.

As the Northwest Indians depended on the salmon, so the Great Plains Indians relied on the buffalo. The region was filled with tens of thousands of the great beasts, roaming the region in herds. Extremely farsighted animals, they were easy prey for hunters, who approached them disguised in buffalo skins and speared cows and calves that strayed to the fringe of the herd.

The teeth of Hohokam skulls are full of cavities because the people ate so much corn.

The Indians of the American Southwest hunted and fished less than their neighbors, but were far ahead of other Native Americans agriculturally. As early as 3500 B.C., domesticated plants started to become a staple of their diets. Generally, farming served as an adjunct to hunting, and was in fact resisted by some communities because it required settling in a single location for a significant period of time.

FURTHER FACTS

The Hohokam were most likely given their name by one of the cultures that replaced them, for it means "things used up," or "the vanished ones."

In Jesus' day, the valley of the Gila River supported the largest population in the Southwest. About 300 B.C., immigrants entered the region from Mexico. While they brought with them unique styles of building and of making pottery, they are best remembered for their sophisticated methods of farming. Known as the Hohokam, they were accustomed to irrigating their crops and soon set to work digging channels parallel to the Gila to divert water to their fields. By 100 B.C., they had put into place an entire network of canals, some of them 30 miles long and 15 feet wide. Neither the Hohokam nor any other Native American farmers invented a plow. Rather, they used digging sticks to put seeds into holes in the ground.

At a glance, it might seem that farming would have given the Hohokam a higher standard of living than other Native Americans enjoyed, but this was not always the case. Problems arose from competition for water and land, from higher rates of disease, and from a diet saturated with carbohydrates. The teeth of Hohokam skulls are full of cavities because the people ate so much corn — far more than hunting populations.

To the north of the Hohokam lived the men and women of the Mogollon culture. Their way of life was very similar to that of the Hohokam: they lived in small villages in houses of wattle and daub, and employed irrigation to bring water to their fields from dams on mountain streams that caught both water and silt.

The Anasazi were on the way to the American Southwest during Jesus' lifetime. They did not arrive and settle permanently, though, until the end of the first century. Today's Pueblo Indians are their descendants.

Like the Hohokam, the Mogollon were among the most sophisticated potters in ancient North America. The figures on this bowl represent the contrast between male and female, night and day, darkness and light, and so on, suggesting that such opposites were integral components in the Mogollon worldview.

CALIFORNIA

California at the time of Jesus was home to many different peoples in many different circumstances. Most dwelt in villages of less than a hundred people and pursued a hunting-and-gathering lifestyle, though a few communities farmed along the Colorado River. Hunters were still using spears to bring down their prey, for the bow and arrow fell into common use only about A.D. 500. Coastal people harvested shellfish, sea mammals, and fish; in the interior men and women depended on the acorns of the California oaks, which the women, using pestle and mortar, ground into flour and baked into bread. These acorns contained poisonous tannic acid that first had to be bleached through boiling. In the Sierras people survived by hunting, for the mountains were still home to a variety of large animals, especially grizzly and black bears. It was usual for men to wear no clothes in the warm months of the year, though when winter came they would don fur garments made by their wives. Women were also skilled in basketry and cordage, and spent a great deal of time gathering the fibers necessary for this craft.

What all these peoples had in common was an extremely traditional way of life. Hereditary chiefs existed in every large village, their importance signified by the number of their wives. They were responsible for making decisions for their subjects, and hence enjoyed special privileges. It was their task to organize war parties against their enemies and to settle any disputes that arose at home, advised by shamans who had contact with the spiritual world. There was fierce competition over hunting grounds among the California Indians; archaeologists estimate that ten percent of the burials between 1000 B.C. and A.D. 500 were of people who died violent deaths.

THE SOUTHEAST

FURTHER FACTS

Ball poles were used in a game called toli, *which had hundreds of players per team, was played on fields several miles long, and often lasted from sunrise until sunset. The modern game of lacrosse is its direct descendant.*

The Native Americans of the Southeast lived in a land that was extremely different from that of their neighbors to the west. Along the coast, the soil was light and sandy, with scrub forests and savannah grasslands; this naturally inclined people to look to the sea for their livelihood. Salt was a major commodity among the Southeast Indians, and shells might have served them as currency, as they did in California. Contacts between the inhabitants of the present United States and the Caribbean were common: since 3000 B.C., Arawak Indians had made their home on the Caribbean islands, having emigrated from the South American coast and hopped from island to island across the sea until reaching Puerto Rico in A.D. 1200.

Those who lived in the interior preferred to settle in the river valleys and rolling hills of the Appalachian Mountains. The Choctaw, Cherokee, and Creek nations made up the largest communities. Their villages tended to be larger than those elsewhere, and were often surrounded by log palisades for defense. They were centered around temples, chiefs' houses, and ball poles, which were used in sporting events. Houses were round, constructed of skins or brush and supported by poles.

Common to the Southeast Native American mentality was the view that death was not a natural event, but something that resulted from an outside force. This was an idea they shared with the Inuits, and with the more distant Australian Aborigines. The soul of a deceased person, they believed, could not rest until the cause of death was discovered and dealt with. Even slain animals needed to have their spirits appeased. Shamans were kept constantly busy with the many ceremonies that accompanied death.

Hell's Half Acre in present-day Wyoming was the site of at least one buffalo drive. This complicated method of hunting involved constructing a large network of cairns in the shape of a bottleneck. Gradually, sometimes over several days, a herd of buffalo was lured into this trap and then chased off a cliff. Injured by their fall, the animals were then easy prey for hunters waiting below.

In summary, Native American culture during the first century was paradoxically diverse yet unchanging. While each culture developed its own way of life, these individual cultures were often similar to one another, and they changed little over centuries or even millennia. Since none of them developed a system of writing to record their history, it is left to modern anthropologists to reconstruct the past. What they have discovered suggests that it would not have been easy for Jesus' message to take root in Native American society. Jesus emphasized the existence of a single God who created the universe and sought a personal relationship with his creation. The spiritual world of the Native Americans was pantheistic: it teemed with life and all was sacred — plants, animals, and humans shared a common existence. The distinction Jesus drew between God and the world that God created would have been alien to the Native Americans, whose shamans saw good and evil spirits in everything.

Chapter Fourteen

Central America

ARCHAEOLOGISTS ESTIMATE that Native Americans first crossed the Rio Grande into modern Mexico approximately twenty thousand years ago. They arrived in pursuit of the large animals they were accustomed to hunting farther north, and for the next ten thousand years there was enough game to sustain them. But the climate change that affected much of North America stretched into Central America as well, gradually killing off the large animals and forcing hunters to alter their methods and lifestyles accordingly. This brought about the beginning of Central American civilization.

FARMERS OF CENTRAL AMERICA

The next step in the evolution of life in Central America occurred a thousand years later, with the advent of farming on the Mexican plateau. It was probably women who noticed that a portion of wild seed could be put into the ground, where it germinated and could eventually be harvested. By 4500 B.C., a variety of beans, squash, pumpkins, and chili peppers were being cultivated for food, as was a species of cotton whose fibers could be woven into cloth. In order to prepare their fields,

↑

Because many of them are wearing helmets, some archaeologists surmise the Olmec heads depict the stars of a ball game the Olmecs enjoyed.

men girdled trees with stone axes to kill them, then set them on fire so that the ash would increase soil fertility. After several years, the soil lost its nutrients, and the process was repeated in new fields. This method of agriculture, known as slash-and-burn, was certainly prevalent in Jesus' time throughout the agricultural regions of Mexico and Central America, and is practiced in tropical countries to this day.

The most important discovery of Central American farmers was that corn could be domesticated. This may have happened as late as 3500 B.C. Already a hybrid when farmers first planted it, early species of corn had very few kernels on each ear. Over time, by careful selection of the best plants, the kernels increased in number and size. Women took the kernels and ground them into flour for making tortillas, the staple of the Mexican diet at the time of Jesus.

It was corn that allowed people to settle permanently in Mexico. Because it was developed so slowly, perhaps over a period of about a thousand years, the first permanent villages in Mexico date from about 2500 B.C. Evidence of pottery and the bones of dogs, turkeys, and ducks show that settled existence had by then become common. Farmers' houses were far from sturdy, made of brush, bark, and clay over a framework of poles. Thatch covered the roofs.

THE OLMECS

Civilization in the Americas began with the Olmecs, a people long gone by the time Jesus walked the earth. Although they disappeared well before the first century, their influence was felt by all subsequent civilizations in Central America. Their religion in particular, with its worship of a god who was part man and part jaguar, lived on long after they were gone.

The first identifiable site of an Olmec town is at a location now known as San Lorenzo. Up to a thousand people lived here because of its importance as a religious and economic center. Here a temple served by the priests attracted pilgrims from all over the region. Farming was the mainstay of the economy, though the Olmecs' location along the hot, humid Atlantic coast of Mexico made it a difficult occupation at best. Those who opted out of farming generally became merchants, exporting the obsidian and jade that were in high demand for making tools, jewelry, and figurines.

Although we can only guess at its rules today, stakes were high in the ball games the Olmecs played. The coaches of losing teams were decapitated and sacrificed to the gods.

Olmec artisans are best remembered for their enormous carvings of human heads, some of which surpassed nine feet in height. Lacking metal tools, sculptors used stone hammers to chisel the heads out of solid basalt. Quarried from rock some fifty miles distant, the stone had to be put on rafts and floated down to San Lorenzo. A huge labor force must have been required to move the rock; some of the heads weigh up to forty-four tons. Today, unfortunately, the purpose of the heads is a mystery; because many are wearing helmets, some archaeologists surmise they are heroes of a ball game that the Olmecs enjoyed.

By the time of Jesus, San Lorenzo had been destroyed and abandoned, its survivors absorbed into neighboring populations. The Olmecs, however, were not entirely gone; they opened new religious sites at other locations throughout Mexico. Here they carried on their ceremonies to the jaguar-men gods first worshiped at San Lorenzo, and constructed mounds in the shape of pyramids which were to make a lasting impression on Mexican religious architecture. At some point they instigated the tradition of incorporating human sacrifice into their worship; they were the first Central Americans to do so. At Monte Alban, a flourishing religious center in Jesus' time, there is a fresco depicting many contorted figures that archaeologists believe represent those slaughtered in a religious ceremony.

TEOTIHUACÁN

Agriculture did not reach central and southern Mexico until about 1500 B.C. When it did, though, the population soared; Cuicuilco, the largest settlement, soon became home to three thousand men and women. The town's builders erected a pyramid seventy-five feet tall, the first of its kind in the Valley of Mexico. Despite its promising beginnings, though, Cuicuilco was not to last: around 150 B.C., a volcanic eruption destroyed it.

For several years thereafter, the valley was deserted. But eventually memory of the disaster began to fade, and people again were willing to settle there. About thirty miles northeast of present-day Mexico City, they founded a town called Teotihuacán, "the place the gods call home." Its beginnings date from about a hundred years before the birth of Jesus. Teotihuacán was a planned city, and home to the largest religious complex ever constructed in the Americas. Two grand avenues divided it into quarters, probably meant to reflect the universe as its inhabitants saw it, and its leaders were so confident of their security that they found no need to surround the city with a wall. In the heart of the city, an elite group of priests conducted religious ceremonies to honor the city's gods and goddesses.

Most of the extant monuments of Teotihuacán were built after Jesus' birth, but even in this early period the city must have held the prototypes of what later became the awesome Pyramids of the Sun and Moon. Here the feathered serpent god, Quetzalcoatl, and the rain god, Tlaloc, made their homes among humankind. Like the jaguar-men gods before them, these deities demanded that they be nourished with human blood.

A number of parallels exist between Jesus and the god Quetzalcoatl. Both were considered to be humans who ascended into heaven: Jesus to sit at the right hand of God, Quetzalcoatl to become the morning star. Both were tempted by evil powers: Jesus by Satan, Quetzalcoatl by the god Tezcatlipota. And followers of both believed they would one day return to earth to claim their kingdoms. In this carving, Quetzalcoatl bursts from the jaws of a serpent and ascends to become the morning star.

The Pyramid of the Sun in Teotihuacán was part of the largest religious complex ever constructed in the Americas.

According to the people of Teotihuacán, without these sacrifices the gods would die, and if the gods died, the universe would come to an end. For six centuries after its founding, Teotihuacán was the largest, most renowned pilgrimage site in all the Americas. It was destroyed, however, in A.D. 750; archaeologists have yet to fully explain how or why.

THE MAYANS

To the south of Teotihuacán was the homeland of the Mayans. Living in a land of rain forests, the Mayans over time became expert farmers, developing and mastering the techniques necessary for tropical agriculture. Irrigation ditches brought water to the cornfields, providing enough surplus to sustain a population boom that began around 300 B.C. and did not end for over five centuries. Fascinated by the passage of time, the Mayans developed a remarkably accurate calendar, a hieroglyphic script, and the concept of the zero. The first recorded date on their calendar corresponds to 36 B.C., proving that at the time of Jesus the creativity of the Mayan people was already flourishing.

Like all other Central American peoples, the Mayans built pyramids

→

The Mayan calendar was based on the movements of the moon, Venus, and other heavenly bodies, and was accurate enough to measure the solar year to within minutes. This circular calendar has a series of dates around the ends and the figure of a ball player in the center.

for the worship of their gods and goddesses. These pyramids were of stepped construction, built on stone platforms with cores of rubble and earth and extravagantly decorated exteriors of stucco. At the time of Jesus' birth, work had begun on the great Mayan temple at Tikal in modern Guatemala. Other temples were under construction as well in the first century, but the golden age of the Maya did not arrive until after A.D. 250.

DAILY LIFE

If Jesus had grown up in a Mayan culture, he would have received a formal education only if he were training to be a priest. Then he would have learned history, writing, medicine, divining, and the complex Mayan calendar system.

Since the Mayans had developed a system of writing by Jesus' time, it is conceivable that he would not have been forgotten after his death. But in a religious milieu that placed such striking emphasis on human sacrifice, it is hard to envision a place for his message — the demands of the Central American deities seem at direct odds with his reverence for human life. Jesus taught that his death would offer new life to humanity, not that an endless succession of slaughter was necessary to propitiate bloodthirsty gods. If he had been born and raised among the Mayans, it is difficult to imagine that he would ever have developed the idea of a loving, forgiving God that Christians believe stands at the center of his teachings.

Chapter Fifteen

South America

AT THE TIME OF JESUS, the Indians of South America were living in what archaeologists have named the First Intermediate period. The first civilization on the continent, known as Chavín, had disappeared about three hundred years earlier, and it would be another three hundred years before a successor, the Moche civilization, would arise to take its place. The inhabitants of South America, therefore, were scattered throughout the continent, isolated in small, family-based groups whose lifestyles varied according to the region in which they lived. Some made their homes in the cold, dry areas that hugged the steep cliffs of the Andes Mountains, while others delved into the wet, humid rain forests that surrounded the world's mightiest river, the Amazon.

Archaeologists still debate as to when humankind first arrived in South America. Certain, though, is the fact that they came in pursuit of the large animals that then inhabited the continent: the mastodon, the giant sloth, and a variety of deer. Like other early Americans, hunters gradually had to turn to smaller prey — particularly rabbits and, in the rain forests, monkeys — as the larger beasts died out. Many centuries passed before men and women reached the southern tip of South America, Tierra del Fuego. Here the first human evidence dates from about 8000 B.C.

↑

Gold beads such as these, depicting a jaguar and a monkey respectively, are the only artifacts left to identify many South American cultures.

PERU

The Andean region of Peru was especially favorable for human settlement. Thanks to a deep upwelling off the coast of cold, nutrient-rich water, it is a coast that teems with fish, sea mammals, and shellfish, which, in turn, attract millions of birds. Early settlers were more than content to make their home amid such bounty, thriving on fish, birds, and the numerous local plants they discovered could be domesticated. Agriculture commenced in the Andes about the same time it began in the Valley of Mexico, with farmers growing squash, tomatoes, peppers, peanuts, and, most importantly, a wide array of potatoes, both white and sweet. Few foods were as nutritious and as easy to grow in the cool coastal climates. Farmers also discovered how to grow the cotton that was native to the region, and about 2500 B.C. they were introduced to corn, probably through contacts with Mexicans who traveled down the coast in

boats. Faced with huge amounts of surplus, artisans had no choice but to develop pottery that could be used as storage.

But while many plants were available for food, South America was home to very few animals that could be domesticated: guinea pigs, dogs, and ducks. Only the llama and its cousin the alpaca could be kept as beasts of burden, and even they were too small to carry really heavy loads.

The largest villages of Peru flanked the coast, an almost rainless region sustained by a number of rivers that pass through on their way to the Pacific. These rivers deposit a layer of fertile silt in flood plains that would otherwise remain lifeless deserts. Here the ancient Peruvians made a life for themselves, combining farming and fishing with hunting birds and sea lions. By 500 B.C., political leaders had come to power in Peru, and society was sufficiently stable that they could oversee large-scale irrigation projects to expand the amount of arable land. These same

chiefs, seeking to foster devotion to their gods, ordered the construction of stone platforms upon which temples were erected, requiring tons of stone to be quarried and transported.

CHAVÍN CIVILIZATION

From these humble beginnings the first civilization in South America was born. Overcoming extremes of both geography and climate, the people founded a city at Chavín de Huántar in the Peruvian highlands. By 850 B.C., they had constructed a stone temple so large for its time that archaeologists call it the Castillo, "castle." Archaeologists have discovered there a cult object, a twelve-foot-high smiling god, part jaguar and part human, with claws and hair in the shape of snakes. So similar is the statue to those found in Central America that some scholars theorize that the cult was brought from there into Peru. Pilgrims must have come from miles around to worship at Chavín, setting a pattern that continued for several centuries.

FURTHER FACTS

Although it is unknown how Chavín civilization came to an end, archaeologists know it was very sudden: findings suggest that a number of major building projects were simply abandoned midway and never completed.

Strangely, about three centuries before Jesus was born, Chavín civilization came to a sudden end that today is unexplainable. For a time, art and architecture served as memories of its existence, but eventually these too died out. At the time of Jesus, each village had its own style of pottery and textile weaving, and these are the only artifacts that can be used to identify them today.

The flute the shaman in this ceramic sculpture is playing suggests that music was an important part of worship at Chavín. Similar figurines have been discovered that depict shamans with mucus streaming out their noses, indicating that hallucinogenic snuffs also played a role in their religious ceremonies.

OTHER SOUTH AMERICAN CULTURES

In the region that is now Colombia and Ecuador, the discovery of gold prompted settlers to develop mining, hammering, and smelting techniques; their jewelry and ornaments identify them to modern archaeologists. Along the north shore of Lake Titicaca, at an altitude of over twelve thousand feet, builders at the time of Jesus were constructing a temple and sunken court to serve as places of worship for local peoples, and sculptors were preparing statues to decorate it. The inhabitants of the Amazon rain forest in Jesus' time were still hunters and gatherers, but they were so adept at their lifestyle that they had learned to make tapioca from the manioc root, a tuber that is poisonous unless it is bleached. Farmers in what is now Chile and Argentina imported crops from the Peruvians, and families in Tierra del Fuego were sustained by the fish and shellfish that nature offered them. None of these peoples established nations or systems of government; all of them were, however, remarkably well adapted to their environments.

The manioc is similar to the potato, but poisonous until peeled, grated, compressed, and sun-dried.

Clearly we would not know Jesus today had he lived and taught in South America. The same factors that would have impeded his message in other parts of the Americas were not only present, but more extreme: no systems of writing, no major cities, and a concept of the gods nothing like his vision of a God of love. Perhaps he would have shared his teachings with those around him, but to us, two thousand years later, his message would be utterly lost.

Index

Photo credits

2 Lions Gate, Mycenae. Charles Frazee.
15 Ruins at Delos. © Roger Wood / Corbis / Magma
18 Caesar Augustus. Musei Vaticani.
22 Livia Drusilla. Charles Frazee.
26 Roman mosaic. Gilles Mermet / Art Resource, NY.
33 Pharos. Phoenix Data Systems.
40 Cleopatra Coin. Werner Forman / Art Resource, NY.
45 Cleopatra's Needle. Phoenix Data Systems.
53 Asklepion at Pergamum. Photo by the author.
64 Alexander Jannaeus coin. Erich Lessing / Art Resource, NY.
76 Glass beaker. The Newark Museum / Art Resource, NY.
82 Cremation urn. Werner Forman / Art Resource, NY.
83 Stone axes and hammers. Erich Lessing / Art Resource, NY.
88 Gold torques. Erich Lessing / Art Resource, NY.
90 Mamertine Prison, Forum Romanum, Rome. Erich Lessing / Art Resource, NY.
94 Stonehenge. © Robert Holmes / Corbis / Magma.
96 Broch. © Wolfgang Kaehler / Corbis.
97 Celtic bronze helmet. Erich Lessing / Art Resource, NY.
114 Meroen pyramids. Werner Forman / Art Resource, NY.
117 Terracotta Nok head. Werner Forman / Art Resource, NY.
122 Women preparing silk. Museum of Fine Art, Boston.
130 Clay soldiers. Erich Lessing / Art Resource, NY.
132 Elegy of Ni Kuan. Werner Forman / Art Resource, NY.
135 Bronze Mirror. © Royal Ontario Museum / Corbis / Magma
142 Dolmen. Charles Frazee.
144 Shinto temple. Charles Frazee.
152 Great Wall. © Keren Su / Corbis / Magma.
156 Bronze appliqués. Réunion des Musées Nationaux / Art Resource, NY.
162 Mohenjo-Daro. Photo by the author.
169 Arjuna's Penance. Michael © Macduff Everton / Corbis / Magma.
174 Bust of Buddha. Réunion des Musées Nationaux / Art Resource, NY.
177 Stupa. Scala / Art Resource, NY.
180 Head of Brahma. Réunion des Musées Nationaux / Art Resource, NY
184 Dong-son sculpture. Giraudon / Art Resource, NY.
190 Petroglyph. Werner Forman / Art Resource, NY.
194 Ayers Rock. © Paul A. Souders / Corbis.
197 Aboriginal bark painting. Werner Forman / Art Resource, NY.
202 Model umiak. Werner Forman / Art Resource, NY.
203 Dorset mask. Werner Forman / Art Resource, NY.
205 Seal oil lamp. Werner Forman / Art Resource, NY.
212 Toad pipe. Werner Forman / Art Resource, NY.
215 Hopewell pot. Werner Forman / Art Resource, NY.
218 Salmon rattle. Werner Forman / Art Resource, NY.
222 Mogollon bowl. Werner Forman / Art Resource, NY.
224 Hell's Half Acre. Werner Forman / Art Resource, NY.
226 Olmec head. Charles Frazee.
229 Quetzalcoatl. Werner Forman / Art Resource, NY.
230 Pyramid of the Sun, Teotihuacan. Photo by the author.
231 Mayan calendar. Werner Forman / Art Resource, NY.
234 Jaguar bead. Werner Forman / Art Resource, NY.
235 Monkey bead. Werner Forman / Art Resource, NY.
236 Shaman. Werner Forman / Art Resource, NY.